MW01075644

A Thousand Ways to Please a Husband

with Bettina's Best Recipes

Louise Bennett Weaver
and
Helen Cowles LeCron

Decorations by Elizabeth Colbourne

Dover Publications, Inc.
Mineola, New York

Bibliographical Note

This Dover edition, first published in 2012, is an unabridged republication of the work originally published by Britton Publishing Company, Inc., New York, in 1917. The original tinted endpapers have been reproduced here in black and white.

Library of Congress Cataloging-in-Publication Data

Weaver, Louise Bennett.
  A thousand ways to please a husband with Bettina's best recipes / Louise Bennett Weaver and Helen Cowles LeCron ; decorations by Elizabeth Colbourne.
      p. cm.
  Originally published: New York : Britton, 1917.
  Includes index.
  ISBN-13: 978-0-486-48871-4
  ISBN-10: 0-486-48871-3
  1. Cooking, American. I. LeCron, Helen Cowles. II. Title. III. Title: 1,000 ways to please a husband with Bettina's best recipes.

TX715.W36 2012
641.5973—dc23

2012007619

Manufactured in the United States by LSC Communications
48871303   2018
www.doverpublications.com

A DEDICATION

To every other little bride
  Who has a "Bob" to please,
And says she's tried and tried and tried
  To cook with skill and ease,
And can't!—we offer here as guide
  Bettina's Recipes!

To her whose "Bob" is prone to wear
  A sad and hungry look,
Because the maid he thought so fair
  Is—well—she just can't cook!
To her we say: do not despair;
  Just try Bettina's Book!

Bettina's Measurements Are All Level

C = cup
t = teaspoon
T = tablespoon
lb. = pound
pt. = pint
B.P. = baking-powder

CONTENTS

Contents

Contents

Contents

Contents

JUNE.

No, you cannot live on kisses,
Though the honeymoon is sweet,
Harken, brides, a true word this is,—
Even lovers have to eat.

CHAPTER I

HOME AT LAST

"**H**OME at last!" sighed Bettina happily as the hot and dusty travelers left the train.

"Why that contented sigh?" asked Bob. "Because our wedding trip is over? Well, anyhow, Bettina, it's after five. Shall we have dinner at the hotel?"

"Hotel? Why, Bob! with our house and our dishes and our silver just waiting for us? I'm ashamed of you! We'll take the first car for home—a streetcar, not a taxi! Our extravagant days are over, and the time has come to show you that Bettina knows how to keep house. You think that you love me now, Bobby, but just wait till you sit down to a real strawberry shortcake made by a real cook in a real home!"

Half an hour later Bob was unlocking the door of the new brown bungalow. "Isn't it a dear?" cried Bettina proudly. "When we've had time to give it grass and shrubs and flowers and a vegetable garden, no place in town will equal it! And as for porch furniture, how I'd like to get at Mother's attic and transform some of her discarded things!"

"Just now I'd rather get at some of Mother's cooking!" grinned Bob.

"Oh, dear, I forgot! I'll have supper ready in ten minutes. Do you remember my emergency shelf? Why, Bob—Bob, they must have known we were coming! Here's ice—and milk—and cream—and butter—and bread—and rolls, and even a grape fruit! They knew, and didn't meet the train because they thought we would prefer to have our first meal alone! Wasn't that dear of them? And this will save you a trip to the corner grocery!"

Bettina fastened a trim percale bungalow apron over her traveling suit, and swiftly and surely assembled the little meal.

"I like that apron," said Bob. "It reminds me of the rainy day when we fixed the emergency shelf. That was fun."

"Yes, and work too," said Bettina, "but I'm glad we did it. Do you remember how much I saved by getting things in dozen and half dozen lots? And Mother showed me how much better it was to buy the larger sizes in bottled things, because in buying the smaller bottles you spend most of your money for the glass. Now that you have to pay my bills, Bob, you'll be glad that I know those things!"

"I think you know a great deal," said Bob admiringly. "Lots of girls can cook, but mighty few know how to be economical at the same time! It's great to be your——"

"Dinner is served," Bettina interrupted. "It's a 'pick-up meal,' but I'm hungry, aren't you? And after this, sir, no more canned things!"

And Bob sat down to:

Creamed Tuna on Toast Strips
Canned Peas with Butter Sauce
Rolls   Butter
Strawberry Preserves
Hot Chocolate with Marshmallows

BETTINA'S RECIPES

(All measurements are level)

Creamed Tuna on Toast Strips (Two portions)

1 T-butter	½ slice pimento
1 T-flour	1 C-milk
¼ t-salt	3 slices of bread
½ C-tuna	

Melt the butter, add the flour, salt and pimento. Mix well. Gradually pour in the milk. Allow the mixture to boil one minute. Stir constantly. Add the fish, cook one minute and pour over toasted strips of bread.

Hot Chocolate (Three cups)

1 square of chocolate	2 C-milk
3 T-sugar	¼ t-vanilla
2/3 C-water	3 marshmallows

Cook chocolate, sugar and water until a thin custard is formed. Add milk gradually and bring to a boil. Whip with an egg beater, as this breaks up the albumin found in chocolate, and prevents the coating from forming over the top. Add vanilla and marshmallows. Allow to stand a moment and pour into the cups.

Strawberry Preserves (Six one-half pt. glasses)

4 lbs. berries	3lbs. sugar
3 C-water	

Pick over, wash and hull the berries. Make a syrup by boiling the sugar and water fifteen minutes. Fill sterilized jars with the berries. Cover with syrup and let stand fifteen minutes to settle. Add more berries. Adjust rubbers and covers. Place on a folded cloth in a kettle of cold water. Heat water to boiling point and cook slowly one hour. Screw on covers securely.

On Bettina's Emergency Shelf

6 cans pimentos (small size)	6 cans tomatoes
6 cans tuna (small size)	6 pt. jars pickles
6 cans salmon (small size)	6 pt. jars olives
6 jars dried beef	6 small cans condensed milk
12 cans corn	6 boxes sweet wafers
12 cans peas	1 pound box salted codfish
6 cans string beans	3 pkg. marshmallows
6 cans lima beans	3 cans mushrooms
6 cans devilled ham (small size)	2 pkg. macaroni

CHAPTER II

BETTINA'S FIRST REAL DINNER

"SAY, isn't it great to be alive!" exclaimed Bob, as he looked across the rose-decked table at the flushed but happy Bettina. "And a beefsteak dinner, too!"

"Steak is expensive, dear, and you'll not get it often, but as this is our first real dinner in our own home, I had to celebrate. I bought enough for two meals, because buying steak for one meal for two people is beyond any modest purse! So you'll meet that steak again tomorrow, but I don't believe that you'll bow in recognition!"

"So you marketed today, did you?"

"Indeed I did! I bought a big basket, and went at it like a seasoned housekeeper. I had all the staples to get, you know, and lots of other things. After dinner I'll show you the labelled glass jars on my shelves; it was such fun putting things away! June is a wonderful month for housekeepers. I've planned the meals for days ahead, because I know that's best. Then I'll go to the market several times a week, and if I plan properly I won't have to order by telephone. It seems so extravagant to buy in that way unless you know exactly what you are getting. I like to plan for left-overs, too. For instance, the peas in this salad were left from yesterday's dinner, and the pimento is from that can I opened. Then, too, I cooked tomorrow's potatoes with these to save gas and bother. You'll have them served in a different way, of course. And—— Oh, yes, Bob," Bettina chattered on, "I saw Ruth down town, and have asked all five of my bridesmaids to luncheon day after tomorrow. Won't that be fun? But I promise you that the neglected groom shall have every one of the good things when he comes home at night!"

"It makes me feel happy, I can tell you, to have a home like this. It's pleasant to be by ourselves, but at the same time I can't help wishing that some of the bachelors I know could see it all and taste your cooking!"

"Well, Bob, I want you to feel free to have a guest at any time. If my dinners are good enough for you, I'm sure they're good enough for any guest whom you may bring. And it isn't very hard to make a meal for three out of a meal for two. Now, Bobby, if you're ready, will you please get the dessert?"

"What? Strawberry shortcake? Well, this is living! I tell you what, Bettina, I call this a regular man-size meal!"

It consisted of:

Pan-Broiled Steak	New Potatoes in Cream
Baking-Powder Biscuits	Butter
Rhubarb Sauce	Pea and Celery Salad
Strawberry Short-cake	Cream
Coffee	

BETTINA'S RECIPES

(All measurements are level)

Pan-Broiled Steak (Two portions)

1 lb. steak	⅛ t-pepper
1 T-butter	2 T-hot water
1 t-salt	1 t-parsley chopped

Wipe the meat carefully with a wet cloth. Remove superfluous fat and any gristle. Cut the edges to prevent them from curling up. When the broiling oven is very hot, place the meat, without any fat, upon a hot flat pan, directly under the blaze. Brown both sides very quickly. Turn often. Reduce heat and continue cooking about seven minutes, or longer if desired. Place on a warm platter; season with salt, pepper and bits of butter. Set in the oven a moment to melt the butter. If salt is added while cooking, the juices will be drawn out. A gravy may be made by adding hot water, butter, salt, pepper and parsley to the pan. Pour the gravy over the steak.

New Potatoes in Cream (Two portions)

4 new potatoes 1 qt. water
1 t-salt

Scrape four medium sized new potatoes. Cook in boiling water (salted) until tender when pierced with a fork. Drain off the water, and shake the kettle over the fire gently, to allow the steam to escape and make the potatoes mealy. Make the following white sauce and pour over the potatoes.

White Sauce for New Potatoes (Two portions)

2 T-butter 1 c-milk
2 T-flour ½ t-salt
¼ t-paprika

Melt the butter, add the flour, salt and paprika. Thoroughly mix, slowly add milk, stirring constantly. Allow sauce to cook two minutes.

Strawberry Shortcake (Two portions)

2 T-lard	1/3 t-salt
1 T-butter	4 t-baking powder
2 c-sifted flour	1 qt. strawberries
¾ C-milk	2/3 C-sugar

Cut the fat into the flour, salt and baking powder until the consistency of cornmeal. Gradually add the milk, using a knife to mix. Do not handle any more than absolutely necessary. Toss the dough upon a floured board or a piece of clean brown paper. Pat into the desired shape, and place in a pan. Bake in a hot oven for 12 to 15 minutes. Split, spread with butter, and place strawberries, crushed and sweetened, between and on top. Serve with cream.

CHAPTER III

BETTINA'S FIRST GUEST

"HELLO! Yes, this is Bettina! Why, Bob, of course! Is he a real woman-hater? No, I've never met any, but I'll just invite Alice, too, and tomorrow you won't be calling him that. Six-thirty? Yes, I'll be ready for you both; I'm so glad you asked him. He'll be our first guest! Goodbye!"

Bettina left the telephone with more misgivings than her tone had indicated. She couldn't disappoint Bob, and she liked unexpected company, but the dinner which she had planned was prepared largely from the recipes filed as "leftovers" in her box of indexed cards.

"Well, Bob will like it, anyhow," she declared confidently, "and if Alice can come, we'll have enough scintillating tabletalk to make up for disappointments."

Alice accepted with delight, promising to wear "a dream of a gown that just came home," and confessing to a sentimental feeling at the thought of dining with such a new bride and groom.

"Let's see," said Bettina in her spick and span little kitchen, "there is meat enough, but I must hard-boil some eggs to help out these potatoes. 'Potatoes Anna' will be delicious. Goodness, what would my home economics teacher have said if she had heard me say 'hard-boil'? They mustn't really be boiled at all, just 'hard-cooked' in water kept at the boiling point. There will be enough baked green peppers for four, and enough of the pudding, and if I add some very good coffee

17

I don't believe that Bob's Mr. Harrison will feel that women are such nuisances after all! It isn't an elaborate meal, but it's wholesome, and at any rate, our gas bill will be a little smaller because everything goes into the oven."

When Alice arrived, Bettina was putting the finishing touches on her table. "Alice, you look stunning!"

"And you look lovely, which is better! And the table is charming! Those red clover blossoms in that brown basket make a perfect center-piece! How did you think of it?"

"Mother Necessity reminded me, my dear! My next door neighbor has roses, but I covet some for my luncheon tomorrow, and did not like to ask for any today. So I had to use these red clover blooms from our own back yard. They are simple, like the dinner."

"Don't you envy me, Harrison?" asked Bob at the table. "This is my third day of real home cooking! You were unexpected company, too!"

The dinner consisted of:

Boubons with Tomato Sauce

Potatoes Anna   Baked Green Peppers Stuffed

Bread   Butter

Cottage Pudding   Lemon Sauce

Coffee

BETTINA'S RECIPES

(All measurements are level)

Boubons (Four portions)

1 C-cooked meat ground fine (one or more
  kinds may be used)
2 T-fresh bread crumbs
¼ t-pepper
½ C-milk
1 T-green pepper or pimento chopped fine
¼ t-celery salt
1 egg
½ t-salt
1 t-butter (melted)

Beat the egg, add milk, seasonings, melted butter, breadcrumbs and meat. Mix thoroughly. Fill buttered cups three-fourths full of mixture. Place in a pan of boiling water, and bake in a moderate oven fifteen minutes. The mixture is done as soon as it resists pressure in the center. Allow them to remain in the pans a few minutes, then remove carefully upon a serving plate. They may be made in a large mould or individual ones. Serve with the following sauce.

Tomato Sauce (Four portions)

1 C-tomatoes	½ t-sugar
1 slice onion	½ C-water
4 bay leaves	2 T-butter
4 cloves	2 T-flour
½ t-salt	

Simmer the tomatoes, onion, bay leaves, cloves, sugar and water for fifteen minutes, rub through the strainer. Melt butter, add flour and salt, add strained tomato juice and pulp. Cook until the desired consistency.

Potatoes Anna (Four portions)

1½ C-cooked diced potatoes	½ t-celery salt
2 hard-cooked eggs	¼ t-onion salt
1 C-thin white sauce	

Place alternate layers of diced cooked potatoes and sliced hard-cooked eggs in a baking dish. Season. Pour a thin white sauce over all of this. Place in a moderate oven fifteen minutes.

Stuffed Green Peppers (Four portions)

4 green peppers   4 C-boiling water

Remove the stems of the peppers and take out all the contents. Remove small slices from the blossom end so they will stand. Cover peppers with boiling water, allow to stand five minutes and drain. Fill with any desired mixture. Bake in a moderate oven twenty-five minutes, basting frequently with hot water.

Filling for Peppers (Four portions)

1 C-fresh bread crumbs	½ t-salt
1 t-chopped onion or ¼ T-onion salt	1 T-melted butter
1/3 C-chopped ham, or 1 T-salt pork	⅛ t-paprika
2 T-water	

Mix thoroughly and fill the pepper cases.

Baked Cottage Pudding (Four portions)

1 C-flour	1/3 C-sugar
1 2/3 t-baking powder	2 T-melted butter
¼ t-salt	½ C-milk
1 well-beaten egg	¼ t-vanilla or lemon extract

Mix dry ingredients, add egg and milk. Beat well and add melted butter and extract. Bake twenty-five minutes in a well buttered mould. Serve hot with the following sauce:

Lemon Sauce (Four portions)

½ C-sugar	1 t-butter
1½ T-flour	1 t-lemon extract or ½ t-lemon juice
1 C-hot water	½ t-salt

Mix sugar, flour and salt. Slowly add the hot water. Cook until thick, stirring constantly. Add flavoring and butter.

CHAPTER IV

BETTINA GIVES A LUNCHEON

"O YOU darling Bettina! Did you do it all yourself?"
Mary exclaimed impulsively, as the girls admired the
dainty first course which their hostess set before them.
"Everything is pink and white, like the wedding!"

"Yes," said Bettina, "and those maline bows on the basket
of roses actually attended my wedding. And after this is over,
you may see that maline again. I expect to press it out and
put it away for other pink luncheons in other Junes! Today,
since my guests were to be just my bridesmaids, I thought that
a pink luncheon would be the most appropriate kind."

"Isn't it fine to be in Bettina's own house? I can't realize
it!" said Ellen. "And the idea of daring to cook a whole
luncheon and serve it in courses all by herself! Why, Bettina,
how did you know what to have?"

"Well," said Bettina, "I went to the market and saw all the
inexpensive things that one can buy in June! (They had to
be inexpensive! Why, if I were to tell you just what this
luncheon cost, you'd laugh. But I want you to like it all before
I give that secret away.) And then in planning my menu, I
thought of pinky things that went together. That was all, you
see."

"But didn't it take hours and hours to prepare everything?"

"Why, no. I thought it all out first, and wrote it down, and
did most of it yesterday. I've found that five minutes of
planning is worth five hours of unplanned work. I haven't
hurried, and as Bob will have this same meal as his dinner
tonight, I didn't have to think of him except to plan for more.

21

You see, I estimated each portion as carefully as I could, for it isn't necessary to have a lot of left-over things.   Tonight I'll wear this same pink gown at dinner so that Bob will get every bit that he can of my first luncheon except the silly girls who flattered the cook."

"Bettina, there are so many things I'd like to ask you!" said Ruth, who was a little conscious of the shining ring on her left hand.   "Tell me, for instance, how you shaped these cunning timbales.   With your hands?"

"With a conical ice-cream mould.   It is so easy that way."

"And this salad!   Fred is so fond of salad, but I don't know a thing about making it."

"Well, I washed the lettuce thoroughly, and when it was very wet I put it on the ice in a cloth.   I poured boiling water over these tomatoes to make the skins peel off easily.   And, oh, yes, these cucumbers are crisp because I kept the slices in ice water for awhile before I served them.   Good salad is always very cold; the ingredients ought to be chilled before they are mixed."

"These dear little cakes, Bettina!   How could you make them in such cunning shapes?"

"With a fancy cutter.   And I dipped it in warm water each time before I used it, so that it would cut evenly.   I'd love to show you girls all that I know about cooking.   Do learn it now while you're at home; it will save much labor and even tears! Why, Bob said——"

"I knew that was coming!" laughed Alice.   "Girls, in self-defense, let's keep the conversation strictly on Betty's menu, and away from Betty's husband!"

And so they discussed:

Strawberries au Naturel

Kornlet Soup   Whipped Cream

Croutons

Salmon Timbales with Egg Sauce

Buttered Beets   Potato Croquettes

Pinwheel Biscuit   Butter Balls

Vegetable Salad   Salad Dressing

Wafers

Fancy Cakes   Coffee

BETTINA'S RECIPES

(All measurements are level)

Strawberries au Naturel (Ten portions)

2 quarts strawberries   1 C-powdered sugar

Pick over selected berries, place in a colander and wash, draining carefully. Press powdered sugar into cordial glasses to shape into a small mould. Remove from glasses onto centers of paper doilies placed on fruit plates. Attractively arrange ten berries around each mound. Berries should be kept cool and not hulled. Natural leaves may be used very effectively on the doily.

Croutons for the Soup (Ten portions)

4 slices bread   2 T-butter (melted)
½ t-salt

Cut stale bread in one-third inch cubes. Brown in the oven. Add melted butter and salt. Mix and reheat the croutons.

Salmon Timbales (Eight portions)

1 C-salmon flaked   2/3 C-milk
¼ C-bread crumbs   1 T-lemon juice
1 slightly beaten egg   ⅛ t-paprika
¼ t-salt

Mix ingredients in order named. Fill small buttered moulds or cups one-half full. Set in a pan of hot water, and bake twenty minutes in a moderate oven. Serve with following sauce:

Egg Sauce (Eight portions)

3 T-butter   ½ t-salt
3 T-flour   ¼ t-pepper
1½ C-milk   1 egg yolk

Melt the butter, stir flour in well, and slowly add the milk. Let it boil about two minutes, stirring constantly. Season, add yolk of egg, and mix well. (The oil from the salmon may be substituted for melted butter as far as it will go.)

White Cakes (Sixteen cakes)

1/3 C-butter   3 t-baking powder
1 C-sugar   ½ t-lemon extract
2/3 C-milk   ½ t-vanilla
2 C-sifted flour   3 egg whites

Cream butter, add sugar, and continue creaming. Alternately add the dry ingredients mixed and sifted. Add the milk. Beat well, add flavoring. Fold in the stiffly beaten whites. Spread evenly, two-thirds of an inch thick, on waxed paper, placed in a pan. Bake twenty minutes in moderate oven. Remove from oven, allow cake to remain in pan five minutes. Carefully remove and cool. Cut with fancy cutters.

White Mountain Cream Icing for Cakes

1 C-granulated sugar ¼ C-water
⅛ t-cream tartar 1 egg white
½ t-vanilla

Boil the sugar, water and cream of tartar together without stirring. Remove from fire as soon as the syrup hairs when dropped from a spoon. Pour very slowly onto the stiffly beaten egg whites. Beat vigorously with sweeping strokes until cool. If icing gets too hard to spread, add a little warm water and keep beating. Add extract and spread on cakes. Decorate with tiny pink candies.

CHAPTER V

BOB HELPS TO GET DINNER

"**G**UESS who!" said a voice behind Bettina, as two hands blinded her eyes.

"Why, Bob, dear! Good for you! How did you get home so early?"

"I caught a ride with Dixon in his new car. And I thought you might need me to help get dinner; it's nice to be needed! But here I've been picturing you toiling over a hot stove, and, instead, I find you on the porch with a magazine, as cool as a cucumber!"

"The day of toiling over a hot stove in summer is over. At least for anyone with sense! But I'm glad you did come home early, and you *can* help with dinner. Will you make the French dressing for the salad? See, I'll measure it out, and you can stir it this way with a fork until it's well mixed and a little thick."

"I know a much better way than that. Just watch your Uncle Bob; see? I'll put it in this little Mason jar and shake it. It's a lot easier and—there you are! We'll use what we need tonight, put the jar away in the ice-box, and the next time we can give it another good shaking before we use it."

"Why, Bob, what an ingenious boy you are! I never would have thought of that!"

"You married a man with brains, Betty dear! What is there besides the salad?"

"Halibut steak. It's Friday, you know, and there is such good inexpensive fish on the market. A pound is plenty for us. The potatoes are ready for the white sauce, the beans are in the fireless cooker, and for dessert there is fresh pine-apple sliced. The pineapple is all ready. Will you get it, dear? In the ice-box in a covered jar."

"Why didn't you slice it into the serving dish?"

"Because it had to be covered tight. Pineapple has a pene-trating odor, and milk and butter absorb it in no time."

"What else shall I do, Madam Bettina?"

"Well, you may fix the lemon for the fish. No, not sliced; a slice is too hard to handle. Just cut it in halves and then once the other way, in quarters; see? You may also cut up a little of that parsley for the creamed new potatoes. That reminds me that I am going to have parsley growing in a kitchen window box some day. Now you can take the beans out of the cooker, and I'll put butter sauce on them. No, it isn't really a sauce,—just melted butter with salt and pepper. There, Bobby dear! Dinner is served, and you helped! How do you like the coreopsis on the table?"

"You always manage to have flowers of some kind, don't you, Betty? I'm growing so accustomed to that little habit of yours that I suppose I wouldn't have any appetite if I had to eat on an ordinary undecorated table!"

"Don't you make fun of me, old fellow! You'd have an appetite no matter when, how or what you had to eat! But things are good tonight, aren't they?"

Bob had helped to prepare:

Halibut Steak	New Potatoes in Cream
String Beans	Butter Sauce
Bread	Butter
Tomato, Cucumber and Pimento Salad	French Dressing
Sliced Fresh Pineapple	

BETTINA'S RECIPES

(All measurements are level)

Halibut Steak (Two portions)

2/3 lb. Halibut Steak	½ t-salt
3 T-flour	¼ t-paprika

Wash one pound of Halibut steak and wipe **dry**. Cut **in** two pieces. Roll in flour, and cook ten minutes in a frying pan in hot fat. Brown on one side, and then on the other. Season with salt and paprika. Serve very hot.

String Beans with Butter Sauce (Two portions)

1½ C-string beans 1 T-butter
2 C-water 1 t-salt
¼ t-paprika

Remove ends and strings from green beans. Add water and cook over a moderate fire for twenty-five minutes. Drain off the water, add butter, salt and paprika. Reheat and serve.

Tomato, Cucumber and Pimento Salad (Two portions)

1 tomato sliced 1 t-salt
½ C-sliced cucumbers ¼ t-paprika
1 T-pimento cut fine 2 pieces lettuce

Arrange lettuce on serving dishes. Place portions of tomato, cucumber and pimento on the lettuce. Sprinkle with salt and paprika. Serve with French dressing.

French Dressing (Two portions)

4 T-olive oil ½ t-salt
2 T-vinegar ¼ t-paprika

Mix ingredients, which have been thoroughly chilled, and beat until the mixture thickens. Pour over the vegetables.

Pineapple Sliced (Two portions)

1 pineapple ½ C-sugar

Remove the skin and eyes from the pineapple. Cut crosswise in half-inch slices, and the slices in cubes, at the same time discarding the core. Sprinkle with sugar and stand in a cold place for an hour before serving.

CHAPTER VI

COUSIN MATILDA CALLS

"HELLO, is this you, Bettina? This is Mother! I'll have to speak in a low voice. Who do you think is here? No,—Cousin Matilda! Just between trains, but she says she must see how you are 'situated'! Clementine has such a wonderful establishment now, you know! No, of course not, but I want her to see how happy you are. She seems to have the idea that an 'establishment' is necessary! Just to see the house, you know! I know the porch isn't ready, but don't worry! About three, then. Good-by!"

That afternoon Bettina looked anxiously through the living room window across the bare little front yard. If only critical Cousin Matilda had waited a few months before coming! But then, the only thing to do was to be as cheerful about it as possible——

"So this is little Bettina!" said a majestic voice at the door. "And how is love in a cottage? How charmingly simple everything is!"

"They planned it all just as they wanted it," explained Bettina's mother proudly. "On a small scale, of course, but perhaps some day——"

"But I couldn't ever be happier than I am right now, Cousin Matilda. What do you think of our big living room? Browns and tans seemed best and safest in a little house like this, and I knew I shouldn't tire of them as of any other color! I do so dislike going into a bungalow with one little room in blue, another in pink, and so on. The walls are all alike, even in

28

the bedrooms. And the curtains are just simple cotton voiles, ecru in the living and dining rooms, and white in the bedrooms. No side curtains to catch the dust and keep out the air. But I beg your pardon for seeming too complacent; I love it all so that I just can't help boasting."

"What is this, my dear? A wedding gift?"

"Yes, isn't it lovely? It is a sampler in cross-stitch that Bob's great-great-grandmother made! His Aunt Margaret had it put under the glass cover of this tea cart, and gave it to us for a wedding present. See, the cart is brown willow, and I think it looks well with our furniture, don't you? This is to be a living porch, but we haven't furnished it yet except for this green matting rug. And Bob brought that hanging basket home from the florist's the other day. . . . Oh, yes, this is my Japanese garden! Bob laughs at me, I have so much fun watching it."

"What a lovely table decoration those red cherries make in your dining room, my dear! Like a picture, in that piece of dull green pottery!"

"Yes, Bob says I decorate the table differently for every meal! We use this breakfast alcove for breakfast, Sunday evening tea, or any informal meal when we are alone. You see how convenient it is! I do want to put a round serving table with leaves on our living porch. Then we can eat there on warm evenings in summer."

"Bettina is very accomplished in economy," said her mother. "You must let her tell you some of her methods."

"Clementine would be interested, I'm sure," said Cousin Matilda in her languid way. "Is this your guest room?"

"Yes, and Bob and I are proud of that. We white enameled the furniture ourselves! It is some that we found in a second-hand store, and it was certainly a bargain, though it didn't look it at the time. I sewed the rags together for these blue and white rugs. Bob made that little open desk out of a small table that we found somewhere. Now that it is white, too, I think it is cunning. And, Cousin Matilda, I give you three guesses as to the place in which I keep my sewing machine!"

"Why, I haven't seen it yet. In the kitchen?"

"Goodness, no! Well, I'll tell you! This looks like a dressing table, but is merely a shelf with a mirror above it. The shelf has a cretonne cover and 'petticoat' that reaches the floor. And underneath it—behold the sewing machine! Bob made the shelf high enough and wide enough to let the sewing machine slip under it! But, Cousin Matilda, you must be tired of Bettina's economies! Please sit down with mother in the living room and I will get the 'party.' "

And Bettina wheeled her tea cart into the kitchen, returning with luncheon napkins, plates, glasses, a pitcher of iced fruit juice, a plate of little chocolate cakes, and several sprays of wild roses.

"What delicious little cakes, Bettina! At least you can't be called economical when you serve such rich and dainty food as this!"

"I must plead guilty still, Cousin Matilda. I made these little cakes partly from dry bread crumbs. The fruit juice is mostly from the pineapple which Bob had for dessert last night. I cooked the core with about two cups of water and added it to the lemonade."

"Bettina, Bettina! How did you learn these things? Robert is certainly a lucky man, and I'm sure that some day he will be a wealthy one! You must give me the recipes you used!"

And Bettina wrote them down as follows:

BETTINA'S RECIPES

(All measurements are level)

Little Chocolate Cakes (Twelve cakes)

2 eggs	1 C-dry bread crumbs
¼ C-butter	3 T-flour
½ C-sugar	1 t-vanilla
	3 squares chocolate

Cream the butter, add sugar, and cream the mixture. Add the beaten eggs and stir well. Add melted chocolate, bread crumbs, flour and flavoring. Spread the mixture very thinly on a buttered pan, and bake twenty minutes in a slow oven. Shape with a tiny biscuit cutter, and put together in pairs with mountain cream icing between and on top. (Icing recipe already given.)

Fruit Juice (Eight glasses)

1 C-sugar   2 C-water
1½ C-lemon juice

Boil sugar and water ten minutes without stirring, add lemon juice, and any other fruit juices. Cool and bottle. Keep on ice and dilute with ice water when desired for use. Serve mint leaves with the fruit juice.

JULY.

The market is full of delights in July:
    Fresh vegetables, berries, red cherries for pie!
Good housewives and telephones seldom agree,
    So market yourself! You can buy as you see!

CHAPTER VII

A NEW-FASHIONED SUNDAY DINNER

"YOU will go to church with us this morning, Bettina?" asked Bob's cousin Henry, known also as the Rev. Henry Clinkersmith, as he came into Bettina's immaculate kitchen one Sunday.

"Yes, indeed, I will go!" Bettina answered him. "Is it nearly ten o'clock? Oh, yes, nine forty-five. I'll go at once and get ready."

Cousin Henry had arrived late Saturday evening. He was filling the pulpit of a friend that Sunday morning.

Bettina finished arranging the low bowl of pansies which was to be her table decoration. "For the dinner table," she explained to Cousin Henry.

"And Bob," she said as they walked to church (Cousin Henry was ahead with an old friend), "I do believe he was worried about dinner. There wasn't a trace of any preparation to be seen! You know I made the cake and the salad dressing yesterday, and the lettuce was on the ice. The sherbet was on the porch (I bought it, you know), and the lamb and potatoes were in the cooker."

"Well, let him worry! How long will it take to get it ready after we get home?"

"About fifteen minutes. The table is set, but I'll have to warm the plates and take things up. Then there's the gravy to make, of course."

"All I can say is this," said Cousin Henry at dinner, as he passed his plate for a second helping, "since you've explained the mysteries of the fireless cooker, I realize how it would have helped those cold Sunday dinners of the past generation. The women could have obeyed the fourth commandment and given their families a good Sunday dinner, too!"

That day they had:

Leg of Lamb with Potatoes	Lamb Gravy
Head Lettuce	Thousand Island Dressing
Mint Sauce	
Bread	Butter
Pineapple Sherbet	Bettina's Loaf Cake
Coffee	

BETTINA'S RECIPES

(All measurements are level)

Roast Leg of Lamb with Potatoes (Ten portions)

A 4-lb. leg of lamb	¼ t-paprika
6 large potatoes	1 T-salt
2 T-lard	

Wash the lamb with a damp cloth. Wipe dry and sprinkle with two teaspoons of salt. Place the lard in a frying-pan. When hot, add the lamb, and brown well on all sides. Place the meat in the fireless utensil. Sprinkle the potatoes with salt and paprika. Arrange these about the leg of lamb. Place the disks, heated for baking, over and under the baking pan. Cook three hours in the fireless. Use the drippings for gravy.

Lamb Gravy (Four portions)

4 T-drippings	2 T-flour
2/3 C-water	½ t-salt

Place half of the drippings in a sauce-pan. Add the flour, and allow it to brown. Add slowly the water, salt and the rest of the drippings (two tablespoonsful). Boil one minute.

Mint Sauce (Four portions)

¼ C-mint leaves	4 T-vinegar
½ C-boiling water	⅛ t-paprika
2 T-sugar	¼ t-salt

Chop the mint leaves very fine. Add the boiling water and sugar. Cover closely and let stand one-half hour. Add the vinegar, pepper and salt.

Loaf Cake (Bettina's Nut Special) (Twelve pieces)

1/3 C-butter	3 t-baking powder
1 C-"C" sugar	¼ C-nut-meats, cut fine
1 egg	¼ t-salt
1½ C-flour	2/3 C-milk
½ t-cinnamon	1 t-vanilla
½ t-lemon extract	

Cream the butter, add the sugar and the egg. Mix well. Add the flour, baking powder, cinnamon, nut-meats, salt, milk, vanilla and lemon extract. Beat two minutes. Pour into a loaf-cake pan prepared with waxed paper. Bake thirty minutes in a moderate oven.

CHAPTER VIII

CELEBRATING THE FOURTH

"**N**OW, boys, run and play while Alice and I set the picnic table!" said Bettina to Bob and Mr. Harrison. "See if the fish are biting! Cultivate your patience as well as your appetites and we'll surprise you soon!"

"Bettina, let me help you unpack. Everything looks so dainty and interesting!" said Alice, as Bob and Mr. Harrison strolled off toward the river. "You ought to have allowed me to bring something, although I'll admit that I do enjoy being surprised. You were a dear to bring me with you!"

"I?" said Bettina. "Of course I'm glad to have you here—no one is better fun—but I wish you had heard something that Bob told me. He and Harry Harrison were planning to go fishing today, all by themselves, until Harry suggested that Bob might like to bring me along. And then he added as an afterthought, that as three is a crowd, Miss Alice might be induced to come too. (Why is it that 'Miss Alice' or 'Miss Kate' or 'Miss May' always sounds so like a confirmed bachelor?) Bob chuckled when he told me how careless and offhand Harry tried to be!"

"Betty, how pretty those pasteboard plates are with the flag-seals pasted on them!"

"I saw some ready-made Fourth of July plates, but it was more economical to make my own. And how do you like the red, white and blue paper napkins and lunch cloth? 'Lunch paper,' I ought to say, I suppose. Alice, you arrange the fruit in the center in this basket, with some napkins around it, and with these little flags sticking out of it in every direction. But first, my dear, please tell me why you changed the subject when I was speaking of Mr. Harrison?"

"Those devilled eggs wrapped in frilled tissue-paper look just like torpedoes."

"Alice, Alice, I learned something new about you today. Harry said that society girls got on his nerves, but that 'Miss Alice' seemed sensible enough!"

"Goodness, Betty, he has disagreed with every single thing I've said, so far! If he is being pleasant behind my back, I don't see why he should be so disapproving in his manner to me! But if he is really beginning to think me sensible, let us by all means encourage him! Hide my frivolous new hat in the lunch-basket, and give me something useful to be doing. Can't I appear to be mixing the salad? . . . Honestly, Betty, I do get tired of society as a single interest. But what else is there for me to do? Go into settlement work? I'd be a joke at that! Learn to design jewelry? Take singing lessons?"

"Try the good old profession of matrimony. Why are you so fickle, Alice, my dear?"

"I'm not; it's the men! Every sensible one I meet is—well, disagreeable to me!"

"Meaning Harry Harrison? He appears to be taking quite an interest, at least!"

"That is merely his reforming instinct coming to the surface. But—is everything ready now? We'll sing a few bars of the Star Spangled Banner, and I'm sure the men will come immediately!"

The lunch table was set with:

Lobster and Salmon Salad

Ham Sandwiches   Nut Bread Sandwiches

Pickles   Radishes

Potato Chips   Devilled Eggs

Moist Chocolate Cake

Bananas   Oranges

Torpedo Candies

Lemonade

BETTINA'S RECIPES

(All measurements are level)

Lobster and Salmon Salad (Four portions)

1 C-salmon	6 sweet pickles cut fine
½ C-lobster	3 hard-cooked eggs, sliced
1 C-diced cucumber or celery	1 t-salt
½ C-salad dressing	

Mix the ingredients in the order given. Use a silver fork for mixing. Garnish with lettuce leaves.

Ham Sandwiches (Four portions)

½ C-chopped ham	1 T-chopped olives
2 T-pickles	3 T-salad dressing
12 slices bread	

Mix ham, olives and pickles with salad dressing and spread on lettuce or nasturtium leaves between buttered slices of bread. Trim off the crusts, and cut the sandwiches in fancy shapes.

Devilled Eggs (Six eggs)

6 hard-cooked eggs	1 t-melted butter
1 t-vinegar	¼ t-chopped parsley
¼ t-mustard	¼ t-salt

Shell the eggs, cut lengthwise in half, remove yolks, mash them and add vinegar, mustard, melted butter, parsley and salt. Refill the whites and put pairs together. Wrap in tissue paper with frilled edges to represent torpedoes.

Moist Chocolate Cake (Ten portions)

1/3 C-butter	1 C-flour
1 C-sugar	1¾ t-baking powder
2 eggs	½ t-cinnamon
½ C-hot mashed potatoes	¼ t-clove
1 ounce melted chocolate	½ t-nutmeg
¼ C-milk	1 t-vanilla

Cream the butter, add the sugar. Mix well. Add the egg yolks, slightly beaten, and the potato. Stir, add the chocolate, milk and then all the dry ingredients which have been mixed and sifted together. Fold in the white of the eggs beaten stiffly. Add the vanilla. Pour into two layer-cake pans which have been prepared with waxed paper. Bake in a moderate oven for thirty minutes. Ice with white mountain cream icing.

CHAPTER IX

UNCLE JOHN AND AUNT LUCY MAKE A VISIT

UNCLE JOHN and Aunt Lucy had driven Bob and Bettina home from a Sunday spent in the country.

"Do come in," begged Bettina, "and have a little lunch with us. After such a bountiful dinner, we really ought not to be hungry, but I confess that the lovely drive home has given me an appetite. And you've never been here for a meal! Don't be frightened, Uncle John, I really thought of this yesterday, and my cupboard isn't entirely bare. It would be so much fun to show you our things and the house!"

"I'm not afraid I won't be fed well," said Uncle John, "but those clouds are black in the east. If it should rain we'd have trouble getting home. Besides, I don't like to have the car standing out in a storm."

"I don't believe it'll rain, John," said comfortable Aunt Lucy. "And if it does, well, we'll manage somehow. I, for one, would like to see Bettina's kitchen—and all the rest of her house," she added.

Bettina arranged the dainty little meal on the porch table, and Aunt Lucy and Uncle John sat down with good appetites.

"This looks almost too pretty to eat," said he as he looked at his plate with its slice of jellied beef on head lettuce, served with salad dressing, and its fresh crisp potato chips. And the nasturtium and green leaf lay beside them.

"Have a radish and a sandwich, Uncle John," said Bettina. "We have plenty, if not variety. Our only dessert is fresh pears."

"But it all tastes mighty good!" said Uncle John. "Say, Bob, it is beginning to rain, I believe!"

39

"Sure enough, a regular storm! We must put the car in the empty garage across the street. I'm sure we can get permission." And he and Uncle John hurried out.

"It will blow over, I'm sure," said Aunt Lucy.

"But if it doesn't—why, Aunt Lucy, stay here all night! We'd love to have you! The guest room is always ready. I know you'll be comfortable, and they can manage without you at home for once, I'm sure."

"Of course they'll be all right, and it would be quite exciting to be 'company' for a change. If only Uncle John thinks he can do it!"

"It looks as if there'll be nothing else to do," said Uncle John, when he and Bob returned. "Not but what I'd enjoy it—but I haven't been away from home a night for—how long is it, Lucy?"

"Seven years last May, John. All the more reason why this'll do you good."

"Oh, I'm so glad you'll really stay!" said Bettina. "Now tell me what you like for breakfast!"

"Anything you have except those new fashioned breakfast foods," Uncle John replied. "I might feed 'em to my stock, now, but not to a human being. But don't you worry about me, Betty! Because I don't worry about the breakfast proposition. Bob here is a pretty good advertisement of the kind of cooking you can do!"

The lunch that night consisted of:

Jellied Beef		Potato Chips
	Radishes	
	Peanut Butter Sandwiches	
Iced Tea		Fresh Pears

BETTINA'S RECIPES

(All measurements are level)

Jellied Beef (Four portions)

1 C-cold chopped cooked beef	1 T-chopped parsley
½ T-chopped onion	1 T-lemon juice
1 T-chopped pimento	2 t-granulated gelatin
½ t-salt	1 T-cold water
¾ t-pepper	½ C-boiling water

Soak the gelatin in one tablespoon cold water for three minutes. Add the boiling water and dissolve thoroughly. Add the meat, onion, pimento, salt, pepper, lemon juice and parsley. Stir well together and turn into a mould that has been moistened with cold water. (A square or rectangular mould is preferable.) Stand in a cold place for two hours. When cold and firm, unmould on lettuce leaves and cut into slices. Salad dressing may be served with it.

Radishes (Four portions)

12 radishes	1 C-chopped ice

Wash the radishes thoroughly with a vegetable brush. Cut off the long roots and all but one inch of green tops. These tops make the radishes easier to handle and more attractive. Serve in a bowl of chopped ice.

Peanut Butter Sandwiches (Twelve sandwiches)

4 T-peanut butter	1 T-salad dressing
⅛ t-salt	12 slices of bread
1 t-butter	12 uniform pieces of lettuce

Cream the peanut butter, add the butter. Cream again, add the salt and salad dressing, mixing well. Cut the bread evenly. Butter one side of the bread very thinly with the peanut butter mixture. Place the lettuce leaf on one slice and place another slice upon it, buttered side down. Press firmly and neatly together. Cut in two crosswise. Arrange attractively in a wicker basket.

CHAPTER X

RUTH INSPECTS BETTINA'S KITCHEN

"MAY I come in?" said a voice at the screen door. "I came the kitchen way because I hoped that you would still be busy with the morning's work, and I might learn something. You see" (and Ruth blushed a little), "we are thinking of building a house and we have lots of ideas about every room but the kitchen. Neither Fred nor I know the first thing about that, so I told him that I would just have to consult you."

"How dear of you, Ruth!" said Bettina, as she put away the breakfast dishes. "Well, you shall have the benefit of everything that I know. Bob and I began with the kitchen when we planned this little house. It seemed so important. I expected to spend a great deal of time here, and I was determined to have it cheerful and convenient. I never could see why a kitchen should not be a perfectly beautiful room, as beautiful as any in the whole house!"

"Yours is, Bettina," said Ruth, warmly, as she looked around her. "No wonder you can cook such fascinating little meals. It is light, and sunny and clean looking—oh, immaculate!—and has such a pleasant view!"

"I wanted it to have lots of sunshine. We had the walls painted this shade of yellow, because it seemed pretty and cheerful. Perhaps you won't care to have white woodwork like this, but you see it is plain and I don't find it hard to keep clean out here on the edge of town! I think it is so pretty that I don't expect to regret my choice. Another thing, Ruth, do get a good grade of inlaid linoleum like this. I know the initial expense is greater, but a good piece will last a long time, and will always look well."

"How high the sink is, Bettina!"

"Thirty-six inches. You see, I'm not very tall and yet I have always found that every other sink I tried was too low for solid comfort. The plumbers have a way of making them all alike—thirty-two inches from the floor, I think. They were scandalized because I asked them to change the regulation height, and yet, I find this exactly right. And isn't it a lovely white enameled one? I am happy whenever I look at it! Don't laugh, Ruth; a sink is a very important piece of furniture! I had always liked this kind with the grooved drainboard on each side, sloping just a little toward the center. And see how easily I can reach up and put away the dishes in the cupboard, you see. I don't like a single dish or utensil in sight when the kitchen is in order. This roll of paper toweling here by the sink is very convenient for wiping off the table or taking grease off pans and dishes or even for drying glass and silver. A roll lasts a long time, and certainly does save dishcloths and towels.

"Do you use your fireless cooker often?"

"Every day of the year—I do believe. I cook breakfast food in it, and all kinds of meats except those that are boiled or fried. Then it is splendid for steaming brown bread and baking beans, and oh, so many other things! Mother keeps hers under the kitchen table, but I find it more convenient here at the right of the stove—on a box just level with the stove. Next, O Neophyte, you may observe the stove. The oven is at the side, high up so that one need not stoop to use it. It has a glass oven door through which I can watch my baking."

"I like this white enameled table. And the high stool must be convenient, too."

"It is splendid. Ruth, haven't you an old marble topped table at home? It would be just the thing for pastry making."

"Yes, I do know of one, I think, and I'll have the lower part enameled white."

"Fred can do it himself. Let him help to fix things up, and he'll be all the more interested in them, and in helping you use them."

"Bettina, this is an adorable breakfast alcove! What fun

you must have every morning! If we have one, I don't believe we'll ever use the dining room. How convenient! Here come the waffles—hot from the stove! Fred, do have a hot muffin!"

"Not at the same meal, Ruth!"

"No, he'll be fortunate if he gets anything to eat at all! He isn't marrying a Bettina. But he says he's satisfied. Bettina, does Bob help get breakfast?"

"Indeed he does. He loves to make coffee in the electric percolator and toast on the toaster. He says that an electric toaster and plenty of bath towels are the real necessities of life, but I say I cannot live without flowers and a fireplace. Oh, you will have such fun, Ruth! Let Fred help you all he will."

"I'm hearing all this advice!" suddenly shouted a big voice in her ear. "Look here, Mrs. Bettina, does Bob know that you are advising your friends to train their husbands just as you are training him?"

"Fred, you old eavesdropper! I hope that Ruth makes you get breakfast every single morning to pay for this! Aren't you ashamed? Don't you know that listeners never hear any good of themselves?"

"I suppose Fred knew he needn't worry," said rosy Ruth, as she took his arm. "Look, Fred, isn't it a dear little house? May he see it all, Bettina?"

"Yes, if he'll explain how a busy man can get away at this hour of the morning."

"Well, you see I was on my way to the office when I caught a glimpse of Ruth's pink dress at your back door. I happened to think that she said she didn't get a recipe for those "skyrocket rolls" that you had at your party the other day. I just thought I'd have to remind her, for the sake of my future."

"What under the shining sun! Oh, pinwheel biscuits!"

"Yes,—that's it!"

"Why—all right. I have it filed away in my card-index. Here—with a picture of them pasted on the card. I cut it out of the magazine that gave the recipe. They are delicious."

BETTINA'S RECIPES

(All measurements are level)

Pinwheel Biscuits (Fifteen biscuits)

2 C-flour	¾ C-milk
4 t-baking powder	1/3 C-stoned raisins
3 T-lard	2 T-sugar
½ t-salt	2 T-melted butter
½ t-cinnamon	

Sift together the flour, baking powder, and salt, work in the lard with a knife, add gradually the milk, mixing with the knife to a soft dough. Toss on a floured board, roll one inch thick, spread with butter, and sprinkle with the sugar and cinnamon, which have been well mixed. Press in the raisins. Roll up the mixture evenly as you would a jelly roll. Cut off slices, an inch thick—flatten a little and place in a tin pan. Bake in a hot oven for fifteen minutes. (These are similar to the cinnamon rolls made from yeast sponge.)

CHAPTER XI

BETTINA'S BIRTHDAY GIFT

"YOUR set, Bob," said Bettina, as she gathered up the tennis balls. "But please say you think I'm improving! Oh, there'll come a time when I'll make you a stiff opponent, but I'll have to work up my service first! It's time to go home to breakfast now, but hasn't it been fun?"

"Fine, Betty! We'll do it again! I don't object at all to getting up early when I'm once up! And we ought to get out and play tennis before breakfast every day."

"I knew you'd like it when you'd tried it once. But it took my birthday to make you willing to celebrate this way."

"Just you wait till you see what I have for you at home! I made it all myself, with a little help from Ruth!"

"Oh, Bob, is that what you've been doing all these evenings? I'm so anxious to see it! I've begrudged the time you've spent all alone hammering and sawing away down in the basement, but I didn't let myself even wonder what it was you were making, since you had asked me not to look."

"Well, while you're beginning the breakfast, I'll be bringing your birthday gift upstairs. Then I can help you."

In a short time, when Bettina was arranging the cheerful hollyhocks on the table, she heard a low whistle behind her. There stood Bob—looking like a sandwich-man, with a brightly flowered cretonne screen draped about him.

"Well, how do you like it?"

"Oh, Bob, it's the sewing-screen I've been wanting, and it just matches the cretonne bedroom hangings! Here are the little pockets for mending and darning materials—and the

46

larger ones for the unfinished work! How beautifully it is made—and won't it be convenient! It will be useful as a screen, and also as a place for those sewing things, for I have no good place at all in which to keep them!˙ It will be decorative, too! And how light it is! I can carry it so easily, and work beside it on the porch or in the living room!"

"Glad you like it! Ruth designed it, and made the pockets. I did the carpenter work."

"Bob, it's a lovely birthday gift, and I appreciate it all the more because you made it yourself. How pretty it is with all the woodwork enameled white!"

"I wanted it to match the bedroom things. Well, is that coffee done yet? Tennis certanly does give me an appetite!"

Breakfast consisted of:

Iced Cantelope

Poached Eggs on Toast

Toast   Apple Sauce

Coffee

BETTINA'S RECIPES

(All measurements are level)

Poached Eggs (Two portions)

2 eggs   1 t-salt
1 t-butter   1 pt. water, boiling

Butter the bottom of a saucepan or frying-pan. Fill half full of boiling water. Break the eggs one at a time in a sauce dish, and slip them very gently into the pan of boiling water. The eggs will lower the temperature of the water to a point below the boiling point. Keep the water at this point (below boiling). Allow the eggs to remain in the water four to six minutes, or until the desired consistency. Remove from the water with a skimmer and serve on slices of toast which are hot, buttered, and slightly moistened with water. The proper length of time for poaching eggs is until a white film has formed over the yolks and the white is firm. A tin or aluminum egg poacher is very convenient. When using rings, butter the rings, fill each compartment with an egg, and dip into the boiling water. These are inexpensive, and economical, as no part of the egg is wasted.

Toast (Four Pieces)

4 slices bread   2 T-butter

Toast slices of bread one-half an inch thick on the broiler directly under the flame, or on a toaster fitted for a burner on top of the stove. Brown on one side, then turn and brown on the other. When both sides are an even golden brown, butter one side, care being taken to butter the edges. Set the toast on an enamel plate or tin pie-pan in the oven, until all the pieces are ready for serving. Always serve toast very hot.

Apple Sauce (Two portions)

4 apples   4 T-sugar
1/3 C-water   ½ t-cinnamon

Wash, peel and core the apples. Add water and cook slowly in a covered utensil until tender. Remove cover, add the sugar and cook two minutes. Sprinkle cinnamon on the top.

CHAPTER XII

BETTINA'S FATHER TRIES HER COOKING

"SO she is about to try her cooking on me, is she?" said Bettina's father to Bob, as he sat down at the table. "Well, I'll admit that I have looked forward to this all day. But there was a time when I was a little more skeptical of Bettina's culinary skill. You know, when mother was in California two years ago last winter——"

"Now, Charlie, you know that all girls have to learn at some time or other," interrupted Bettina's mother. "And I believe that Bob has fared pretty well, considering that Bettina is just beginning to keep house——"

"I should say so!" said Bob, heartily. "Why, I'm getting fat! I was weighed to-day, and——"

"Don't say any more, Bob! We'll rent the house and take to boarding! If you get fat——"

"No boarding-houses for mine! Not after your cooking, Bettina! I had enough of boarding before I was married. Say—how long ago that does seem."

"Has the time dragged as much as that? Well, I'll change the subject. Dad, how do you like my Japanese garden? I think it's pretty, don't you?"

"I certainly do, my dear. What are those feathery things?"

"Why, don't you know that, Father? And when you were a boy, you worked on a farm one summer, too! There's a parsnip and a horse radish, and a beet. Then there are a few parsley seeds and grass seeds on a tiny sponge! And see the little shells and stones that Bob and I collected for it."

"Yes, we found that pink stone up the river on a picnic a

49

year ago last May, before we were engaged, or were we engaged then, Bettina? And the purple one——"

"Oh, you needn't reminisce," Bettina interrupted hastily. "Eat your dinner."

> *"Every little stone*
> *Has a meaning all its own,*
> *Every little shell——*
> *But it wouldn't do to tell."*

"I composed that poem just this minute," said Bob, undisturbed.

"Will you help me get the dessert now, Robert? Are you ready, Mother? And Father?"

"Yes, indeed. A very fine dinner, Bettina. We never have steak fixed this way at home; do we, Mother? Can we try it some day soon?"

"I have something for dessert that you like, Dad. Guess what!"

"What is it? Oh, lemon pie! That is fine, I can tell you! But I know already that it won't be as good as your mother's! Still, we'll try it and see!"

That evening for dinner, Bettina served:

Devilled Steak   New Potatoes in Cream
Baking-powder Biscuits   Jelly
Cucumber and Radish Salad
Lemon Pie
Coffee

BETTINA'S RECIPES

(All measurements are level)

Devilled Steak (Four portions)

2 T-butter	½ t-pepper
1 T-onion	⅛ t-paprika
1½ lb. flank steak ¾ inch thick	1 t-mustard
2 T-flour	1 T-vinegar
1 t-salt	1 T-flour
	2 C-water

Melt the butter in a frying-pan, slice the onion in it and sautè gently until golden brown in color. Remove the onion from the butter, cut the flank steak into pieces three by two inches. Dredge these lightly in one tablespoon flour and sautè in the butter until well browned. Remove the meat from the drying-pan; add the salt, pepper, paprika, mustard, vinegar and flour. Mix all together and add the water slowly. Replace the steak in the pan, cover closely and simmer one hour, or until the steak is tender. Serve on a warm platter and pour the gravy over it.

Baking Powder Biscuit (Fifteen biscuits)

2 C-flour	¼ t-salt
4 t-baking powder	3 T-lard
2/3 C-milk	

Mix and sift the flour, baking powder and salt; cut in the lard with a knife until the consistency of cornmeal. Add the milk, mixing with a knife. Pat into a rectangular shape, one-half inch thick, on a floured board. Cut with a biscuit cutter one and one-half inches in diameter. Place side by side in a tin pan. Bake in a moderate oven fifteen minutes.

Cucumber and Radish Salad (Four portions)

1 C-diced cucumbers	1 t-salt
½ C-diced radishes	¼ t-pepper
2 t-chopped onion	4 T-salad dressing
4 lettuce leaves	

Mix the cucumbers, radishes, onions, salt and pepper. Add salad dressing. Serve on lettuce leaves.

Lemon Pie

Filling	2 eggs (yolks)
1 C-sugar	1½ C-water
½ t-salt	1 t-grated rind
juice 1 large lemon	½ C-flour
1 t-butter	

Beat the egg yolks, add the sugar gradually and beat; add the flour, salt, water, lemon juice and rind. Cook in a double boiler until it thickens. Pour into the pastry shell, cover with meringue and bake in a moderate oven until the meringue is brown.

Pie Crust

1 C-flour	⅛ t-salt
1/3 C-fat	2 T-cold water

Cut the fat into the flour and salt with a knife. Add the water gradually, lifting with a knife that portion that was moistened first and pushing it to one side of the bowl, wet another portion and continue until all is moistened, using just enough water to hold together. Put together and place on a floured board. Roll the crust to fit the pan. Press the crust firmly into the bottom of the pan. Prick the sides and bottom with a fork. Crinkle the edges of the crust; have the crust extend above the edge of the pan to make a deep shell for the filling. Bake the crust first to make it more crisp. Do not butter the pan. Bake from five to six minutes in a hot oven. When the crust is done, add the filling and cover this with the meringue.

Meringue

2 egg whites beaten stiff	5 T-sugar (powdered preferred)
	½ t-lemon extract

Do not beat the egg-whites until ready for use. Then beat until stiff and add the sugar, beating only a minute. Pile the meringue lightly on top of the filling, and bake the whole slowly. If baked too quickly, the meringue will rise and then fall. Bake only until it turns a golden brown.

CHAPTER XIII

BOB HELPS WITH THE DINNER

"HERE, Bettina, let me mash those potatoes! It's fine exercise after a day at the office!" And Bob seized the potato masher with the same vigor that he used to handle a tennis racquet.

"Good for you, Bob! They can't have a single lump in them after that! About the most unappetizing thing I can think of is lumpy mashed potato, or mashed potato that is heavy and unseasoned. More milk? You'd better use plenty. Here! Now watch me toss them lightly into this hot dish and put a little parsley and a lump of butter on the top. There, doesn't that look delicious?"

"I should say so! And look at the fancy tomatoes, each one with a cover! What on earth is inside?"

"Just wait till you taste them; they're a new invention of mine, and I do believe they'll make a splendid luncheon dish for the next time that Ruth is here, or Alice brings her sewing over. I'm practising on you first, you see, and if you survive and seem to like them, I may use them for a real company dish."

"You can't frighten me that way! Creamed chicken?"

"Creamed veal. Don't you remember what we had for dinner last night? There were two chops left and I made it of them. I know it is good when made of cold veal roast, but I had never tried it with cold veal chops—so again I am experimenting on you, Bobby!"

"You don't frighten me so easily as that! I've just caught a glimpse of something that looks like cocoanut cake, and I'll be happy now, no matter how the rest of the dinner tastes!"

"There, everything is on, Bob! Let's sit down to dinner, and you tell me all about your day!"

Dinner consisted of:

Creamed Veal   Mashed Potatoes
Stuffed Tomatoes Bettina
Bread   Butter
Sliced Peaches   Cream
Cocoanut Cake
Iced Tea

BETTINA'S RECIPES

(All measurements are level)

Creamed Veal (Two portions)

1 C-cooked veal chopped   ½ C-white sauce (medium)
3 rounds of toast

Mix the veal and sauce. Heat and serve hot on rounds of toast.

Mashed Potatoes (Two portions)

4 potatoes   ½ T-butter
2 C-water   ½ t-salt
1 t-salt   ¼ t-paprika
1 T-milk

Wash and peel medium-sized potatoes; cook in boiling water (salted) until tender. (About twenty minutes.) Drain and shake over the fire a minute or two until they are a little dry. Either mash with potato masher, or put through potato ricer. Add butter, salt, paprika and milk. Beat till very light, fluffy and white. Reheat by setting the saucepan in a larger kettle containing boiling water. Place over flame. More milk may be needed. Pile them lightly on the hot dish in which they are to be served.

Stuffed Tomatoes Bettina (Two portions)

2 firm, good-sized tomatoes
3 T-fresh bread crumbs
2 T-left-over cooked vegetables (peas, beans, celery or corn)
1 T-chopped cooked ham or cooked bacon
⅛ t-paprika
1 T-egg
1 t-melted butter
½ t-salt

Wash the tomatoes thoroughly and cut a slice one inch in diameter from the blossom end, reserving it for future use. Carefully scoop out the pulp, being careful to leave the shell firm. To the tomato pulp, add bread crumbs, left-over vegetables, chopped meat, egg, melted butter, salt and paprika. Cook the mixture four minutes over the fire. Fill the shells with the cooked mixture. Put the slices back on the tomatoes. Place in a small pan and bake twenty minutes in a hot oven.

CHAPTER XIV

A SUNDAY EVENING TEA

"WHAT kind of tea is this?" Ruth inquired one Sunday evening on the porch.

"Why, this is a mixture of green and black tea," said Bettina. "I like that better for iced tea than either kind alone."

"I like tea," said Fred, "although perhaps that isn't considered a manly sentiment in this country. I hope you do too, Ruth. Nothing seems so cozy to me as tea and toast. And I like iced tea like this in the summertime. An uncle of mine is very fond of tea, and has offered to send me some that he considers particularly fine. I believe that Orange Pekoe is his favorite."

"I think that has the best flavor of all," said Bettina, "though just now we are using an English breakfast tea that we like very much. And the green tea mixed with it for this is Japan tea."

"I've heard my uncle say that 'Pekoe' means 'white hair,' and is applied to young leaves because they are covered with a fine white down. Uncle also says that black teas are considered more wholesome than green because they contain less tannin. I tell you, he's a regular connoisseur."

"I see that I must become an expert tea-maker!" said Ruth. "I'm learning something new about Fred every day. Bettina, do tell me exactly how you make tea. Fred can listen, too, unless he already knows."

"Well, let's see, Ruth. I take a level teaspoonful of tea to a cup of water. I put the tea in a scalded earthenware tea-pot—that kind is better than metal—and pour boiling water over it

56

—fresh water. Then I cover it and allow it to steep from three to five minutes. Then I strain and serve it. You know tea should always be freshly made, and never warmed over. It shouldn't be boiled either, not a second. Boiling, or too long steeping, brings out the tannin."

"But how about iced-tea? That has to stand."

"It shouldn't steep, though. I make it just like any tea and strain it. Then I let it cool, and set it on the ice for three or four hours. I serve it with chipped ice, lemon and mint."

"Mother always added a cherry to her afternoon tea," said Ruth.

"That would be great," said Bob. "I don't care much for hot tea, but I believe I would be willing to drink a cup for the sake of the cherry."

"Ruth," said Bettina, "I know now what I will give you for an engagement present since Fred likes tea, too. A silver teaball. Surely that will symbolize comfort and fireside cheer."

"Speaking of firesides," asked Bob, "what material have you decided upon for your fireplace? It seems to me that we're talking too much about tea-making, and not enough about house-building."

That evening Bettina served:

Salmon Salad with Jellied Vegetables
Boston Brown Bread Sandwiches
Sliced Fresh Peaches
One Egg Cake   Chocolate Icing
Iced Tea

BETTINA'S RECIPES

(All measurements are level)

Salmon Salad with Jellied Vegetables (Four portions)

1 C-cooked mixed diced vegetables (string
   beans, carrots, peas or celery)
1 C-meat stock or water (hot)
2 t-granulated gelatin
1 t-salt
1 T-chopped pimento
3 T-cold water
1 t-lemon juice

Cooked vegetables may be combined for this salad. Soak the gelatin in cold water a few minutes, add the meat stock or water and stir until the gelatin is thoroughly dissolved. If it is not completely dissolved, heat over a pan of hot water. Add the vegetables in such proportions as desired or convenient. Add the salt, lemon juice and pimento; turn the mixture into a moistened mould. (A ring mould is attractive.) Allow to stand for one hour or more in a cold place. When ready to serve, remove from mould to a chilled plate. If a ringed mould is used, the center may be filled with flaked salmon over which salad dressing has been poured. If the vegetable part is used as a salad, salad dressing may be placed around the vegetables.

One Egg Cake (Ten portions)

4 T-butter	½ C-milk
½ C-sugar	1⅛ C-flour
1 egg	2½ t-baking powder
	1 t-vanilla

Cream the butter, add the sugar gradually, and the egg well beaten. Mix and sift the flour and baking powder and add alternately with the milk. Add the vanilla. Bake in a loaf-cake pan twenty-five minutes in a moderate oven.

Chocolate Icing for Cake

1 square of chocolate, melted	1½ powdered sugar
3 T-boiling water	½ t-vanilla

Melt the chocolate, add a little powdered sugar, then water and flavoring and sufficient sugar to allow the icing to spread on cake. Usually one and one-half cups is the necessary amount. Spread on the cake.

CHAPTER XV

A MOTOR PICNIC

"HELLO, Bettina; this is Bob. What are you having for dinner to-night?"

"It's all in the fireless cooker! Why?"

"Couldn't you manage to make a picnic supper of it? One of the men at the office has invited us to go motoring to-night with him and his wife, and, of course, I said we'd be delighted. They're boarding, poor things, and I asked if we couldn't bring the supper. He seemed glad to have me suggest it. I suppose he hasn't had any home cooking for months. Do you suppose you could manage the lunch? How about it?"

"Why, let me think! How soon must we start?"

"We'll be there in an hour or a little less. Don't bother about it—get anything you happen to have."

"It's fine to go, dear. Of course, I'll be ready. Good-bye!"

Bettina's brain was busy. There was a veal loaf baking in one compartment of the cooker, and on the other side, some Boston brown bread was steaming. Her potatoes were cooked already for creaming, and although old potatoes would have been better for the purpose, she might make a salad of them. As she hastily put on some eggs to hard-cook, she inspected her ice box. Yes, those cold green beans, left from last night's dinner, would be good in the salad. What else? "It needs something to give it character," she reflected. "A little canned pimento—and, yes—a few of the pickles in that jar."

Of course, she had salad dressing—she was never without it. Sandwiches? The brown bread would be too fresh and soft for sandwiches, but she could keep it hot, and take some butter along. "I'm glad it is cool to-day. We'll need hot coffee in the thermos bottle, and I can make it a warm supper—except for the salad."

She took the veal loaf and the steamed brown bread from the cooker, and put them into the oven to finish cooking.

"How lucky it is that I made those Spanish buns! And the bananas that were to have been sliced for dessert, I can just take along whole."

When Bettina heard the auto horn, and then Bob's voice, she was putting on her hat.

"Well, Betty, could you manage it?"

"Yes, indeed, dear. Everything is ready. The thermos bottle has coffee in it, piping hot; the lunch basket over there is packed with the warm things wrapped tight, and that pail with the burlap over it is a temporary ice box. It holds a piece of ice, and beside it is the cream for the coffee and the potato salad. It is cool to-day, but I thought it best to pack them that way."

"You are the best little housekeeper in this town," said Bob as he kissed her. "I don't believe anyone else could have managed a picnic supper on such short notice. Come on out and meet Mr. and Mrs. Dixon. May I tell them that they have a fine spread coming?"

"Don't you dare, sir. It's a very ordinary kind of a supper, and even you are apt to be disappointed."

But he wasn't.

Bettina's picnic supper that cool day consisted of:

Warm Veal Loaf	Cold Potato Salad
Fresh Brown Bread	Butter
Spanish Buns	Bananas
Hot Coffee	

BETTINA'S RECIPES

(All measurements are level)

Veal Loaf (Six to eight portions)

2 lbs lean veal	4 t-onion salt
½ lb. salt pork	1 T-salt
6 large crackers	½ t-pepper
2 T-lemon juice	4 T-cream

Put two crackers in the meat grinder, add bits of meat and pork and the rest of the crackers. The crackers first and last prevent the pork and meat from sticking to the grinder. Pack in a well-buttered bread-pan. Smooth evenly on top, brush with white of an egg and bake one hour in a moderate oven. Baste frequently. The meat may be cooked in a fireless cooker between two stones. It is perfectly satisfactory cooked this way, and requires no basting.

Boston Brown Bread (Six portions)

1 C-rye or graham flour	¾ C-molasses
1 C-cornmeal	¼ C-sugar
1 C-white flour	1½ C-sour milk or 1¼ C-sweet
1 t-salt	milk or water
1 t-soda	2/3 C-raisins

Mix and sift dry ingredients, add molasses and liquid. Fill well-buttered moulds two-thirds full, butter the top of mould, and steam three and one-half hours. Remove from moulds and place in an oven to dry ten minutes before serving. 1—If sweet milk is used, 1 T-vinegar to 1¼ C will sour the milk. 2—Baking powder cans, melon moulds, lard pails or any attractively shaped tin cans may be used as a mould. 3—Two methods of steaming are used: (a) Regular steamer in which the mould, either large or individual, is placed over a pan of boiling water. Buttered papers may be tied firmly over the tops of uncovered moulds. (b) Steaming in boiling water. The mould is placed on a small article in the bottom of a pan of boiling water. This enables the water to circulate around the mould. Care must be observed in keeping the kettle two-thirds full of boiling water all of the time of cooking. (Bettina used the method in the fireless cooker.) She started the brown bread in the cooker utensil on the top of the stove. When the water was boiling vigorously, she placed it over one hot stone in the cooker. The water came two-thirds of the distance to the top of her cans. In the cooker, she did not have to watch for fear the water would boil away. After fastening the lid tightly on the cooker-kettle in which the bread was to steam, she did not look at it again for four hours. (It takes a little longer in the cooker than on the stove.)

CHAPTER XVI

BETTINA HAS A CALLER

THE next morning Bettina was alone in her little kitchen when the door bell rang.

"Why, Mrs. Dixon; how do you do?" she said, as she opened the door and recognized the visitor. "Won't you come in?"

It must be admitted that Bettina was somewhat embarrassed at the unexpected call at so unconventional a time. Mrs. Dixon was dressed in a trim street costume, but under her veil Bettina could see that her eyes were red, and her lips quivered as she answered:

"Forgive me for coming so early, but I just had to. I know you'll think me silly to talk to you confidentially when I met you only yesterday, but I do want your advice about something. You mustn't stop what you are doing. Couldn't I come into the kitchen and talk while you work?"

"Why, my dear, of course you can," said Bettina, trying to put her at her ease. "You can't guess what I was doing! I was washing my pongee dress; someone told me of such a good way!"

"Why, could you do it all yourself?" said Mrs. Dixon, opening her eyes wide. "Why not send it to be dry-cleaned?"

"Of course I might," said Bettina, "but it would be expensive, and I do like to save a little money every month from my housekeeping allowance. There are always so many things I want to get. You see I'm doing this in luke-warm, soapy water—throwing the soap-suds up over the goods, then I'll rinse it well, and hang it in the shade to drip until it gets dry.

I won't press it till it is fully dry, because if I do, it will be spotted."

"How do you learn things like that?"

"Oh, since I've been married, and even before, when I thought about keeping house, I began to pick up all sorts of good ideas. I like economizing; it gives me an opportunity to use all the ingenuity I have."

"Does it? I always thought it would be awfully tiresome. You see, I've lived in a hotel all my life; my mother never was strong, and I was the only child. I liked it, and since 'I've been married, we've lived the same way. I never thought of anything else and I supposed Frank would like it, too—but lately—oh, all the last year—he's been begging me to let him find us a house. And then"—(Bettina saw that her eyes had filled with tears)—"he has been so different. You have no idea, my dear. Why—he hasn't been at home with me two evenings a week—and——"

"You must be dreadfully unhappy," interrupted Bettina, wondering what she could say, since she disliked particularly to listen to any account of domestic difficulties. "But why not try keeping house? Maybe that would be better. Why, Bob doesn't like to be away from home any evenings at all."

"But you've just been married!" said Mrs. Dixon, tactlessly. "Wait and see how he'll be after a few years!"

"Well, that's all the more reason for trying to make him like his home. Have you thought of taking a house?"

"That was just the reason I came to you. You seem to be so happy living this way—and it surprised me. I knew last evening what Frank was thinking when he saw this little house —and then when you unpacked the lunch—tell me honestly, did you cook it yourself?"

"Of course," said Bettina, smiling.

"Wasn't it hard to learn? Why, I can't cook a thing—I can't even make coffee! Frank says if he could only have one breakfast that was fit to eat——" and she buried her face in her handkerchief.

"Why, Mrs. Dixon!" cried Bettina, cheerfully, though her heart was beating furiously. "Your trouble is the easiest one in the world to remedy! Your husband is just hungry—that's all! I'll tell you—we'll make this a little secret between us, and have such fun over it! You do just as I tell you for one month and I'll guarantee that Frank will be at home every single minute that he can!"

"Do you suppose I can learn?"

"I'll show you every single thing. We'll slip out this very day and look for a little house—to surprise Frank! And I'll teach you to cook by easy stages!"

"Oh, will you?" smiled Mrs. Dixon, showing an adorable dimple in her round cheek. "You don't know how much better I feel already! When can we begin?"

"Right now—with coffee—real, sure 'nough coffee that will make Frank's eyes stick out! Have you a percolator?"

"No, but I can get one."

"It isn't necessary at all. I'll tell you how to do without it, and then using one will be perfectly·simple."

BETTINA'S RECIPES

(All measurements are level)

Coffee (Four cups)

7 T-coffee	½ T-egg white
3 T-cold water	4½ C-boiling water

Scald the coffee pot, add the coffee, cold water and egg-white. Mix thoroughly, add the boiling water. Boil two minutes. Allow to stand in the pot one minute. Serve.

Twin Mountain Muffins

2 C-flour	1 egg
4 t-baking powder	1 C-milk
¼ t-salt	1 T-melted butter
¼ C-sugar	

Mix and sift together the flour, baking powder, salt and sugar. Beat the egg, add the milk; add these liquid ingredients to the dry ones. Beat two minutes. Add the melted butter. Fill well buttered muffin pans one-half full. Bake in a moderate oven twenty minutes.

CHAPTER XVII

BOB GETS BREAKFAST ON SUNDAY

"NOW, Bettina, you sit here and direct me, but don't you you dare to move. I'm going to get breakfast myself."

"Fine for you, chef! Have it on the porch, will you? It's the most beautiful morning of the year, I do believe! But you must give me something to do. Let me set the table, will you?"

"Well, you can do that, but get me an apron first. Be sure you get one that'll be becoming!"

Bettina went to a deep drawer in the pantry, of which the breakfast alcove was a part, and selected a white bungalow apron with red dots.

"Here, put your arms through this! There, how 'chic' you look! Bob, do you realize that this is our first breakfast on the porch? I must get some of those feathery things growing out there; I want them for the table. We must celebrate!"

"If having flowers on the table is celebrating, you celebrate every day!"

"Of course, my dear! Our married life is just one long celebration. Haven't you discovered that yet?"

Bettina had thus far no flower garden, but she was never without flowers. The weeds and grasses in her backyard had a way of turning themselves into charming centerpieces, and then, too, red clover was always plentiful.

Bob moved the coffee percolator and the electric toaster to the porch and attached them while Bettina spread the luncheon cloth upon the small table. "Aren't you glad we thought to

65

plan it so that we might have the percolator and the toaster out here?" she said. "That was your idea, wasn't it?"

"Aren't you glad you married me?" said Bob enthusiastically. "I'll bet I'm the only man on this street who can frizzle dried beef and cream it! And make coffee!"

"Who taught you that, I'd like to know? Give some credit to your wife who forces you to do it! Here, Bridget! The grapefruit is in the ice box; did you see it? And the oatmeal in the cooker is waiting to be reheated. Set it in a kettle of water over the fire, so that it won't burn. There are rolls in the bread-box. Put them in the oven a minute to warm up. If they seem dry, dip them quickly in water before heating them. Now shall I be making some toast-rounds for the chipped beef?"

"Well, you might be doing that. I'm getting dizzy with all these orders, ma'am. You can hunt up the cream and the milk and the butter, too, if you will. Now for the beef! Say, but this is going to be a good breakfast! 'Befoh de wah' I used to sleep late on Sundays, but not any more for me! I like to cook!"

"There's someone at the door. I'll go; you're busier than I am."

There on the doorstep beside the Sunday paper stood a little four-year-old neighbor, her hands full of old-fashioned pinks.

"My mother sent these to you," she said.

"Oh, lovely, dear! Thank you! Won't you come in?"

"No'm! My daddy has to shine my shoes for Sunday school."

"Bob, aren't these pretty with the white feathery weeds? I do love flowers!"

"They don't look half so pretty as this 'ere frizzled beef does! Breakfast is all ready!"

Bettina sat down to an open-air breakfast of

	Grapefruit	
Oatmeal		Cream
Creamed Beef		Toast Rounds
Rolls		Butter
	Coffee	

After a jolly and leisurely meal, Bob announced that he was ready to wash the dishes.

"Ever since I've seen that nice white-lined dishpan of yours, I've wanted to try it. It's oval, and I never saw an oval one before."

"I like it because it fits into the sink so well, and fills all the space it can."

"See how efficient I am! I put on the water for the dishes when we sat down to eat! Now I'll have nice hot, soapy water, and lots of it, to rinse them!"

"But don't rinse the glasses, dear. See how I can polish glass and silver that has just come out of that clean soapy water! Look! Isn't that shiny and pretty? There, you can scald everything else!"

"There's the telephone! It's Mrs. Dixon! What on earth can she want? She asked for you!"

Bettina talked for a few moments in monosyllables and then returned to the dishes. "What did she have to say?" Bob asked.

"She asked me not to tell you, Bob. Nothing much. Perhaps you'll know some day."

Bob looked puzzled and slightly hurt. It was the first time that Bettina had kept anything from him and he could not help showing some displeasure.

Bettina saw this, and said: "Bob, I don't want to have any secret from you, and I'd like you to know that this is nothing that I wouldn't tell you gladly if I were the only one concerned. I promised, that's all. You'll smile when you know all about it."

And Bob was mollified.

BETTINA'S RECIPES

(All measurements are level)

Oatmeal (Four portions)

¾ C-rolled oats   2 C-hot water
½ t-salt

Put the hot water in the upper part of the double boiler.

When boiling, add salt and oats. Boil the mixture for three minutes. Cover and place the upper part in the lower part of the double boiler. Cook over a moderate fire for one hour. Stir occasionally.

Creamed Beef (Four portions)

¼ lb. diced beef thinly sliced	2 T-flour
2 T-butter	1 C-milk

Place the butter in a frying-pan, and when the pan is hot and the butter is melted, add the beef separated into small pieces. Allow it to frizzle. Add the flour, mix thoroughly with beef and butter, allowing the flour to brown a little. Add the milk slowly, cooking until thick and smooth. Pour over rounds of toast. Garnish with parsley.

CHAPTER XVIII

BETTINA GIVES A PORCH PARTY

"I 'M so glad that you girls have come, for I've been longing to show you the porch ever since Bob and I put on the finishing touches."

"O Bettina, it's lovely!" cried all the guests in a chorus. "But weren't you awfully extravagant?"

"Wait till I tell you. Perhaps I ought not to give myself away, but I am prouder of our little economies than of anything else; we've had such fun over them. This is some old wicker furniture that Mother had in her attic, all but this chair, that came from Aunt Nell's. Bob mended it very carefully, and then enameled it this dull green color. I have been busy with these cretonne hangings and cushions for a long time, and we have been coaxing along the flowers in our hanging baskets and our window boxes for days and days, so that they would make a good impression on our first porch guests. Bob made the flower boxes himself and enameled them to go with the furniture. This high wicker flower box was a wedding gift, and so was the wicker reading lamp. This matting rug is new, but I must admit that we bought nothing else except this drop-leaf table, which I have been wanting for a long time. You see it will make a good serving table, and then we expect to eat on it in warm weather."

"What are we to make today, Bettina? The invitation has made us all curious.

"'The porch is cool as cool can be,
So come on Thursday just at three,
To stay awhile and sew

69

On something useful, strong, and neat,
Which, with your help, will quite complete
Bettina's bungalow!' "

"What about the little sketches of knives and forks and spoons in the corners?"

"Bob did that. He wrote the verse, too, or I'm afraid I should have telephoned. Are we all here? Wait a minute."

And Bettina wheeled out her tea-cart, on which, among trailing nasturtiums, were mysterious packages wrapped in fringed green tissue paper.

"What is in them? Silver cases—cut and ready to be made! Oh, how cunning! Shall we label them, too? What is the card?

" 'I'll not incase your silver speech,
For that is quite beyond my reach!' "

"Did Bob do that, too? The impudence!" and Ruth threaded her needle in preparation.

"You see," said Bettina, "I hadn't found time to make cases for my silver, so I just decided to let you girls help me! The card tells what to label them, in outline stitch in these bright colors. I used to open ten cases at home before I found what I wanted, so I am insuring against that."

Talk and laughter shortened the afternoon, but at five o'clock Bettina wheeled out her tea-cart again. The dainty luncheon was decorated with nasturtiums. The girls laid aside their work while Bettina served:

Sunbonnet Baby Salad	Nut Bread Sandwiches
Iced Tea	Mint Wafers
Lemon Sherbet	Tea Cakes

BETTINA'S RECIPES

(All measurements are level)

Sunbonnet Baby Salad (Ten portions)

10 halves pears	10 thin slices pimento
20 cloves, whole	10 T-salad dressing
20 almonds	10 pieces lettuce

Arrange the halves of canned pears, round side up, on lettuce leavès, which curl closely about the pear and have the effect of a hood. Place cloves in the pear for eyes, blanched almonds for ears, and slip thin slices of canned pimento into cuts made for nose and mouth. The expression may be varied. Put salad dressing around the outside of the pear to represent hair and arrange a bow of red pimento under the chin of the sunbonnet baby. These salads are very effective and easy to make.

Nut Bread (Twenty-four sandwiches)

1½ C-graham flour	2 t-salt
2 C-white flour	1½ C-milk
4 t-baking powder	2/3 C-chopped nut ineats, dates
1 C-"C" sugar	or raisins

Sift together all the dry ingredients, add the nut meats and fruit. Add the milk. Stir well, and pour into two well-buttered loaf pans. Allow to stand and rise for twenty minutes. Bake three-fourths of an hour in a moderate oven. Use bread twenty-four hours old for the sandwiches. "C" sugar is light brown sugar and gives food a delicious flavor.

Lemon Sherbet (Ten portions)

4 C-water	¼ C-lemon juice
2 C-sugar	1 egg white

Boil sugar and water ten minutes. Cool, add lemon juice and strain. Freeze, and when nearly stiff, add beaten egg white and finish freezing.

Icing (White Mountain Cream)

2 C-sugar	2 egg whites
½ C-water	½ t-lemon extract

Boil the sugar and water without stirring until it threads when dropped from the spoon. Pour slowly into the whites' of the eggs beaten stiffly. Beat until it holds its shape. Add the flavoring and spread on the cake.

Bettina's Suggestions

Arrange the sunbonnet babies on a salad platter, and let the guests help themselves. The salad is light and attractive. The stem end of the pear represents the neck. Cream the butter to be used for sandwiches. It spreads more evenly and goes farther. Sandwiches taste better if allowed to stand for several hours, wrapped securely in a napkin which has been well dampened (not wet). Cut the slices very thin and press together firmly. Cut into fancy shapes.

CHAPTER XIX

BETTINA AND THE EXPENSE BUDGET

"RUTH asked me today how we manage our finances," said Bettina over the dinner table. "She said that she and Fred were wondering what plan was best. I'm so glad I have a definite household allowance and that we have bulgeted our expenses so successfully. The other day I was reading an article by Carolyn Claymore in which she says that three-fourths of the domestic troubles are caused by disagreements about money."

"Then we haven't much to quarrel about, have we, Betty? That is true in more than one sense. But I'm sure that this way seems to suit us to a T."

"I'm even saving money, Bob."

"I don't see how you can when you give me such good things to eat, and when we have so much company."

"Well, I plan ahead, you know—plan for my left-overs before they are left, even. I do think that an instinct for buying and planning is better than an instinct for cooking. And either one can be cultivated. But it was certainly hard to get that budget of expenses fixed satisfactorily, wasn't it? I told Ruth that no two families are alike, and that I couldn't tell her just what they ought to spend for clothes, or just what groceries ought to cost. After all, it is an individual matter which things are necessities and which are luxuries. The chief thing is to live within your means, and save as well as invest something—and at the same time be comfortable and happy. I told Ruth we started with the fixed sums and the absolute neces-

73

sities, and worked backward. I told her they must absolutely be saving something, if only a quarter a week. Then, that Fred must manage the budget of expenses that comes within his realm, and not interfere with hers, and that she must do the same with the household expenditures, and not worry him. It takes a lot of adjusting to make the system•work satisfactorily, but it is certainly worth it."

"Did you tell Ruth about the envelope system that my sister Harriet, uses? She says she is so careless naturally that when George gives her her allowance each month, she has to put the actual cash in separate envelopes, and then vow to herself that she will not borrow from the gas money to make the change for the grocer-boy, and so forth. That is the only way she can teach herself."

"My cousin's wife used to keep the most wonderful and complete accounts, but she couldn't tell without a lot of work in hunting up the items how much she already had spent for groceries or clothes or anything. She had to change her method, and it was she who taught me to keep my accounts in parallel columns, a page for a week, because you give me my allowance each week. I like this way so much, for I can tell at a glance how my expenses are comparing with the allotted sum."

"I like to look at your funny, neat little notebook, Bettina, all ruled so carefully for the week, and the headings, such as gas, electricity, groceries, meat, milk, laundry, across the top."

"Don't make fun of my notebook. I couldn't keep house without it. In case of fire, I'd save it first of all, I know! It is almost like a diary to me! I can look back over it and remember, 'That was the day Bob brought Mr. Green home and we almost ran out of potatoes!' Or 'This was the day I thought my brown bread had failed, but Bob seemed to like it!'" she exaggerated.

"Failures in cooking! Why, Bettina, I don't know the meaning of the words! And I don't see how you can feed me so well on the sum I give you for the purpose. I'd feel guilty, only you don't look a bit unhappy or overworked."

"I should say not!"

"You surely don't remember how to cook all the things you give me!"

"No, indeed, Bob, not definitely, that is. You see, on the shelf by my account book, which you smile over, I have my card index with lots and lots of recipes filed away. Then I have notebooks, too, with all sorts of suggestions tucked in them just where I can lay my hand on them."

"Betty dear, you've given me a real glimpse into your business-like methods! Some men seem to think that it doesn't take brains to run a house well, but they don't know. It requires just as much executive ability and common sense as it does to manage a big business."

That night the dinner for two consisted of:

BETTINA'S RECIPES

Cold Ham   Green Peppers Stuffed with Rice
Light Rolls   Peach Butter
Hot Fudge Cake

(All measurements are level)

Light Rolls

2 T-sugar	¾ C-flour
¼ t-salt	2 T-melted butter
½ C-scalded milk	1 egg, well-beaten
½ yeast cake	2 T-lukewarm water
flour	

Add the sugar and salt to the scalded milk and when lukewarm, add the yeast dissolved in the lukewarm water, and three-fourths of a cup of flour. Cover and set in a warm place to rise. Then add the melted butter, the well-beaten egg, and enough flour to knead. Let rise in a warm place. Roll to one-half an inch in thickness and shape with a biscuit cutter. Butter the top of each. Fold over, place in a buttered pan, close together. Let rise again for forty-five minutes and then bake in a quick oven for twenty minutes.

Green Peppers Stuffed with Rice

6 green peppers	1 T-chopped green pepper
1 C-white sauce	3 onions cooked and cut fine
½ C-cooked rice	½ t-paprika

Cut the stem ends from the peppers, and remove all seeds; add one-eighth of a teaspoonful of soda to each pepper, fill with water and allow to stand one-half hour. Mix one cup of white sauce with the rice, onions, chopped pepper and paprika. Fill the pepper cases and bake thirty minutes in a moderate oven.

Hot Fudge Cake

1/3 C-butter	½ C-hot water
1 C-sugar	2 C-flour
2 egg yolks	1 t-cinnamon
2 squares (or ounces) of chocolate, melted	1 t-soda
	1 t-baking powder
½ C-molasses	¼ t-salt
½ C-sour milk	1 t-vanilla
2 egg whites	

Cream the butter, add the sugar and continue creaming. Add the egg yolks, melted chocolate, molasses, sour milk, hot water, flour, cinnamon, soda, baking powder, salt and vanilla. Beat two minutes, and add the stiffly beaten egg whites. Fill well-buttered muffin pans one-half full, and bake in a moderate oven for twenty-five minutes. Serve hot as a dessert, with whipped cream.

CHAPTER XX

MRS. DIXON AND BETTINA'S EXPERIMENT

"I'M so happy!" said Mrs. Dixon, as she stopped at Bettina's door one cool morning. "But I'm nervous, too! What if Frank shouldn't like it?"

"Oh, but he will!" Bettina assured her. "He'll think he's the luckiest man in town, and I almost believe that he is! He'll love that dear little white house with the screened porch! Why, the very grass looks as if it longed to spell 'Welcome' like some of the door mats I've seen! And think of the flower boxes! You were very fortunate to rent it for a year, furnished so nicely, and probably when that time is up you'll be ready to build or buy one of your own."

"You are a dear to cheer me up this way, but I'm nervous in spite of you. Perhaps I should have consulted Frank before I promised to take the house."

"But he has been urging you to keep house for so long! And I know he'll be grateful to you for sparing him the worry of hunting one himself. Besides, he'll like being surprised."

"Well, I'll go back to the hotel for luncheon with him, and then I'll phone him later to meet me at the house. I won't tell him a thing; I'll just give him the address. I'll say it's very, very important. That will surprise him and perhaps will frighten him a little. He never does leave his office during business hours, but it will take only a few minutes for him to run out here in the car. Goodness, I'm forgetting what I came for! Do you suppose I am too stupid to try to make those Spanish buns Frank liked so much? We had them at the picnic, you know. I have three hours after luncheon until he comes, and I just long to give him some good coffee and some

77

Spanish buns that I've made myself! That little kitchen looks as if it would be so nice to work in! I tried coffee a little while ago over at the house, and really—it was fine! It looked just like yours! I was so surprised! To think of my doing such things!"

"Of course you could make Spanish buns; it would be fine if you would. I'll tell you,—why not let me come over for an hour right after luncheon and superintend? Then I'll slip home so that you can be alone when Frank comes. I could tell you some other things about cooking while we're there together,—things you may write down in your new notebook. For example, I've often wondered that so few housekeepers can make good white sauce."

"What in the world is that?"

"It's used in cream soups, and it's the cream part of creamed vegetables and meat and fish, and then there is a thicker white sauce that is used to bind croquettes—that is, hold the ingredients together. There are really four kinds of white sauces and they are very simple to make. I think everyone should know the right way to make them, for they are useful in preparing so many good things."

"I'm glad we'll be near you because I can ask you so many questions."

"And I'm glad that it is summer, because you can have so many things that require little or no cooking, and by fall, I'm sure you will be an accomplished housekeeper."

"Will you come over at two, then, or earlier if you can?"

"Of course I will!"

And as Mrs. Dixon hurried away Bettina felt a sympathetic thrill at the happiness two other people were about to find.

BETTINA'S RECIPES

(All measurements are level)

Spanish Buns (Twelve Buns)

½ C-butter	3 t-baking powder
1 C-sugar	1 t-cinnamon
2 egg yolks	¼ t-powdered cloves
½ C-milk	2 egg-whites beaten stiffly
1¾ C-flour	1 t-vanilla
½ C-currants	

Cream the butter and sugar, add the egg yolks. Mix and sift the flour, baking powder, cinnamon and cloves; add these and the milk to the first mixture. Beat one minute. Add the vanilla and the stiffly beaten egg whites. Bake in well buttered muffin pans twenty minutes in a moderate oven. Ice with confectioner's icing.

Confectioner's Icing (Twelve portions)

3 T-cream   1 t-vanilla
1 C-powdered sugar

Mix the cream and vanilla, add sugar slowly until the consistency to spread (more sugar may be needed). This is a most satisfactory frosting and is easily and quickly made. It is suitable for hot weather.

White Sauces (Four portions)

1—Soup

1 T-flour   1 C-liquid
1 T-butter   ¼ t-salt

This is the consistency for creamed soups.

2—Vegetable Sauce

2 T-butter   1 C-milk
3 T-flour   ¼ t-salt

This white sauce is used for creamed vegetables, creamed fish, etc. This amount is required for two cups of vegetables.

3—Pattie Sauce

3 T-butter   1 C-milk
3 T-flour   1/3 t-salt

This sauce is used for oyster or other patties.

4—Croquette Sauce

3 T-butter   1 C-milk
4 T-flour   1/3 t-salt

This is called a binding white sauce and is used to hold other ingredients together.

Method of Preparing White Sauces

Melt the butter in a saucepan and add the flour and salt, stirring constantly. When well mixed add the liquid, a little at a time. Bring to a boil, stirring constantly. This is far better than mixing the flour with a little of the liquid when cold, as so many people do when creaming potatoes or other things. If the white sauce seems too thick for the purpose, thin with a little more liquid before removing from the fire.

CHAPTER XXI

A RAINY-DAY DINNER

THE rain had been falling all day in a heavy downpour, and Bettina had ventured out only to gather some red clover blooms for the porch table, which she was now setting for dinner. In spite of the rain, it was not cold, and she liked the contrast of the cheerful little table, with its white cloth and bright silver, and the gray day just outside the screen.

"If Bob would only come home early, how nice it would be!" she thought. "Perhaps that's he at the telephone now."

However, it proved to be Mrs. Dixon. "I phoned to ask you if I should throw away the yolks of two eggs. I've just used the whites."

"Oh, no, Mrs. Dixon! Beat them up well, and add a little cold water to them. Then set them in the ice-box. They will be just as good later as they would be now. You may want them for salad dressing or something else."

"If I ever have the white of the egg left, shall I treat that the same way?"

"No, don't beat that up at all, nor add any water. Just set it in the refrigerator as it is. I'm so glad you called up, Mrs. Dixon. Will you and your husband take dinner with us next Sunday? Perhaps we might all go to church first."

"We'd love to do that! I've just been worrying over Sunday dinner, and you've restored my peace of mind. But won't it be a great deal of work for you?"

"I won't let it be. I don't believe in those heavy, elaborate Sunday dinners that take all the morning to prepare. We'll just come home from church and have it in half an hour. You may help me."

"We'd love to come. I have so much to tell you. I've been very busy, but Frank has helped, and it has been such fun! You don't know how he enjoys the little house! Well, goodbye till tomorrow!"

"Boo!" shouted Bob in her ear, as she hung up the receiver. "I discovered your dark secret this morning! Frank Dixon told me!"

"Well, what did you think of it?"

"The only possible solution in that case. You are their good angel—that is, if she doesn't poison Frank with her cooking, or burn the house down when she's lighting the fire."

"She won't, don't worry! She takes to housekeeping as if she had always done it. Her house is immaculate; she has been cleaning and dusting and polishing from morning to night. I'm almost ashamed of mine!"

"I'm not!" said Bob, decidedly. "I don't see how you can keep it clean at all with a man like me scattering papers and cigar ashes everywhere. And I'm always losing my belongings, and always will, I suppose."

"That's only a sign that we haven't discovered the proper place for them all yet. But we'll work it out in time. Well, are you hungry?"

"Hungry? I should say so! Why, I could almost eat you!"

"Well, Bob, we have a rainy-day dinner tonight that I hope you'll enjoy. Hash! Does that frighten you?"

"Not your hash, Betty."

"Well, everything is ready."

The rainy evening menu consisted of:

Browned Hash	Creamed Cauliflower
Date Muffins	Butter
Apple Sauce Cake	Chocolate

BETTINA'S RECIPES

(All measurements are level)

Browned Hash (Two portions)

1 C-chopped cold cooked beef	¼ t-pepper
1 C-cold boiled potatoes diced	1 T-milk
a few drops of onion juice	1 T-fat (lard, butter or one-
2/3 t-salt	half of each)

Mix all the ingredients thoroughly. Spread the mixture evenly in a hot frying-pan in which the fat has been placed. Cook without stirring until a crust is formed on the bottom; fold over like an omelet and place on a hot platter.

Creamed Cauliflower (Two portions)

1 head cauliflower	1 t-salt
4 C-water	1 C-vegetable white sauce

Separate cauliflower into sections, wash well and cook in boiling salted water until tender. (About half an hour.) Drain and cover with vegetable white sauce.

Date Muffins (Ten muffins)

¼ C-sugar	¾ C-milk
¼ C-dates cut fine	1¾ C-flour
1 egg	4 t-baking powder
¼ t-salt	2 T-butter (melted)

Mix the sugar, dates, baking powder, flour and salt. Add milk in which one egg has been beaten. Beat two minutes. Add butter, melted. Fill well-buttered muffin pans half full of the mixture, and place in the oven. Bake twenty minutes. Serve hot or cold.

Apple Sauce Cake (Ten portions)

½ C-butter	½ t-powdered cloves
1 C-sugar	1 C-hot, thick, strained, sweet-ened apple sauce
1 egg, beaten light	
1¾ C-flour	1 C-mixed, chopped raisins, nut meats and dates
1 t-soda	
1½ t-cinnamon	1 t-vanilla

Cream the butter, add the sugar gradually. Stir well. Add the well-beaten egg. Mix the soda and apple-sauce, and add to the first ingredients. Alternately with the flour and spices, add the vanilla and fruit. Beat for two minutes. Turn into a square pan, and sift granulated sugar over the top. Bake in a moderate oven one-half hour.

CHAPTER XXII

BUYING A REFRIGERATOR

"SOMETHING in refrigerators?" said the clerk politely to Mrs. Dixon and Bettina.

"You talk to him," said Mrs. Dixon. "I don't know a thing about a refrigerator; that's why I begged you to come."

"Well," considered Bettina, her red brown head on one side, "we want one that will hold not less than a hundred pounds of ice. The large ones are much more economical in the long run. Here, Mrs. Dixon, is a hundred-pound fellow. May we examine it, please?"

"Certainly, madam."

"No, this won't do. See, Mrs. Dixon, the trap is in the bottom of the food chamber. That is wasteful and inconvenient, because in cleaning it you would have to leave the door of the larger compartment open. That would let the cold air out and waste the ice. Anyhow, you know the trap is the sewer of the refrigerator, and has no business in the food chamber. The trap really ought to be in the bottom of the ice chamber, where it can be cleaned without removing the food, or opening the door of the food compartment. Besides, I prefer to have the ice put in at a door on the side of the front, not on the top. Yes, here is the kind I mean. I like this trap, too. See, Mrs. Dixon, isn't it fine? It has a white enamel lining and shelves of open wire that can be removed."

"It looks nice, doesn't it? And when I get some white shelf paper on those shelves it will be like an attractive cupboard."

"Oh, my dear! You mustn't do that! That would prevent the circulation of air through the ice-box, which is the very

84

thing that makes the food compartment cold. You see, that circulation of air goes on through these open-wire shelves. Another thing, I've seen people cover the ice with newspapers to keep it from melting, as they thought. But they were mistaken. Any friction causes warmth, and ice keeps better when there is nothing touching it."

"Well, if you like this one, I'll ask the price of it."

"It will be expensive, I'm afraid, but the most economical in the long run. Are you staying downtown to meet Mr. Dixon?"

"Yes, I'd like him to see the refrigerator. He takes such an interest in these household things I'm getting."

"Well, good-bye, dear. I must hurry home to get dinner. It won't take long, but I'll have to go, or Bob will get there first, and I'm a little sentimental about being there to greet him at the door."

Bettina's dinner that night consisted of:

Broiled Lamb Chops

Boiled New Potatoes   New Peas in Cream

Vegetable Salad

Bread   Butter

Rhubarb Pudding

BETTINA'S RECIPES

(All measurements are level)

Broiled Lamb Chops (Three portions)

3 chops   1 t-salt

Wipe chops and place in a red-hot frying-pan. As soon as the under surface is seared, turn and sear the other side. Turn down the fire a little, and continue to cook, turning chops often. Cook seven minutes if liked rare. When cooked, sprinkle with salt and spread with butter.

Creamed New Peas (Three portions)

1 qt. peas   ⅛ t-soda

½ t-salt

Shell one quart of peas, cover with cold water and let stand ten minutes, wash well, and drain off the water. Cover with boiled water and cook twenty to fifty minutes, according to age of peas. A pinch of soda may be added to the water. It softens the skins on the peas. Add salt when the peas have cooked twenty minutes.

White Sauce for Peas

1 T-butter	⅛ t-salt
1 T-flour	½ C-milk

Melt the butter, add the flour and salt, mixing well, and the milk, stirring constantly. Cook two minutes. Add the peas.

Rhubarb Pudding (Three portions)

1 C-cooked, sweetened rhubarb sauce	1 T-cold water
2 T-flour	1 egg-white
	⅛ t-salt

Add the water slowly to the flour and mix well. Add the rhubarb sauce and cook until very thick (about five minutes). Add the stiffly beaten white of egg, mix thoroughly and turn into moistened moulds. Serve cold with cream.

CHAPTER XXIII

BETTINA'S SUNDAY DINNER

"THIS seems like old times!" remarked Mr. Dixon, as he and his wife strolled leisurely home from church with Bob and Bettina. "I haven't had this peaceful Sunday feeling since I was a youngster. Then all the Sundays were like this, cool, quiet and sunny—sprinkled all over with little girls in smooth curls and white leghorn hats, and little boys in uncomfortable, hot clothes a size too large, and newly polished shoes. I often recall the plentiful Sunday dinners, too!"

"Don't get your hopes too high!" said Bettina. "Though I will promise you one treat, wild roses on the table. Bob and I walked out into the country last evening and found them."

"What can I do?" inquired Mrs. Dixon, when she and Bettina were alone in the kitchen.

"You can sit here and talk to me while these potatoes are cooking and the veal birds getting done.. You see, the birds have already cooked three-quarters of an hour this morning before I went to church. The waxed beans are in the fireless cooker; I have to make the butter sauce for them. And you see I have the new potatoes all prepared, standing in cold water. I have only to cook them in boiling salted water till they are done. That won't take long, as they aren't large. I set the table on the porch this morning. Bob can make the coffee in the percolator in a little while, when we're ready. He usually starts it when we come to the table, and then it is ready in time to serve last. By the way, if you like the Thousand Island dressing we are to have for the head lettuce, I'd like to give you the recipe. It is a very popular one just now."

"Oh, I've eaten it! Frank is very fond of it, and used to order it every chance he had at the hotel. Will you really tell me how to make it? So many good dinners now end with the salad and cheese and coffee, and I think Thousand Island dressing on head lettuce makes a splendid salad."

"Of course I'll show you. Well, the iced cantaloupe, which is our first course, is in the ice-box. Our dessert today is just cake with chocolate cream frosting, and coffee. It is such a simple Sunday dinner, but that's the kind I believe in!"

BETTINA'S SUNDAY DINNER

Iced Cantaloupe

Veal Birds — Boiled New Potatoes

Gravy

Waxed Beans — Butter Sauce

Bread — Butter

Head Lettuce — Thousand Island Dressing

Salt Wafers

Cake with Chocolate Cream Frosting

Coffee

BETTINA'S RECIPES

(All measurements are level)

Veal Birds (Six portions)

1½ lb. veal steak	½ t-salt
4 slices bacon	¼ t-paprika
1 T-butter	2 T-milk
½ C-crumbs, fresh	2 T-fat

Cut veal from the round (veal steak) into strips, four by two and a half inches. Put the trimming and four slices of bacon through the food chopper. Cook the chopped meat three minutes in the butter. Add to this the fresh bread crumbs, salt, pepper and milk. Spread this mixture on the strips of veal. Roll and tie securely with white cord, roll in flour and sautè until browned a little on both sides, in two tablespoons fat in frying pan. Place in a casserole or small covered pan. Season each bird with salt and a small piece of butter. Pour an inch and a half of water into the pan. Cook an hour, or a little less, in a moderate oven. Gravy may be made by adding four tablespoons of water to two level tablespoons of flour, mixing carefully and gradually pouring into the stock in which the meat has been cooked. Bring to a boil.

Thousand Island Salad Dressing (Six portions)

½ C-olive oil	¼ t-salt
2 T-lemon juice	¼ t-paprika
2 T-orange juice	1 t-Worcestershire sauce
1 t-onion juice	¼ t-mustard
	1 t-chopped parsley

Place all the above ingredients in a pint fruit jar, fit a rubber on the jar cover, and shake vigorously until the dressing is well mixed and creamy. Pour over tomatoes, asparagus, peas, beans, spinach or lettuce. Serve as a salad.

Cake with Chocolate Cream Filling (Six portions)

½ C-butter	2 t-baking powder
1 C-sugar	¼ t-mace
1 beaten egg yolk	½ t-vanilla
1½ C-sifted flour	½ C-milk
	2 egg-whites, stiffly beaten

Cream the butter, add the sugar, yolk of egg, dry ingredients and milk. Stir well, add the flavoring, beat two minutes, cut and fold in the egg white. Bake in a large round buttered pan in a moderate oven for thirty minutes. The pan should be seven inches in diameter. Cover with confectioner's icing.

Confectioner's Icing

2 C-powdered sugar	1 t-vanilla
3 T-milk	12 chocolate creams

Mix vanilla and milk, add powdered sugar. Mix until stiff enough to spread. Cut creams in half and arrange on the cake.

CHAPTER XXIV

BETTINA VISITS A TEA-ROOM

"AREN'T you a bit timid about driving?" asked Bettina, as she stepped into the car beside Mrs. Dixon.

"Not now. You see, I've been practicing every evening with Frank, and he says that I am as good a driver as he is! Oh, Bettina, we are having so much fun these days! The little house is a great success, and I'm really learning to cook! I've had some dreadful failures; but Frank doesn't seem to mind. You see, I know he gets a good meal downtown at noon, and so I don't worry about him."

"Look, Charlotte! What lovely goldenrod! We must stop and get some! Don't you love it?"

"Indeed I do! I have a rough brown waste-paper basket that it looks stunning in. I set the jar of goldenrod right inside! Frank is very fond of it."

"Charlotte, you're just like a bride yourself—thinking about Frank's likes and dislikes."

"Am I?" laughed Mrs. Dixon as her color rose. "Well, lately Frank seems just like his old self! He appreciates everything so, and is so nice at home! And it seems that he can hardly get home quickly enough! We have enjoyed getting things settled and planning our future. Next year we may build a house of our own, but I don't care to have it too large to manage easily."

"Are you going to stop here?" asked Bettina, as Mrs. Dixon slowed down after a peaceful stretch of level road.

"Yes, I want to show you something."

A short path led to a small house close to the road, but almost hidden in a tangle of flowers and wild grapevines. "Isn't this a cunning little rustic place?" asked Charlotte. "Two friends of mine started it. See" (pointing to the sign over the door), "it's called 'The Friendly Inn.' Inside you'll find that quotation about living in a house at the side of the road and being a friend to every man. You know that one. These girls live on that farm over there. When they came home from college they wanted something to do—some way to earn money—but they didn't care to leave home. This is such a splendid road that the autos swarm past all summer long. These girls opened this little tea room, and serve luncheons and tea here all summer. Most of their supplies come directly from the farm. It is just a pleasant drive from the city, and many people like to come out here in the afternoon. I'll introduce you to the girls."

Bettina found the inn-keepers charming, and after a short conversation, she and Mrs. Dixon ordered:

Tomato Cup Salad   Iced Tea
Bread and Butter Sandwiches
Vanilla Ice Cream   Chocolate Sauce
Marshmallow Cakes

BETTINA'S RECIPES

(All measurements are level)

Tomato Cup Salad (Six portions)

6 tomatoes	1 T-chopped onion
1 C-diced cucumbers	1 t-salt
¼ C-chopped green peppers	⅛ t-paprika
¼ C-sliced radishes	6 T-salad dressing

Wash cold firm tomatoes of a uniform size. Cut a slice from the stem end and scoop out seeds and pulp. Save the pulp. Sprinkle the inside with salt. Invert for five minutes. Mix the cucumber, green pepper, radishes, onions, tomato pulp, and salad dressing. Fill with the mixture and refill the shells. Have all of the ingredients cold and serve at once. If the mixture stands in the tomato cups very long it becomes watery. The tomatoes may be prepared and kept cool, and the mixture prepared, all but the onion, and placed in the ice-box until ready for use. Never put anything containing onion in the ice-box. Serve the tomatoes on crisp lettuce leaves.

Chocolate Sauce for the Ice Cream (Six portions)

1 C-sugar	2 T-flour
1 square of chocolate	1 t-butter
⅛ t-salt	1 t-vanilla

2 C-boiling water

Mix the sugar, flour and salt. Add the square of chocolate and boiling water. Allow to boil four minutes, stirring constantly. Add the butter and vanilla. Serve hot or cold with ice cream.

Marshmallow Cake

Use any white cake recipe. Bake in gem pans. Cover with White Mountain cream icing. Just before the icing is ready to spread, add quartered marshmallows. Do not add the marshmallows while the icing is hot, as they will melt, and the little "bumps" are attractive when spread on the cake.

CHAPTER XXV

BETTINA ENTERTAINS ALICE AND MR. HARRISON

"BY the way, Bettina," said Bob, over the phone, "I saw Harrison and asked him out to dinner tonight. He said he was to call on Alice later, so I suggest that you invite her, too."

Bettina smiled to herself at Bob's casual tone. Ought she to ask him not to invite company without consulting her?

"No!" she decided emphatically. "Company or no company, our meals shall be simple, but good enough for anybody. I'll not change my menu for Alice and Mr. Harrison. I'm sure they'll like it just as it is."

"To tell the truth, Bettina," said Alice's vivacious voice over the telephone, "I'd love to come, if it weren't for that—that man!"

"But, Alice, you're going to see him later."

"I know; worse luck! He's the most insufferable person I know! You see, last night we had a little argument, and he was very rude."

"Maybe he's coming to apologize."

"Don't you imagine it! He couldn't. He dislikes society girls above all other people."

"Oh, Alice!"

"Well, he does! He told me so evening before last, out at the park."

"Seems to me you're seeing a good deal of him for a man you feel that way about."

"Well, you started it. You told me that he was a woman-hater, and I thought it would be fun to reform him. At first he thought me fine and sensible, but lately I've been showing him how frivolous I really am. I suppose I hoped that by this time he'd approve of everything I said and did. But he won't. He seems actually to be trying to reform me! And I won't be reformed! I could never be anything but frivolous Alice if I wanted to! I hate those big, slow, serious men, without any fun in them!"

"Cheer up, my dear!" laughed Bettina. "Come tonight, anyhow. I like the frivolous kind, whether he does or not."

That evening, much to Bettina's secret amusement, Mr. Harrison and Alice met on the doorstep.

"Don't think we came together," explained Alice, flippantly. "A dinner and an evening of me are about all Mr. Harrison can endure!"

"I couldn't have spared the time, anyhow, Miss Alice. You see, I'm a busy man, and the people who are doing worthwhile things in this world are obliged to overlook some of the amenities."

It was on Bettina's tongue to inquire how a busy man found time to make so many calls as he was making now. But she refrained, knowing well that lively Alice could hold her own with any man in the universe, even though she might not be doing the things that Mr. Harrison considered worth while.

"A fine dinner," said he to Bettina, as they sat down at the table. "I admire a woman who knows how to prepare and serve food. She is paying her way in the most dignified and worth-while profession of all—that of a home-maker."

"Mr. Harrison," asked Alice severely, "may I inquire whether or not you know how to drive insects out of cabbage before serving it?"

"I'm afraid I don't."

"Well, I'm surprised, for even I know that. Bettina just told me. You place the cabbage, head downward, in cold water, to each quart of which has been added a tablespoonful of vinegar."

"Silly Alice!" said Bettina. "Don't tease! Look at my lovely pansies. Alice, I believe you gave me that flower-holder when I announced my engagement."

"When I announce my engagement——" said Alice.

Bettina saw a strange and startled look come over Mr. Harrison's face, which immediately departed when Alice added:

"Which will be years hence, no doubt—I hope my friends will give me nothing useful. I love to come here, Bettina, but I'm not a natural-born housekeeper like you. I shall marry an idle millionaire, and we will do nothing but travel aimlessly about from one end of the world to the other. That is my idea of perfect happiness!"

That night for dinner Bettina served:

Pork Chops   Potatoes Maitre d'Hotel Butter
Bread   Butter
Cabbage Salad Served in Lemon Halves
Cocoanut Blanc Mange   Custard Sauce
Iced Tea

BETTINA'S RECIPES

(All measurements are level)

Pork Chops (Four portions)

4 chops	½ t-salt
¼ C-water	¼ t-paprika

Wipe the chops, sprinkle with salt and pepper. Place in a hot frying-pan (no fat added), brown on one side and then turn on the other side, cooking over a moderate fire. Add the water and immediately place the cover on the frying-pan. The steam cooks the pork more quickly and prevents over-browning. Cook twenty-five minutes.

Maitre d'Hotel Butter Sauce (Four portions)

3 T-butter	½ t-salt
1 T-lemon juice	⅛ t-pepper
½ t-parsley	

Cream the butter, add the lemon juice, salt, pepper and finely chopped parsley. Pour this over new potatoes which have been boiled. Garnish with parsley.

Cocoanut Blanc Mange (Four portions)

¼ C-cornstarch	2 C-milk
¼ C-sugar	2/3 C-cocoanut
½ t-salt	3 egg whites
2 T-cold water	½ t-vanilla

Mix the cornstarch, sugar and salt with the cold water. Add the milk slowly, stirring well. Cook twenty minutes in a double boiler, stirring occasionally, or ten minutes over the flame, stirring constantly. Cool slightly and add the shredded cocoanut and the stiffly beaten whites of the eggs. Add the vanilla. One-fourth of a cup of nuts, candied cherries or preserved pineapple may be added if desired. Chill in moulds wet with cold water. Serve with cream or custard sauce made from the egg yolks.

Custard Sauce (Four portions)

3 egg yolks	1 T-flour
1/3 C-sugar	2 C-milk
⅛ t-salt	1 t-vanilla

Beat the eggs, slowly add the sugar and the flour well blended, the salt and the milk. Cook in a double boiler until thick enough to coat a silver spoon. Add the flavoring and serve cold.

CHAPTER XXVI

OVER THE TELEPHONE

BOB and Bettina were at breakfast one morning when the telephone rang. "It's Mrs. Dixon, Bettina," said Bob, his hand over the mouthpiece. "Much excited. Panicky. House afire. Hurry."

"Hello, Charlotte!" said Bettina, quickly. "What in the world is the trouble?"

"The worst yet!" came a nervous voice. "Frank's Aunt Isabel is to be at our house tonight! Oh, I wish you knew her! She never did approve of me!"

"Oh, Charlotte, you just imagine that! She wouldn't come if she disliked you so!"

"That's just it! She didn't approve of me when we lived at the hotel, and now that we've taken a house, she wants to see how things are."

"Well, things are fine! Doesn't Frank say so?"

"Yes, of course. But the meals! Two company meals to get, and for a critical person like her, too! What on earth shall I do?"

"Now, don't be nervous, Charlotte! It's easy! We'll think up a delicious little dinner that you can prepare mostly beforehand. When does she arrive?"

"Five o'clock, and leaves just after breakfast."

"Good! Two simple meals and all day in which to get them ready. Let's see. The weather is warm, so you will prefer a dinner that is partly cold. Watermelon that has been in the refrigerator all day would be a simple dessert, with no cake or anything else to think of. How about cold boiled

97

tongue for your main dish? Sliced thin and garnished with parsley. You might also have a very good salad. Apple, celery and green pepper salad would be delicious and economical also. Then you might have corn on the cob. I've had it recently and know how good it is. That would be the only thing you would have to think of at meal time, and it is very easy to cook. You would serve it in a napkin to keep it hot. Then I want to send you some peach butter that I made the other day; that would go beautifully with your dinner. There you have it all! If I were doing it, I should add iced tea to drink, served very daintily, with sliced lemon and mint leaves."

"Oh, Bettina, how good it sounds! Will you repeat that menu for me?"

Cold Boiled Tongue
Apple, Celery and Green Pepper Salad
Golden Bantam Corn on the Cob
Bread   Butter   Peach Butter
Iced Tea   Lemon
Sliced Watermelon

"Now, if you'll get a pencil and paper, I will give you some directions about cooking."

BETTINA'S RECIPES

(All measurements are level)

Boiled Tongue (Four portions)

A fresh beef tongue of two pounds   1 T-vinegar

Wipe the tongue well. Place in a kettle and cover with cold water. Add the vinegar. Bring to a boil, and boil slowly until it seems tender when pierced with a fork. (It should boil at least two hours.) Take the tongue from the water, and remove the skin and roots while it is still warm. Cool, and slice thin. This may easily be cooked in the fireless cooker, in which case the water with which the tongue is covered must be brought to a good boil on the stove, and then removed to the cooker. If the tongue is very salty, soak in cold water for two hours.

Apple, Celery and Green Pepper Salad (Four portions)

1 pt. tart apples cut in ½-inch cubes
2 T-lemon juice
1 C-celery (diced)

1 large green pepper (cut in strips)
1 t-salt
½ t-paprika
6 T-salad dressing

Mix the lemon juice and apples to prevent discoloring. Add the celery, salt, paprika seasoning and salad dressing. Serve cold on lettuce leaves.

Corn on the Cob (Four portions)

8 ears corn

Carefully remove husks and all silk from the corn. Cover with boiling water. Cook ten minutes, or longer if the corn is old. If salt is added to water, it turns the corn yellow and toughens the husks. Very tender young corn needs little cooking. Salt may be added (one teaspoon to a quart of water) two minutes before removing from the fire.

Peach Butter (One and one-half pints)

2 C-peaches   1 C-sugar

Peel peaches and slice very fine. Add one pint of sugar to every quart of peaches. Let stand twenty minutes. Mix well, and cook quickly for twenty-five minutes. Put in glasses and seal.

CHAPTER XXVII

BETTINA HAS A BAKING-DAY

"WHY, Ruth, I didn't hear you come in!"

"The door was partly open—Bob must have left it that way—and I slipped in quickly to see what you were up to. It's raining as if it never intended to stop. I called to Bob on his way downtown, and asked what you were doing today. He said that wonderful baking preparations were going on because you expected his sister Polly and her three children tomorrow. That sounded like a deluge—all those lively youngsters, and Polly livelier yet—so, I came over to see if I couldn't help."

"Indeed you can, Ruth! That was dear of you! We'll have a houseful, won't we? I have planned to put Polly and Dorothy and the baby in the guest room, but Donald will have to sleep on the davenport. And I'm planning to do most of the cooking today, so that tomorrow we can visit and see people and show the children the sights. They are coming this afternoon, and will be here Sunday and Monday at least. As soon as I finish filling these salt-shakers, I'll begin the baking. Goodness, it will certainly be a help to have you here, Ruth! You were such a dear to come in all this rain!"

"Oh, I like it! I always learn so much from you, Bettina. But what on earth are you doing with that rice?"

"Just putting a few grains in the shakers. You know salt gets damp on a rainy day like this, and the rice loosens it and absorbs the moisture. I'm doing it first because I might forget."

"What are you going to make?"

"Well, I'll cook some potatoes and beets to warm up or make salad of, and I'll make a veal loaf and a white cake, I think. Then some salad dressing, and a berry pie and some sour cream cookies. Oh, yes, some nut-bread and some tomato gelatin, too."

"Goodness! Can you use all those things?"

"Yes, indeed! For tonight's dinner I'll have lamb chops, and some of the cooked potatoes, creamed, and tomato gelatin, and the blackberry pie. (You know berry pies ought to be eaten soon after they are made.) If tomorrow is a nice day, we'll eat our dinner in the park, and in any case, I'll be prepared, for I'll have the veal loaf, and the beets to warm up, and the rest of the potatoes to cream or make salad of, and the nut-bread for sandwiches if we need them, and the cake and some sliced peaches for dessert."

"And the cookies?"

"Well, children always want cookies. I'll bake these on my big baking sheets just the size of the oven, and I'll put lots of raisins on top."

"Bettina, what fun it would be to visit you! But we must get at our work or Polly and family will be here before this big baking is done!"

BETTINA'S BAKING DAY RECIPES
(All measurements are level)

Berry Pie (Four portions)

1½ C-berries (black or blue ber-   2 T-flour
ries)   ⅛ t-salt
½ C-sugar   1 T-lemon juice

Wash the fruit, mix with the sugar, flour, salt and lemon juice. Line a deep pie tin with a plain pie paste and sprinkle one tablespoon sugar over bottom crust. Add the berry mixture. Wet the lower crust slightly. Roll out the upper crust and make slits in the middle to allow the steam to escape. Place on the lower crust, pinching the edges together. Bake in a moderately hot oven forty minutes.

Tomato Jelly (Six portions)

2 C-tomatoes   1 bay leaf
½ C-water   3 cloves
1 T-sugar   1 t-salt
        3 T-gelatine

Simmer tomatoes, water, sugar, bay leaf, cloves, and salt

for ten minutes. Strain. Soak the gelatin in two tablespoons cold water, and add the hot vegetable mixture. Pour into small wet moulds. Chill for two hours and serve with salad dressing.

Boiled Salad Dressing (One cup)

2 egg yolks	⅛ t-paprika
2 T-flour	½ t-butter
1 t-salt	1/3 C-vinegar
1 t-mustard	1/3 C-water
2 T-sugar	

Beat egg-yolks thoroughly and add the dry ingredients (mixed and sifted). Gradually add the vinegar and water. Cook in a double boiler until thick and creamy, or directly over small flame, stirring constantly. If whipped cream is to be used, no butter need to be added. If not, add butter the last thing. Beat with a Dover egg beater until creamy. Keep in a cool place.

Sour Cream Cookies (Three dozen)

1 C-sugar	½ t-soda
½ C-butter (or lard and butter mixed)	½ t-salt
	2 t-grated nutmeg
2 eggs	about 2 C-flour, or as little as
½ C-sour cream or sour milk	possible

Cream the fat, add the sugar. Cream again. Add the eggs well beaten, sour milk, one cup flour, soda, salt and nutmeg mixed and sifted together. Add the rest of the flour. Roll out to one-third of an inch thickness, cut any desired shape, and bake in a moderately hot oven for fifteen minutes. Sugar mixed with a little flour may be sifted over the dough before cutting. Raisins may also be pressed into the top of each cooky.

Doughnuts (Thirty)

¼ C-sugar	2 C-flour
1 egg beaten	½ t-salt
2/3 C-milk	¼ t-cinnamon
2 t-baking powder	

Mix the beaten egg and sugar, add the milk, flour, salt, cinnamon and baking powder, sifted together. Take one-half of the dough, and roll out one-third of an inch thick. Cut with a doughnut cutter. Roll and cut the other half. Put the scraps together and roll again. Fry in deep fat, turning until a delicate brown. Drain on brown paper.

CHAPTER XXVIII

POLLY AND THE CHILDREN

"WILL you look at the way that child eats her cereal!" ejaculated Polly at the breakfast table. "And I simply can't get her to eat it at home! In fact, on warm days like this, she won't eat any breakfast at all."

"I like Aunt Betty's cereal; it looks so pretty," explained little Dorothy gravely, looking down at her plate of moulded cereal surrounded by plump red raspberries.

"I hope you don't mind my serving it cold today," said Bettina. "It seemed so warm yesterday that I cooked the cereal and put it in moulds in the refrigerator."

"No indeed! The change is a regular treat for the children. They like fixed-up things like this, and it certainly does give anyone an appetite."

"Well, in hot weather, no one feels much like eating, anyhow, so I try to make things as attractive as I can. And I want the children to have just what they like. . . . You needn't be afraid of this cream, Polly. We buy it from a neighbor, and I am absolutely sure that it is both clean and good. I'm ashamed to say that we have no certified milk in th town. Isn't that dreadful? And people keep on buying it of dairies that they don't know one thing about! Why, I've seen women who had just moved to town, and who knew nothing about conditions here, begin housekeeping by cleaning house thoroughly from top to bottom, and at the same time, leave an order for milk with the first dairy wagon that happened to drive down their street! And they buy groceries and meat from the nearest stores without knowing that three blocks away there may be other stores that are better, cleaner and less expensive. Shouldn't you think that women would insist upon knowing all about the food they are giving their children? It seems to me that much common sense in a housewife is a great deal more important even than knowing how to cook and sew."

"I think that knowing how to plan and buy is more important than knowing how to do things with your hands," said Polly. "After all, it's the result that counts. You're a wonder, Bettina, because you have a useful head and useful hands, too, but I haven't. So I try to know as much as possible about every article of food and clothing that I buy, and to be sure that I am getting the very best value from Tom's money, but I don't know how to cook or sew or trim hats or embroider. I like friends and babies and outdoor exercise, but I'll confess that I don't like housework."

"Well, Tom and the children seem to be perfectly contented and happy, and so do you. Therefore, you are a successful housekeeper."

"You are the right kind of a sister-in-law to have, Betty! I quite approve of Bob's choice!"

The breakfast that morning consisted of:

Moulded Cream of Wheat
Raspberries
Sugar   Cream
Poached Eggs on Toast
Coffee

BETTINA'S RECIPES

(All measurements are level)

Wheat Cereal (Three portions)

1 C-wheat   2 T-cold water
1/3 C-raspberries

Cook the wheat according to the instructions on the package, only cook twice as long as the directions suggest. Mix cereal and cold water. Add boiling water slowly. This method prevents lumping. Wet individual moulds with cold water, place raspberries around the inside of the mould and fill with the wheat. Allow to remain in mould for fifteen minutes.

Remove from mould, surround with more berries and serve. If desired cold, chill in the refrigerator. Cereals may be cooked in a double boiler or a fireless cooker.

Method of Cooking Cereals

Put the water and salt in the upper part of double boiler and place directly over the flame. When the water boils, add the cereal very slowly, stirring constantly. Cook for five minutes directly over the fire. Place the upper part in the lower part of the double boiler containing boiling water, and cook the required time. All cereals must be thoroughly cooked.

AUGUST.

Twenty little jelly-glasses, twenty pots of jam,
  Twenty jars of pickles and preserves,
*Making other wealth than this appear a stupid
    sham,——*
  Ah, you dears! What color, gleam and curves!

CHAPTER XXIX

BETTINA PUTS UP FRUIT

"HONK! Honk!" sounded an auto horn at Bettina's door one cool morning, as a crowd of lively voices also summoned her.

"Bettina, O, Bettina! We've come to get you to play tennis with us this morning. You must! You've been neglecting us for Bob and we're jealous."

"Oh, girls, I simply can't! I have just bought quarts and quarts of cherries and currants of a boy who came to the door, and I must take today to put them up!"

"That's easy! Leave 'em till tomorrow!" said Alice cheerfully.

"I can't do that, because they're just at the canning point and it isn't a good thing to have them a bit over-ripe. Then these are freshly picked, and that is the best way to have them."

"I'll stay and help; may I?" said Ruth, who had suddenly developed a deep interest in things domestic.

"Why, of course I'd love to have you, Ruth, but seeding cherries is slow work, and I believe that playing tennis would be more exciting."

"But not half so interesting as to hear you tell me how you do things. I love to listen."

"We'll all stay," suggested Mary. "It'll do us good. But you'll have to lend us big aprons; can you?" And she looked down at her white middy, skirt, and shoes.

"Come on!" shouted Elsie. "You can lecture as we seed cherries, Bettina. How are you going to put them up?"

"Well, Bob likes plain currant jelly, and plain canned cherries awfully well. I may preserve some cherries with currant juice, too, but I think I'll not do anything very elaborate today."

"Goodness, that sounds elaborate enough to suit me! Will you be looking over the currants while we are stoning cherries?"

"Leave the stones in half of them, girls; many people like them that way better."

"What were you doing to all those jars?"

"Just getting ready to sterilize them. You see I'll put them on a folded cloth, in this big kettle of cold water. Then I'll slowly heat the water to the boiling point, and fill the jars immediately with the fruit and syrup. I must scald the rubber rings, too, before I use them."

Bettina was rapidly looking over currants as she talked. "Girls, do you notice my jelly strainer? See, it's a piece of cheese-cloth fastened into a wire strainer. It can be attached to any kettle. I haven't used it yet, but I know that it will be very convenient. You know it's best to strain the juice through the cheese-cloth without pressure. If I have the cloth double, the juice will be quite clear. If I wanted an especially clear jelly, I could even have the juice pass through a flannel or felt bag."

"How on earth can you tell when the jelly jells?" asked Ruth.

"Well, I test it this way. I take up, in a cold silver spoon, a little of the mixture that is cooking. If it jells and breaks from the spoon, it has been cooking long enough. Of course I remove the rest from the fire while testing it, because it might be done."

"Bettina, cooking and jelly-making and things like that seem to be so natural for you!" cried Ruth. "I get so frightened sometimes when I think what if I should be a poor house-keeper and make Fred unhappy!"

"Alice," said Mary, "Heaven forbid that either of us should ever be talking like that about a man!"

"Goodness, I should say so!" declared Alice emphatically, a little too emphatically, thought Bettina.

BETTINA'S RECIPES
(All measurements are level)
Currant Jelly

2 qts. currants   sugar

Pick over currants, but do not remove the stems. Wash and drain. Mash a few with a vegetable masher in the bottom of a porcelain-lined or granite kettle. Add more currants and mash. Continue adding currants until all are used. Bring to a boil slowly and let simmer without stirring until the currants appear white. Strain through a coarse strainer, and allow juice to drain through a jelly bag. Measure the juice, and boil ten minutes. Gradually add an equal amount of heated sugar, stirring occasionally to prevent burning, and continue boiling until the test shows that the mixture has jelled. When filling sterilized glasses, place them in a pan containing a little boiling water. This keeps the glasses from breaking when hot jelly is poured in. Fill and set the glasses of jelly aside to cool. Cover with hot melted paraffin.

Canned Cherries

6 qts. cherries   1½ qts. sugar
½ pt. water

Measure the cherries after the stems have been removed. Stone if desired. If they are stoned, be sure to save the juice. Put the sugar and water in a kettle and stir over the fire until the sugar is dissolved. Add the cherries and heat slowly to the boiling point. Boil ten minutes skimming carefully. Put into sterilized jars, filling the jars to overflowing with the syrup. Seal securely. (When filling the jars stand them in a pan containing boiling water. This keeps them from breaking.)

Bettina's Jelly-Making Suggestions

1. Use a porcelain-lined or a granite kettle.
2. Let juice drip from a cheese cloth or flannel bag.
3. Measure equal quantities juice and sugar.
4. Boil juice ten minutes, add heated sugar. (Heated by being placed in warm oven.)
5. Boil until it drops thick from a cold silver spoon, or jells on a plate.
6. The smaller the quantity of jelly made at a time, the clearer it is.
7. Cook no more than three cups of juice at a time.
8. Skim carefully.
9. Boil regularly.
10. Pour in sterilized glasses.
11. Let stand in bright sun twenty-four hours.
12. Cover with very hot paraffin. This kills any bacteria that may have collected.
13. Keep jelly in a cool, dark, dry place.

CHAPTER XXX

A COOL SUMMER DAY

"WHY, hello, Ruth!" cried Bettina at the door one afternoon. "I haven't seen you for weeks, it seems to me! What have you been doing? Come in and give an account of yourself!"

"First let me deliver these nasturtiums that mother sent," said Ruth. "She always remembers how fond you are of flowers."

"Thank you, they're lovely! I need them tonight for my table, too. Will you come into the kitchen with me while I put these in water?"

"M-m," said Ruth. "Something smells good! In the oven?"

"Yes, pork chops, baked apples and escalloped potatoes. Peek in and see 'em."

"Outch!" cried Ruth, holding her hand in sudden pain. "I forgot that that pan was hot, and started to pull it out to see better! I'm a perfect idiot! I do that every time I have anything in the oven!"

"That's a shame, Ruth, dear! Here, apply a little of this olive oil! It's the nearest remedy I have. Vaseline is good, too, or baking soda. Hold it with the damp cloth to keep out the air."

"It feels better already," said Ruth. "I made some gingerbread last evening for dinner—Fred was there—and burned my hand in the same way exactly. And even at such a cost the gingerbread wasn't very good. I think I didn't bake it quite long enough. How long ought it to be in the oven?"

"Well, gingerbread takes longer than most quick-breads.

Here, let me give you my time-guide for baking, and you can keep it in your card-index. Then it's always at hand when you want to refer to it."

"Thank you, that's a good idea, Bettina. May I sit down here at the kitchen table and copy it?"

"Do, I'll get you a pencil and a piece of paper. Ruth, won't you stay to dinner tonight?"

"I can't possibly, Bettina. I am going out with mother, and should be at home now dressing. Oh, by the way, I had a chance to refer last night to something you made me copy and put with my recipe cards. 'How to Remove Grass Stains'! I got it on my white dress—a dreadful looking stain—and immediately referred to my card-index. It said, 'Moisten with alcohol or camphor, allow to stand five minutes, and wash out with clear water.' The stain came out like magic! I used camphor; we didn't happen to have any alcohol in the house."

"I'm so glad it came out; that is such a pretty white dress. And weren't you glad you knew just where to find a remedy? It seems a little trouble to index things, but it is really worth doing."

"I think so, too. Well, there's Bob, and I must rush off. Bob, you're going to have a good dinner tonight! I've just been investigating!"

Bob had:

Pork Chops		Escalloped Potatoes
	Baked Apples	
Bread		Butter
	Fresh Pears	
	Tea	

BETTINA'S RECIPES

(All measurements are level)

Baked Apples

4 apples	½ C-water
8 T-sugar	½ t-cinnamon
	2 T-butter

Select apples of uniform size. Wash and core. Place in a pan, cover the bottom with water. Fill each cavity with sugar, a dash of powdered cinnamon and a tiny lump of butter. Bake for thirty minutes, basting occasionally. Serve around the platter of pork chops.

Bettina's Time-Guide for Baking Quick Breads

Pop-overs—Thirty minutes in a hot oven.

Baking-powder biscuits—Ten to fifteen minutes in a hot oven.

Corn bread—Twenty-five to forty minutes in a moderate oven.

Muffins—Twenty to twenty-five minutes in a moderate oven.

Gingerbread—Thirty to forty-five minutes in a slow oven.

CHAPTER XXXI

BOB AND BETTINA ALONE

"WHY, Bob, look at the front of your Palm Beach suit!" exclaimed Bettina, after she had greeted Bob at the door. "What in the world have you been doing?"

"Pretty bad; isn't it!" said he, ruefully. "Frank Dixon brought me home in his car, and he had some sort of engine trouble. We worked on it for awhile, but couldn't fix it, so he phoned the garage and I came home on the street car. I must have rubbed up against some grease. Do you suppose my clothes are spoiled?"

"No-o," said Bettina, slowly, "not if I get at them. Let me see; what is it that takes out auto grease? Oh, I know! Bob, you go and change your clothes right away while I'm cooking the meat for dinner. Then I'll doctor these."

"What will you do to them?"

"I'll rub them with lard, and let it stay on them for about an hour. Then after dinner I'll wash them out in warm water and soap, and then—well, Bob, I believe they'll be all as good as new."

"I thank you, Mrs. Bettina."

When Bob returned and Bettina was putting the dinner on the table, she smiled to herself over a new idea that had popped into her head.

"Bob, what would you think if I should enter some of my nut-bread at the state fair?"

"Well, is that what you've been smiling at all this time? I think it would be fine. If I were judge you'd get first prize in

a minute! Say, strikes me this is a pretty good dinner!"
It consisted of:

Ham	Mashed Potatoes
Escalloped Onions	
Rolls	Butter
Dutch Apple Cake	Coffee

BETTINA'S RECIPES

(All measurements are level)

Ham (Three portions)

2/3 lb. ham   2 T-water

Wipe a slice of ham (one-third of an inch thick) and remove the rind. Place in a hot frying-pan. Add the water. Cook until brown on both sides (about fifteen minutes).

Escalloped Onions (Two portions)

1 C-cooked onions	3 T-fresh bread crumbs
½ C-vegetable white sauce	2 T-butter

Mix the onions with the white sauce and pour into a buttered baking dish. Melt the butter and add the fresh bread crumbs. Place the buttered crumbs on top of the onions. Brown the mixture in the oven (about fifteen minutes).

Dutch Apple Cake (Two portions)

1 C-flour	1 egg well beaten
¼ t-salt	1/3 C-milk
2 t-baking powder	1 sour apple
1 T-butter	2 T-sugar
½ t-cinnamon	

Mix flour, salt and baking powder. Cut in the butter. Add the milk and egg. Mix well. Spread one-half an inch thick in a shallow pan. Pare and cut the apples in lengthwise sections. Lay in rows in the dough with the sharp edges pressed lightly into the dough. Mix the sugar and cinnamon and sprinkle over the top. Bake thirty minutes in a moderate oven. Serve with lemon sauce.

Lemon Sauce (Two portions)

½ C-sugar	1 C-water
⅛ t-salt	1 t-butter
1 t-flour	Juice of one lemon

Mix the sugar, salt and flour well. Add the water slowly. Cook seven minutes. Add the butter and lemon juice. Serve hot.

CHAPTER XXXII

BETTINA ATTENDS A MORNING WEDDING

"HOW lovely!" Bettina whispered to Bob after the beautiful ceremony had taken place in the rustic grape arbor. "How like Cousin Kate this is! But I had no idea that Frances planned to be married out of doors, had you?"

"She told me that they were hoping for fair weather, but weren't counting on it."

"And this is a regular golden day; isn't it! What a time to remember! Bob, look at Cousin Kate's flowers! A natural altar, without decoration! Poppies, sweet-peas, nasturtiums, cosmos, more kinds than I can count! It's a little earlier than they usually have weddings, too; isn't nine-thirty early?"

"Yes, but Frances thought that this would be the prettiest time for it, and you know they aren't at all conventional."

"What are you two gossiping about?" shouted big Cousin Charles in Bettina's ear: "don't you see enough of each other at home without avoiding the rest of us at a time like this? Go and kiss the bride and congratulate the groom as soon as you can get to them. Fanny wants to see you particularly, Bettina. Breakfast is to be served on the porch; don't forget that you two are to be at the bride's table!"

The wide porch looked very charming. Each table seated four, except the one for the bridal party and near relatives, which was in the center, surrounded by the others. On each table was a basket of pink sweet-peas and trailing greenery. Each simple white place-card held a flower or two, slipped through two parallel cuts across the corner. Frances was seated at the groom's left, and at her left sat her new brother-in-law, who was the best man. Next to him was the minister's wife, then jolly Cousin Charles, the bride's father, then the groom's mother. At the right of the groom sat Anne, Fanny's sister, who was maid-of-honor; and next to her sat the clergyman. Then came the bride's mother and the groom's father. Beyond him sat Bettina, then Bettina's cousin Harry, then Aunt Nell and Bob. That was all, for there were few near relatives and Bettina's father and mother were in California.

"Frances looks well; doesn't she?" said Aunt Nell to Bettina. "No showers, no parties or excitement, and you can see how simple the wedding has been. Cousin Kate is so sensible, and so is Frances. I can tell you already that the breakfast menu will be dainty and delicious, but simple."

She was right, for it consisted of:

Watermelon Cubes
(Served in Sherbet Glasses)
Fried Spring Chicken   New Potatoes
Creamed Peas
Hot Rolls   Butter
Currant Jelly   Peach Ice Cream
Bride's Cake   Coffee
Nuts   Candy

BETTINA'S RECIPES

(All measurements are level)

Fried Chicken

1 2½-lb. chicken	½ t-paprika
4 T-flour	4 T-fat (lard and butter)
2 t-salt	2 T-water

To Prepare the Chicken for Serving and Cooking

Cut the legs from the body, break the joint at the thigh and cut in two. Cut off the neck and wings. Break the breastbone and cut in two lengthwise. Break the back in two pieces lengthwise, if desired. Plunge the pieces into cold water and allow to drain. Sprinkle each piece with salt and paprika, and roll in flour. Place the fat in a frying-pan. When very hot add the chicken. Allow all the pieces to brown thoroughly; cover the pan with a lid and add the water, lower the fire and cook over a moderate fire for thirty minutes. Turn frequently to prevent scorching.

Gravy (Six portions)

3 T-fat from frying-pan	1 t-salt
1 T-butter	¼ t-paprika
6 T-flour	1½ C-milk
1 t-parsley chopped	

Loosen the pieces of chicken which have stuck to the frying-pan, add the butter, stir constantly until the butter "bubbles," add the flour, salt and paprika. Mix thoroughly. Add the milk slowly, cook for two minutes, add the chopped parsley and pour the gravy into a gravy bowl for serving.

Bride's Cake (Thirty pieces)

1½ C-sugar	3 t-baking powder
½ C-butter	¼ t-cream of tartar
2½ C-flour	½ t-almond extract
⅛ t-salt	1 t-vanilla
4 egg whites	

Cream the butter, add the sugar and continue creaming the mixture. Mix and sift three times the flour, salt, baking powder and cream of tartar. Add these dry ingredients alternately with the milk to the first mixture. Add the almond and vanilla extracts. Beat two minutes. Cut and fold in the egg-whites which have been stiffly beaten. Pour the cake batter into a large, round loaf cake pan, having a hole in the center. Bake forty-five minutes in a moderate oven. When the cake is removed from the oven, allow it to stand in a warm place for five minutes, then with a spatula and a sharp knife, carefully loosen the cake from the sides, and turn out onto a cake cooler. When cool, cover with White Mountain Cream Icing.

Suggestions for Serving the Bride's Cake

The Bride's Cake may be baked in this form and placed in the center of the table for the central decoration. A tall, slender vase, filled with the flowers used in decorating, may be placed in the hole in the cake. Place the cake upon a pasteboard box four inches high and one inch wider than the cake.

This gives space to decorate around the cake. The cake and box may be placed on a reflector, which gives a very pretty effect. If cake boxes containing wedding cakes are distributed among the guests as favors, use the one in the round pan for centra. decoration and bake others in square pan. Square pieces may then be cut, wrapped in waxed paper, and placed in the boxes.

CHAPTER XXXIII

AFTER THE "TEA"

"**D**OESN'T it bore you to think of cooking when you've been out all afternoon?" asked Mrs. Dixon, wearily. "And today the refreshments were so elaborate and everything was so stiff and tiresome!"

"I usually anticipate feeling this way," said Bettina, "and plan to have something at home that is already prepared, and that I can get together without much trouble. Then I put on a house dress as quickly as I can, for I can't bear to cook in party clothes. But I'm sure I don't know what I am going to have for dinner tonight. Bob and I had planned to go downtown to dinner with some friends, but just before I went out this afternoon he phoned that the invitation had been withdrawn because of somebody's illness."

"Goodness!" cried Mrs. Dixon, "what will you do? Go downtown yourselves?"

"No; Bob doesn't enjoy that, and neither do I. I can manage somehow, for of course there are always things in the house to get. I'll tell you. I'll phone Bob to bring Mr. Dixon here, and you can see what an emergency supper is like."

"Oh, I couldn't think of it! You're tired, and it's nearly six now!"

"Well, what of that? You can help. And I know you're dreading to get dinner at home. We'll just combine forces."

Bettina went to the telephone and called Bob. "Hello, dear! Please bring Mr. Dixon home to dinner with you; Charlotte is going to stay. And if you come in his car, will you stop on

121

the way and get a watermelon that has been on ice? Be sure it's cold!"

"And now," she said to Mrs. Dixon, "let me get into a house-dress, and then for a sight of the refrigerator."

"Oh, what beautiful glazed apples!" exclaimed Mrs. Dixon ten minutes later.

"They were to have been for breakfast, but I'll have them for dinner instead. Then there are enough cold boiled potatoes for creamed potatoes; and, besides that, we'll have an omelet. And then I'll stir up some emergency biscuit——"

"And you can explain everything that you do!"

"Well, for the omelet—we'll take four good-sized eggs—one for each of us——"

"What else goes in? Milk?"

"No, I think that hot water makes a more tender omelet. Then I'll use a few grains of baking powder to assist in holding it up, though that isn't necessary. We'll beat the yolks and whites separately till they're very light. Goodness! There come the men!"

"Here's your watermelon, Bettina!" called Bob. "A big fellow! Don't forget to save the rind for pickles, will you? Why, hello, Mrs. Dixon! Frank's here!"

The menu that night consisted of:

<table>
<tr><td>Omelet</td><td></td><td>Creamed Potatoes</td></tr>
<tr><td></td><td>Glazed Apples</td><td></td></tr>
<tr><td>Emergency Biscuit</td><td></td><td>Butter</td></tr>
<tr><td></td><td>Watermelon</td><td></td></tr>
</table>

BETTINA'S RECIPES

(All measurements are level)

Omelet (Four portions)

4 eggs	⅛ t-pepper
4 T-hot water	1 T-butter
½ t-salt	a little parsley

Beat the yolks until thick and lemon colored. Add hot water (one tablespoonful to an egg), salt and pepper. Beat the whites till stiff and dry. Cut and fold into the first mixture. Heat the omelet pan, add the butter, turn the pan so that the melted butter covers the sides and bottom of the pan. Turn in the mixture, spread evenly, turn down the fire and allow the omelet to cook slowly. Turn the pan so that the omelet will brown evenly. When well puffed and delicately browned underneath, place the pan on the center shelf in a moderate oven to finish cooking the top of the omelet. Crease across center with knife and fold over very carefully. Allow to remain a moment in pan. Turn gently with a spatula onto a hot platter. Garnish with parsley. An omelet is sufficiently cooked when it is firm to the touch when pressed by the finger.

Creamed Potatoes (Four portions)

2 C·cold diced potatoes	½ t-salt
1 T-chopped parsley	⅛ t-paprika
1 T-chopped pimento	1 C-vegetable white sauce

Add the potatoes, sprinkled with salt and pepper, to vegetable white sauce. Add pimento and parsley. Cook three minutes, stirring constantly.

Emergency Biscuit

2 C-flour	½ t-salt
4 t-baking powder	3 T-fat (lard and butter)
	7/8 C-milk

Mix the dry ingredients and cut in the fat. Add the milk, mixing with a knife. Drop by spoonfuls on a buttered pan, placing one inch apart. Bake twelve minutes in a hot oven.

Glazed Apples (Six portions)

6 apples	1½ C-water
1½ C-"C" sugar	1 t-butter

Boil the sugar and water six minutes in a deep saucepan. Do not stir. Pare and core the apples. Place them in the syrup as soon as pared, to prevent them from discoloring. Cook until apples are tender. Remove the apples from the syrup and boil the sugar and water longer if it is not thick enough. Add the butter to the syrup and pour in and around the apples. Serve hot or cold. Granulated sugar may be used, but "C" sugar gives a better flavor.

CHAPTER XXXIV

BETTINA GIVES A PORCH BREAKFAST

BETTINA had risen early that beautiful July morning, for she had much to do. Bob had insisted upon helping her, and at eight, Ruth was coming.

"Such a simple breakfast after all, Bob! Do you think she'll like it?"

"Sure she will! If she doesn't I'll disown her! Say, Bettina, I haven't had my breakfast yet, and ten o'clock sounds far away. May I have just one doughnut with my coffee?"

"Why, Bobby, Bobby! Did I forget you? Your Aunt Elizabeth and the whole suffrage cause is on my mind this morning, but I didn't think even that could make me forget you. Help yourself to anything you see that looks good!"

The Aunt Elizabeth on Bettina's mind was an aunt of Bob's who was to be in town between nine and twelve, in conference with some of the leading suffragists of the city. She wished to see the bungalow, and at ten o'clock Bettina was giving a breakfast for her and the women with whom she was to confer. It was with fear and trepidation that Bettina had invited them, although she declared to herself that she was sure, sure, sure, of every dish on the menu!

As she arranged the great graceful yellow poppies in the center of the porch table, set for six, she was feeling somewhat nervous.

"Bob, you must go now, or you'll be too late for the train. Take a taxi home, not a street car."

"Taxi! You don't know my Aunt Elizabeth. She'd say, 'Say, young man, if you aren't saving your money any better than this, you ought to be.' And we'd probably end by walking."

"Hurry, dear."

The train proved to be late, and Ruth and Bettina were ready to the last detail. While beautiful, distinguished-looking Aunt Elizabeth was dressing, Bettina was meeting guests at the door. Before she realized it, she had introduced everybody to the guest of honor, and was ushering them out to her charming porch table.

"Oh, Ruth," she said in the kitchen, "isn't my Aunt Elizabeth lovely? I'll say 'mine' now, not Bob's. I was in such a hurry that I forgot to be frightened."

The breakfast consisted of:

Moulded Cereal on Bananas	Whipped Cream
Codfish Balls	Egg Souffle
Green Peas	
Twin Mountain Muffins	Jelly
Doughnuts	Coffee

BETTINA'S RECIPES

(All measurements are level)

Codfish Balls (Four portions)

1 C-raw salt fish	1 egg, well-beaten
2 C-raw potatoes	¼ t-pepper
1 t-butter	more salt if needed
1 C-cracker crumbs	1 T-water

Shred the fish. Pare and quarter potatoes. Place the fish and potatoes in a stewpan and cover with boiling water. Boil twenty-five minutes or till the potatoes are soft. Do not boil too long or they will become soggy. Drain well, mash and beat until light. Add butter, seasoning and egg. Shape, roll in crumbs, egg, more crumbs, and fry in deep fat. These may be shaped into flat cakes, rolled in flour and sautéd in hot fat. Garnish with parsley.

Egg Soufflè (Four portions)

2 T-butter	1 t-salt
2 T-flour	a pinch of cayenne or ¼ t-paprika
2 C-milk	1 C-white sauce
4 eggs	
2/3 C-cooked peas	

Melt the butter, add the flour and gradually add the milk. Cook three minutes, add seasoning and the well-beaten yolks. Fold in the beaten whites and turn into buttered moulds. Set in a pan of hot water and bake in a slow oven until firm (about twenty-five minutes). Serve with a white sauce, highly seasoned, to which has been added one cup of cooked peas. Pour the sauce around the souffle.

Potato Doughnuts (Three dozen doughnuts)

1 C-mashed potatoes, hot	½ C-sweet milk
1½ C-sugar	2 eggs
2 T-melted butter	3 C-flour
3 t-baking powder	⅛ t-grated nutmeg
½ t-salt	½ t-powdered cinnamon
	⅛ t-salt

Beat the eggs, add the sugar. Mash the potatoes and add the butter and the milk. Add this mixture to the eggs and sugar. Add the flour, baking powder, salt, nutmeg and cinnamon sifted together. Roll one-fourth of an inch thick, cut with a doughnut cutter, and fry in hot deep fat.

CHAPTER XXXV

A PIECE OF NEWS

AS Bettina was putting the finishing touches on her porch table, set for dinner, and humming a little song as she tried the effect of some ragged robins in a mist of candy-tuft, all in a brass bowl, she heard a murmur of voices at her front door.

"I'll tell just Betty; no one else must know—yet. But what if I haven't the courage to tell even her?"

"Perhaps she'll suspect anyhow!"

"Goodness, Harry! You make me afraid to go in! Is my expression different?"

The answer was not audible to Bettina, though she was sure that she heard whispers and a little suppressed laughter. Certainly it had sounded like Alice's voice! What? Could Mr. Harrison be with her? For a moment Bettina stood stock still, feeling like an eavesdropper. Then she let out a gasp of amazement. "Well!" was all she said, and sat down to think. When the door-bell rang, she could not at first gain the composure necessary to answer it.

"Why, how are you, Alice? I haven't seen you for ages! And Mr. Harrison! Do come in; you must stay to dinner, for you're just in time. Bob will be home any minute."

"Oh, we couldn't stay!" answered Alice. "Har—Mr. Harrison and I were walking home from town, and when we came to this house, we couldn't help stopping to say 'hello.'"

Bettina was conscious of a strained feeling in the air, which made her want to giggle—or shake Alice. After all, she couldn't help overhearing! And yet she might be mistaken!

127

She found herself saying—she scarcely knew what—to keep up the conversation.

"Do stay! We have a funny little dinner tonight, but I believe you'll like it. Bob had been rather over-worked at the office lately—and I tried today to think of some of his favorite dishes for dinner. I wanted to have a jolly little meal to take his mind off his worries. And it would help a lot if he could see you two people. Do stay! Do you care for blueberry tarts, Mr. Harrison? Well, that's to be our dessert!"

"My, that sounds fine!" said Mr. Harrison. "Couldn't we stay, after all?" he asked, turning to Alice.

"Well, if you really, truly want us," said Alice to Bettina.

"Why, of course I do! I'm delighted to see you! I think we're fortunate. Mr. Harrison, you are usually so busy that we scarcely dare invite you!"

"I suppose I ought to be at work today, but I'm taking a little holiday. I couldn't put my mind on business."

He was actually blushing, Bettina thought. Suddenly she found Alice's arms around her and Alice's laughing face hidden on her shoulder. "Don't, Harry! Let me be the one to tell her!"

And so Bob found them, all laughing and talking at once.

"Hurrah!" said he when he heard the news. "The best possible idea! Is dinner ready, Bettina? Get out some grape juice and we'll drink to the health and future happiness of Alice and Harry! I'm the man that made this match!"

Dinner that night consisted of:

Fish a La Bettina (Four portions)

Fish a la Bettina	Rice Cakes
Stuffed Tomato Salad	
Rolls	Butter
Iced Grape Juice	Blueberry Tarts

BETTINA'S RECIPES

(All measurements are level)

Fish a la Bettina (Four portions)

1 C-medium white sauce	2 T-chopped pimento
1 1/3 C-cooked fish	2 T-chopped sweet pickle
½ t-paprika	

Mix ingredients in order given, heat and serve on wafers.

Rice Cakes (Four portions)

1½ C-boiled rice	1 egg yolk
½ t-salt	6 T-crumbs
4 T-fat (lard and butter mixed)	

Mix the rice and salt with the egg. Shape into flat cakes, two and a half inches in diameter and one-half an inch thick. Roll in bread crumbs and sautè in hot fat until brown on both sides. (About eight minutes.) If the egg does not sufficiently moisten the rice, add one tablespoon of milk.

Stuffed Tomato Salad (Four portions)

4 tomatoes	½ t-salt
1 C-chopped cabbage	¼ t-paprika
4 T-salad dressing	

Stuff fresh tomatoes with cabbage, seasoned, and mixed with salad dressing. Arrange the tomatoes on lettuce leaves and place one tablespoon salad dressing on the top. Add a small piece of green pepper or a sprig of parsley to the salad dressing.

Blueberry Tarts (Four portions)

Fill muffin pans with plain pastry. Place two tablespoons of mixture on each crust. Cover with pastry strips and bake twenty minutes.

Blueberry Mixture

½ C-blueberries	1 T-butter
¼ C-sugar	1 T-vinegar
1 t-cinnamon	

Mix the berries, sugar, butter cut in small pieces, vinegar and cinnamon. Cook, stirring constantly, over a moderate fire for three minutes.

CHAPTER XXXVI

BETTINA ENTERTAINS HER FATHER AND MOTHER

"WE had no such steak as this in California!" declared Bettina's father with satisfaction, as Bob served him a second helping.

"But then," said Bettina's mother, "did you find anything in California that you thought equalled anything in your own state? Father never does," said she, laughing. "He seems to enjoy traveling because it makes him feel that his own home is superior to every other place on earth. And it is," she agreed, looking about her happily. "I can say that after a summer spent in California, I'm more than thankful to be back again."

"I was afraid that you and father would be so anxious to open up the house that you wouldn't agree to come here for your first meal."

"Of course we're anxious to get home," said Mother, "but after you wrote Father that if he would come here to dinner tonight you would have a steak cooked just to suit him, he was as eager as a boy to get here."

"Well, who wouldn't look forward to it, after a summer spent in hotels?" said Father. "And I must say that Bettina's dinner justifies my eagerness. It's exactly right—steak and all."

"Now for dessert!" said Bob. "This coffee that I've been making in the percolator is all ready, Bettina!"

For dinner that night they had:

Pan-broiled Sirloin Steak   Mashed Potatoes
                    Carrots
    Head Lettuce   Thousand Island Dressing
      Sliced Bananas   Quick Cake
                    Coffee

BETTINA'S RECIPES

(All measurements are level)

Pan-Broiled Steak (Six portions)

2 lb. sirloin steak an inch and a   ½ t-salt
  half thick   1 T-parsley
1 T-butter   1 T-lemon juice

Wipe the meat with a damp cloth. Have a tin pan sizzling hot. Place the meat in the pan and cook directly under the broiling flame. Turn frequently with spoons, as a fork will pierce the meat and allow the juices to escape. A steak an inch and a half thick should be cooked from eight to ten minutes. Place the steak on a hot platter. Sprinkle with salt, lemon juice and parsley. Dot with butter. Serve very hot.

Gravy (Six portions)

2 T-drippings from the steak   ½ C-water
2 T-flour   ½ C-milk
                   ¼ t-salt

Pour the drippings from the steak into a pan, add flour and mix well. Allow the flour to brown, add water and milk very slowly to the flour and drippings. Add the salt and allow to cook until the gravy thickens. If there are not two tablespoons of drippings, add sufficient butter to equal the amount.

Carrots (Six portions)

6 medium-sized carrots   ½ t-salt
2 T-butter   ¼ t-pepper

Wash and scrape the carrots, cut into two-thirds inch cubes and cook until tender in enough boiling water to cover. (About fifteen minutes.) Drain, add the butter, salt and pepper. Heat thoroughly and serve. Carrots may be scraped and steamed whole or cooked whole in boiling water.

Quick Cake (Sixteen pieces)

½ C-butter	1 2/3 C-flour
1½ C-brown sugar	3 t-baking powder
1 egg	1 t-cinnamon
½ C-milk	½ t-nutmeg
¼ t-salt	8 dates, cut fine

Cream the butter, add the sugar and mix well. Add the egg and milk, salt, flour, baking powder, cinnamon, nutmeg and dates. Beat for two minutes. Bake in a well-buttered loaf cake pan for thirty-five minutes.

Icing

1 egg white	¾ C-powdered sugar
2 T-cold water	½ t-vanilla

Beat the egg white until very stiff; add water and sugar gradually. Beat thoroughly and add the flavoring. Beat until it will stand alone, then spread on cake. More sugar may be added if necessary.

Thousand Island Salad Dressing (Six portions)

½ C-olive oil	¼ t-paprika
juice of half a lemon	1 t-Worcestershire sauce
juice of half an orange	¼ t-mustard
1 t-onion juice	1 T-chili sauce
¼ t-salt	1 T-green pepper cut fine
	1 t-chopped parsley

Place all the above ingredients in a pint fruit jar, fit a rubber and top tightly on the jar, shake vigorously until well mixed and creamy, and pour over head lettuce, tomatoes, asparagus, peas, beans or spinach. Serve as a salad.

CHAPTER XXXVII

THE BIG SECRET

"COME in, Alice! Now do say that you'll stay to dinner, for we can talk afterward."

"Well, if you'll take me out into the kitchen where you are working. You see, I have all this to learn, and I'm depending on you to help me."

"Of course I'll help, Alice, but you are so clever about anything that you care to do that I know you'll soon outstrip your teacher. Tell me first, does anyone know the Big Secret yet?"

"Not a soul but Bettina, Bob, and my family. That is what I came to talk about."

"Oh, Alice, I'd love to be the one to give the announcement luncheon, or the breakfast, or whatever you prefer to have it!"

"Would you do it, really? Bettina, I've been longing to have you offer, but it is work and trouble, and I didn't want to suggest it."

"Why, Alice, I just enjoy that kind of work! I'd be flattered to be allowed to have it here. Of course, you know that I can't do anything very elaborate or expensive, but I'm sure that between us we can think up just the prettiest, cleverest way of telling it that any prospective bride ever had!"

"Bettina, my faith is in you!"

"When do you plan to be married?"

"Late in October or early in November, I think. And I'd prefer not to have it announced for a month. You see, I don't want to allow time for too many festivities in between."

"Oh, Alice, if you take my advice, you won't have any showers or parties at all. I know you! If you do allow it, you'll have more excitement than any bride in this town!"

"Well, Harry advises me not to, but oh, Betty, you know how it is! I know so many people, and I do like fun, and then Mother likes to think of me as the center of things. She's afraid that when I am married to Harry I'll become as quiet as he is, and then too, I honestly don't think she'd feel that I was really married without it. You know sister Lillian had lots of excitement and more parties crowded into a day than——"

"Yes, and she was so tired that she nearly fainted when she stood up to be married!"

"That's true, but she liked the fun, anyhow. She says that a girl can have that kind of fun only once, and she's silly to deny herself. Well, I'll have a whole month to think it over in. I've been sitting here all this time, Bettina, trying to decide what it is that you are making—those croquettes, I mean."

"They are potato and green corn croquettes, and Bob is very fond of them. I made them because I happened to have some left-over corn. Until I learned this recipe, I didn't know what to do with the ears of cooked green corn that were left."

"And what is the meat dish?"

"Well, that is made of left-overs, too, but I think you'll like it. Creole Lamb, it is called. It is made of a little cold cooked lamb that was left from last night's dinner. The rhubarb sauce that I am serving with the dinner was our dessert last night. But I do have a very good new dessert!"

"New or not, the dinner does sound good. There is Bob, now, and I'm so glad, for I confess that my appetite is even larger than usual!"

The menu that night was as follows:

Creole Lamb
Potato and Green Corn Croquettes
Rhubarb Sauce

Bread		Butter
Head Lettuce		French Dressing
Lemon Pie		Cheese

BETTINA'S RECIPES

(All measurements are level)

Creole Lamb (Three portions)

1 T-butter
1 T-chopped green pepper
½ T-onion, chopped
1 T-flour
¼ C-meat stock or water
¼ C-tomato pulp

½ t-lemon juice
½ t-salt
1/3 t-horseradish
½ C-cold cooked lamb, cut in cubes
3 pieces of toast

Melt the butter, add pepper and onion. Cook two minutes and add flour, stock, pulp, lemon juice, salt and horseradish. Boil two minutes, stirring constantly. Add the lamb. Heat thoroughly, and serve on toast strips.

Potato and Green Corn Croquettes (Three portions)

1 C-hot mashed potatoes
1 C-green corn pulp, cooked with
1 T-butter

½ t-salt
½ t-pepper
1 egg yolk

Mix all ingredients together thoroughly. Shape into cylindrical form, roll in bread crumbs, dip in beaten egg, roll again in crumbs. Deep fry. The egg yolks for croquettes may have a tablespoon of water added for each yolk. The whites as well as the yolks may be used for covering the croquettes. To get the corn pulp, cut the kernels lengthwise of the rows, and press out the pulp with the back of the knife. This recipe is good for left-over corn.

CHAPTER XXXVIII

AFTER THE CIRCUS

"THERE is nothing so exciting as a circus," said Ruth, "but oh, how comfortable and peaceful it seems to get away at last from the crowds and the noise! How quiet and cool this porch is, Bettina. In two minutes I'll get up and help you with dinner, but you made a mistake to put such a comfortable chair here in this particular spot."

"Ruth, stay just where you are! This meal is supper, not dinner, and it will be ready in the shortest possible time. Where are the men?"

"Going over the plans of our house, I suppose. Fred has worn them almost in pieces by exhibiting them so often. There seem to be a great many details to settle at the last minute. As for me, I'm perfectly satisfied, for I'm going to have a kitchen exactly like yours. Bettina, what lovely nasturtiums, and how delicious that cold sliced ham looks with more nasturtiums to garnish it!"

"Yes, and I have nasturtium leaves lining the salad bowl—and see, I'll put one large flower on each plate!"

"Don't nasturtiums always seem cool and appetizing? The whole supper looks that way!"

"Well, circus day is almost invariably warm, and people are tired when they come home, so I planned to have a cold and simple meal."

"Isn't boiled ham hard to prepare?"

"No, indeed, nothing could be simpler. I bought a half of a ham—I like a piece cut from the large end—and I soaked it for an hour in cold water. Then I brought it to a boil in fresh cold water and a little vinegar, and transferred it to the fireless cooker for five hours. Then I baked it for an hour in the cooker, having first trimmed it, and covered it with brown sugar and almost as many cloves as I could stick into it. It is very tender and good, I think—one of the best of my fireless cooker recipes."

"I am planning to have a fireless cooker when I keep house."

"That is fine, Ruth! You have no idea how they save both gas and worry. Some day I'll give you all of my best fireless recipes; I use my cooker a great deal. For instance, this brown bread was steamed in the cooker. A fireless is invaluable for steaming. I usually plan to have Boston Brown Bread, Tuna or Salmon Loaf and a pudding all steaming in the large compartment at once. Then I've learned to bake beautiful beans in the cooker! I wonder what our grandmothers think of Boston Baked Beans and Boston Brown Bread all made in the fireless! I'm sure I could prove to any of them that my way is just as good, besides being much cooler and more economical! Well, shall we call Fred and Bob?"

The circus day supper consisted of:

Cold Sliced Ham

Boston Brown Bread   Butter

Blackberries   Cream

Spiced Cake

Iced Tea   Sliced Lemon

BETTINA'S RECIPES

(All measurements are level)

Spiced Cake (Sixteen pieces)

1/3 C-butter	¼ t-ground cloves
1 C-sugar	¼ t-mace
2 egg yolks	1 t-soda
2/3 C-sour milk	2 C-flour
1½ t-cinnamon	1 egg white
	1 t-vanilla

Cream the butter, add the sugar and egg yolks. Mix well. Mix and sift all dry ingredients. Sift and add alternately with sour milk. Add vanilla and stiffly beaten egg white. Bake in a loaf cake pan, prepared with waxed paper, in a moderate oven for twenty-five minutes. Cover with "C" sugar icing.

"C" Sugar Icing (Sixteen pieces)

1 C-"C" sugar   ⅛ t-cream of tartar
1/3 C-water   1 egg white
½ t-vanilla

Mix the sugar, water and cream of tartar. Cook until the syrup clicks when a little is dropped in cold water. Do not stir while cooking. Have the mixture boil evenly but not too fast. Pour gently over the beaten white of the egg. Stir and beat briskly until creamy. Add vanilla. Place on the cake. If too hard, add a tablespoon of water.

CHAPTER XXXIX

MRS. DIXON ASKS QUESTIONS

"I HAD resolved," said Mrs. Dixon, at Bettina's dinner-table, "not to accept another invitation to come here until you people had eaten again at our house. But your invitations are just too alluring for me to resist, and your cooking is so much better than mine, and I always learn so much that—well—here we are! For instance, I feel that I am about to learn something this very minute! (Now, Frank, please don't scold me if I talk about the food!) Bettina, how did you ever dare to cook cabbage? It looks delicious and I know it is, but I tried cooking some the other day and the whole house has the cabbage odor in no time. Yours hasn't. Now what magic spell did you lay on this particular cabbage?"

"Let me answer that," said Bob. "I want to show off! Bettina cooked that as she always cooks onions and turnips, in a a large amount of water in an uncovered utensil. Isn't that correct, Bettina? Send me to the head of the class!"

"Yes, you're right. I did boil the cabbage this morning, and of course I have a well-ventilated kitchen, but I don't believe the odor would be noticeable if I had cooked it just before dinner."

"I never used to eat cabbage," said Bob, "but I like Bettina's way of preparing it. She never lets it cook until it gets a bit brown, and so it has a delicate flavor. Most people cook cabbage too long."

"Another question, Teacher. How did you manage to bake

these potatoes so that they are so good and mealy? Mine always burst from their skins."

"Well," said Bettina, "I ran the point of the knife around the outside of the potato. This cutting of the skin allows it to swell a little and prevents it from bursting. Then I baked it in a moderate oven. Another thing. I've discovered that it is better not to pierce a potato to find out if it is done. I press it with my fingers, and if it seems soft on the inside, I remove it from the oven and press the skin until it breaks, allowing the steam to escape. If I don't do that, a mealy potato becomes soggy from the quickly condensing steam."

"Oh, Bettina, I'm so glad to know that! I like baked potatoes because I know they are so digestible, but I never can make them like these. Now I won't monopolize the conversation any longer. You men may discuss business, or the war, or anything you choose."

The dinner that night was as follows:

Hamburger Steak   Lemon Butter
Baked Potatoes   Escalloped Cabbage
Bread   Butter
Prune Souffle

BETTINA'S RECIPES
(All measurements are level)
Hamburger Steak (Six cakes)

1 lb. of beef cut from the round   1 t-onion salt or onion juice
¼ t-salt   ⅛ t-pepper

Grind the meat twice and add the seasoning. Shape into cakes two and a half inches in diameter and one inch thick, handling as little as possible. Place on a hot pan and cook under the broiler twelve minutes, turning when brown. Dot with butter and serve hot.

Lemon Butter for the Steak (Four portions)

2 T-butter   ½ T-lemon juice
½ t-salt   ½ T-minced parsley
¼ t-paprika

Mix in order given and spread on hot meat of any kind, broiled steak, chops or fish.

Baked Potatoes (Four portions)

Select potatoes of a uniform size. Wash thoroughly with a vegetable brush. Run the point of the knife around the outside of the potato. Bake in a moderate oven forty to sixty minutes.

Escalloped Cabbage (Four portions)

2 C-cooked cabbage	⅛ t-paprika
1 C-white sauce	¼ C-bread crumbs
1 T-butter	

Remove the outer leaves of a two and a half pound head of cabbage. Cut in half (using but half for dinner). Wash thoroughly and cut in shreds or chop moderately fine. Put in a large kettle of rapidly boiling water. Boil for twenty minutes. Drain well, add one-half a teaspoon salt. Make the white sauce, add the cabbage and paprika, mix well. Place in a buttered baking dish. Cover with buttered crumbs and place in a moderate oven until browned.

Prune Souffle (Four portions)

¼ lb. prunes	1 T-lemon juice or ½ t-lemon extract
6 T-sugar	2 egg whites

Wash the prunes thoroughly, cover with water, and allow to soak three hours. Cook slowly in the same water until soft. Remove the stones from the prunes, and save the pulp and juice. Add sugar, cook until very thick (about three minutes). Stir constantly. Cool, add the lemon juice. Cut and fold in the stiffly beaten egg whites. Fill a well-buttered open tin mould half full of the mixture. Place the pan in another pan filled with boiling water. Cook in a slow oven until well raised, firm, and light brown in color (about twenty-five minutes). Serve with the following custard sauce:

Custard Sauce (Four portions)

2 egg yolks	⅛ t-salt
4 T-sugar	1½ C-milk
1 T-flour	½ t-lemon extract

Beat egg yolks until light, in the upper part of a double

boiler.   Add sugar, flour and salt.   Mix well and slowly add the milk.   Cook over the lower part of the boiler until thick enough to coat a silver spoon.   Beat well, add the extract, and cool.

CHAPTER XL

A TELEGRAM FROM UNCLE ERIC

"WHAT shall I do with this butter, Bettina?" inquired Bob, who was helping to clear off the table after dinner one evening. "Put it in the ice-box?"

"The butter from the table?" asked Bettina. "No, Bob, I keep that left-over butter in a covered dish in the cupboard. You see, there are so many times when I need butter for cake making or cooking, and prefer not to have it very hard. Then I use that cupboard butter. There's the doorbell, Bob. Now who do you suppose that can be?"

"A telegram from Uncle Eric," said Bob, when he returned from the door. "Well, isn't that the limit! He's coming to-night!"

"Tonight!" echoed Bettina.

"Yes, on business. You see, there are so many people in town for the state fair and there are several that he must see. He's a queer old fellow—Uncle Eric is—and he has some queer notions. Doesn't like hotels, or anything but home cooking. He doesn't want anything elaborate, but he's pretty fussy about what he does want. I'm sorry for you, Bettina, but I guess we'll have to make him welcome. He's been pretty good to me, in his funny way, and so I suppose he feels he can descend on us without warning."

"But, Bob—tonight! Why, I'm not ready! I haven't groceries in the house, or anything! And I was planning to give you a cooked cereal for breakfast tomorrow."

"It's too bad, Betty," said Bob sympathetically, "but it seems as if we'll just have to manage some way. Uncle Eric has been good to me, you see. He's an old fogy of a bachelor, but he has a warm heart way down underneath his crusty exterior. And——"

"Don't you worry, Bob," said Bettina heartily. "We will manage. As a rule, I think it's pretty poor taste for anyone to come without warning or an invitation, but maybe Uncle Eric is an exception to all the rules. Tell me about him; do you have time? When does the train get in? Do you have to meet it?"

"I guess I'd better hurry right off now."

"But, Bob, tell me! What must I have for breakfast?"

"Anything but a cereal, Betty! Uncle Eric draws the line at cereals. He has an awful time with his cooks, too. They never suit him."

"Goodness, Bob!" said Betty, in despair. "And I have almost nothing in my cupboard. It's as bare as Mother Hubbard's!"

"Good-bye, dear! I'm off! I know you'll think of something."

Bettina smiled hopelessly at the masculine viewpoint, and as soon as Bob had gone she sat down to think, a dish towel in one hand and a spoon in the other.

"Be a sport, Bettina," she murmured to herself. "If Uncle Eric doesn't like his breakfasts, it's his own fault for coming. Get a pencil and paper and plan several cereal-less breakfasts, so that while he is here you will never be at a loss."

Thus fortified by her common sense and what is less common, her sense of humor, Bettina soon evolved the following breakfast menus for Uncle Eric:

(1)
Cantaloupe
French Toast   Maple Syrup
Broiled Bacon
Coffee

(2)
Fresh Pears
Creamed Beef on Toast
Coffee

(3)
Cantaloupe
Sweet Milk Griddle Cakes
Syrup
Coffee

(4)
Baked Apples
Broiled Ham   Graham Muffins
Coffee

(5)
Fresh Plums
Codfish Balls   Twin Mountain Muffins
Coffee

(6)
Cantaloupe
Waffles   Syrup
Coffee

(7)
Watermelon
Corn Oysters   Syrup
Toast
Coffee

BETTINA'S RECIPES

(All measurements are level)

French Toast (Three portions)

6 slices stale bread	¼ t-salt
2 eggs	T-sugar
2/3 C-milk	

Beat the eggs slightly, add salt, milk and sugar. Place in a shallow dish. Soak bread in the mixture until soft. Cook on a hot, well-greased griddle, browning on one side and then turning and browning on the other. Serve hot with maple syrup.

Sweet Milk Griddle Cakes (Four portions)

2 C-flour	1 C-milk
3 t-baking powder	1 t-salt
1 egg, well-beaten	

Mix the flour, baking powder and salt, add the milk to the well-beaten egg, and pour the liquid slowly into the dry ingredients. Beat thoroughly for one minute. Put a spoonful on a hot, well-greased griddle. When done on one side, turn, and brown on the other. Never turn more than once.

Broiled Bacon (Three portions)

6 slices of bacon

Place bacon slices, which have had the rind removed, on a hot tin pan and set directly under a flame for three minutes. Turn and broil the other side.

Corn Oysters (Three portions)

1/3 C-corn	¼ t-salt
1/3 C-bread crumbs	⅛ t-pepper
1 well-beaten egg	½ t-sugar

Mix the corn, egg, bread crumbs, salt, pepper and sugar. Shape into cakes two inches in diameter and one-half an inch thick. Grease a griddle or a frying-pan thoroughly, and when very hot, place fritters on the pan. When brown on one side, turn over onto the other side. Serve hot, with syrup.

CHAPTER XLI

BETTINA ENTERTAINS STATE FAIR VISITORS

THE next morning when Bob and Uncle Eric had partaken of a cereal-less breakfast, and Uncle Eric had even complimented the cook, Bettina called her mother on the telephone.

"I was about to call you, Bettina. Won't you go to the fair with us this afternoon? You know Cousin Mabel and the children are here from Ford Center, and Cousin Wilfred may arrive some time this morning."

"You do have your hands full this week, don't you, Mother? Uncle Eric is at home only for breakfast, and I called up to ask if you would all come here to dinner tonight."

"Oh, Bettina! I'm afraid it will be too much work for you, dear!"

"I'll plan a simple meal, Mother; one that I can get together in a hurry. In fact I've already planned it."

"But, in that case, you couldn't go to the fair with us this afternoon, could you? And it's said to be especially good to-day."

"Why, yes, I could go. I can get the most of my dinner ready this morning. What time would you start?"

"At two, I think. Well, Bettina, we'll come, but you must make the meal simple, for we won't be back till six."

"Don't worry, Mother."

Bettina hastened to make her preparations, and at half after one her house was in order and she was ready to go. Besides, she was comfortably conscious of a well-filled larder—cold fried chicken ready and waiting, cold boiled potatoes to be creamed, green corn to be boiled, peaches to be sliced, and delicious chocolate cookies to delight the hearts of the children.

"It will take only a few moments," she thought as she arranged the nasturtiums on her dining table, "to set the table, cream the potatoes, boil the corn, slice the peaches and make the tea. And I believe it's the sort of a dinner that will suit them."

The dinner for state fair guests consisted of :

Cold Fried Chicken　　　　Creamed Potatoes
Corn on the Cob
Sliced Peaches　　　　Chocolate Cookies
Tea　　　　　　　　Milk

BETTINA'S RECIPES

(All measurements are level)

Creamed Potatoes as Bettina Served Them (Six portions)

3 C-cold,　cooked　potatoes,	6 T-grated cheese
chopped	1½ C-milk
2 T-butter	½ t-salt
3 T-flour	⅛ t-pepper

Melt the butter, add the flour and seasoning and mix well; gradually add the milk and cheese. Cook until the consistency of vegetable white sauce (about one minute after it boils). Add the potatoes, cook four minutes, stirring constantly. and serve.

Chocolate Cookies (Three dozen)

1 C-sugar	½ t-cinnamon
1/3 C-butter	½ t-salt
1 egg	3 t-baking powder
¼ C-milk	1 square chocolate
2 C-flour	1 t-vanilla

Cream the butter, add the sugar and cream well. Add alternately the sifted flour, salt, baking powder and egg beaten in milk. Add the chocolate and vanilla. Turn out on a floured board and roll a small portion at a time to one-fourth of an inch in thickness. Cut with a floured cooky cutter. Place on a buttered, floured pan and bake in a moderate oven until slightly brown. (About ten minutes).

CHAPTER XLII

UNCLE JOHN AND AUNT LUCY

AS Bettina was standing before a beautiful exhibit of honey in the agricultural building, she was startled by a hand upon her shoulder.

"Gracious, Uncle John!" she exclaimed. "How you frightened me! But I'm so glad to see you! Where is Aunt Lucy?"

"Here, somewhere. You know she took a few prizes herself and is probably hanging around to hear any stray compliments for her butter or preserves."

"Aren't you ashamed, John!" said Aunt Lucy, herself appearing like magic. "I was just looking for the queen bee among the others in this glass case."

"And here she is!" said Uncle John, laying his hand on Bettina's shoulder, and laughing delightedly at his own joke. "You've been looking in the wrong place."

"For that, Uncle John, I'm going to beg you and Aunt Lucy to come home with me to dinner. Won't you? When did you come in?"

"This morning, and we're making a day of it. We'd like to see the fireworks this evening, but perhaps we could go to your house and get back again. For that matter, you and Bob could go with us to see the fireworks. How about it?"

"Oh, that would be splendid! Bob couldn't come to the fair this afternoon, and I came with a friend."

"Well, we'll take you both home in the car. When shall we see you? Five o'clock? Fine! And you and Bob must come back with us this evening."

Dinner that night consisted of:

Broiled Ham
Hashed Brown Potatoes   Pickled Beets
Bread   Butter
Coffee

BETTINA'S RECIPES

(All measurements are level)

Hashed Brown Potatoes (Four portions)

2 C-chopped potatoes	a pinch of pepper
½ t-salt	4 T-fat

Put fat in frying-pan, when very hot, add the potatoes, salt and pepper. Cook three minutes, allowing to cook without stirring for two minutes. Fold as an omelet and turn onto a hot platter. Garnish with parsley.

Pickled Beets (Four portions)

6 beets	2/3 C-vinegar
	2 T-sugar

Wash the medium-sized beets thoroughly, and cook until tender in boiling water. Drain, cover with cold water and slip off the skins. Slice the beets into one-fourth inch slices. Cover with vinegar and sugar. Allow to stand two hours before using.

Brown Betty (Four portions)

2 C-sliced apples	1 t-cinnamon
1 C-fresh bread crumbs	3 T-butter
¼ C-brown sugar	½ C-water

Mix the apples, all but two tablespoons of the bread crumbs, brown sugar, and cinnamon. Add the melted butter and pour into a buttered baking-dish. Pour the water over the whole mixture. Use the remainder of the crumbs and a little melted butter for the top. Bake forty-five minutes in a moderate oven. Serve hot or cold with hard sauce.

Hard Sauce for Brown Betty (Four portions)

4 T-butter	½ t-vanilla extract
1 C-powdered sugar	½ t-lemon extract
	1 t-boiling water

Cream the butter, add the•boiling water, and the sugar gradually. Stir until the sauce is creamy. Add vanilla and lemon extract. Set in the ice-box to harden. Serve cold.

CHAPTER XLIII

SUNDAY DINNER AT THE DIXON'S

"YOU seem to have gained in weight, Frank," said Bob, as he and Bettina sat down to Sunday dinner with the Dixons.

"And what's more, I've gained in spirits! Say, there's nothing like living in a real home! Why, people, just think of having Charlotte say to me as she did yesterday, 'Frank, Bob and Bettina are coming to dinner to-morrow, and I want you to plan the menu!' And here it is! Excuse me for seeming too proud of my own good judgment and my wife's skill in cookery, but——"

"Hush, Frank! Maybe Bob and Bettina won't like your choice of dishes or your wife's cooking!"

"What!" said Bob. "I have yet to meet the person who doesn't like fried chicken! And roasting ears and new potatoes! Sa-ay!"

"It's a man-size dinner all right, isn't it?" said Mr. Dixon. "You know ever since I was a boy my idea of Sunday dinner (at least in the summer) has been fried chicken with gravy, new potatoes, boiled corn on the cob, and ice cream with sliced peaches! Because ice cream is coming, isn't it, Charlotte? At least I ordered it, and this appears to be my lucky day!"

"Indeed, it is coming," said Mrs. Dixon. "You see, Bettina, ever since I came to keep house (thanks to you) I've longed for the time to come when I could let Frank plan a company meal that I could carry out to the last detail. I have tried all these things before, although not all at the same time. I have always suspected that he would order fried chicken and its accessories (a 'little boy dinner' I called this), so when I told him that he might plan the meal, I knew that I could cook it. You see, I have wanted to invite you and Bob—oh, I've been thinking of it for a long time, but you can cook so well that I thought perhaps you'd rather eat at home!"

"Charlotte, this is a perfect dinner—far better than I could get, I know."

"This salad is an acquired taste with me," put in Mr. Dixon. "In my boyhood, my ideal dinner did not include salad, but Charlotte said there must be one, so this was my choice. I mixed the oil-dressing myself," he added with pride.

"It was a simple dinner to get," said Mrs. Dixon. "But now, Frank, we mustn't boast any more about our own dinner, must we? Bob and Bettina will laugh at us. You see, we're regular children since we took the house, but we do have lots of fun. I wouldn't go back to hotel living for anything in the world!"

"And neither would I," said Frank, "if for no other reason than the joy of entertaining our friends at dinner this way!"

Their Sunday dinner consisted of:

Fried Chicken   New Boiled Potatoes

Corn on the Cob

Bread   Butter

Sliced Cucumber, Tomato and Onion Salad

Oil Dressing

Vanilla Ice Cream with Peaches

White Cake   Iced Tea

BETTINA'S RECIPES

(All measurements are level)

Vegetable Salad (Four portions)

2 medium-sized tomatoes   ½ cucumber

1 onion

Dressing

4 T-vinegar   ½ t-salt

2 T-oil   ¼ t-paprika

Cut the peeled tomatoes and cucumber in one-third inch cubes, mix with the onion chopped fine. Add the dressing, which has been well mixed, and allow to stand ten minutes in a cold place. Serve on head lettuce.

Peaches for Ice Cream (Six portions)

2 C-peaches, sliced   2/3 C-sugar

Add the sugar to the peaches and allow to stand in the ice box for ten minutes. Place peaches around the ice cream.

White Cake (Twenty pieces)

½ C-butter	⅛ t-salt
1½ C-sugar	1 C-milk
2 2/3 C-sifted flour	4 egg whites, beaten stiffly
5 t-baking powder	1 t-vanilla
½ t-lemon extract	

Cream the butter, add the sugar, and continue creaming for two minutes. Alternately add all the dry ingredients and the milk. Beat well. Cut and fold in the egg-whites. Add the flavoring. Bake in two buttered layer-cake pans, twenty-five minutes in a moderate oven. Cover with "C" sugar icing.

"C" Sugar Icing (Twenty portions)

3 egg whites	2/3 C-water
3 C-"C" sugar	1 t-vanilla

Cook the sugar and water together without stirring until the icing "clicks" in cold water. Remove from the fire and pour very slowly over the stiffly beaten egg-whites. Beat vigorously and continuously until the icing gets thick and creamy. Add the vanilla. Spread on the cake.

Vanilla Ice Cream (Six portions)

1 qt. cream	1 T-vanilla
¾ C-sugar	⅛ t-salt

Mix cream, sugar, vanilla and salt. Place in a scalded and chilled freezer. Turn until the mixture stiffens. Pack for two hours to ripen.

CHAPTER XLIV

A RAINY EVENING AT HOME

"THIS is just the kind of a cold, rainy evening," said Bob as he pushed back his chair, "that makes me feel like making candy."

"Fine!" said Bettina. "What kind shall it be?"

"Penoche, if you have all the ingredients."

"I think I have. Let's see. It's better when it's made partly with 'C' sugar, and I have that. I wonder if there will be enough milk left for breakfast if we use a little! Well, penoche really tastes exactly as good when it is made with water instead, though, of course, it isn't so rich. But then, I think, we do have enough milk."

"First of all, though," said Bob, "we'll wash these dishes. It was a mighty good dinner tonight, Bettina. The nice kind of a hot meal that it seems good to come home to on a night like this."

"It was an oven dinner, Bob. You see, the meat loaf, the escalloped potatoes, and the rice pudding were all in the oven at once. I always try to use the oven for more than one dish if I am using it at all."

"We seem to have eaten all of this tomato sauce," said Bob, as he carried out the dish, "but there is a good deal of meat left. Will you have to make more sauce?"

"No, I planned just enough for one meal. Then, tomorrow, I'll serve the rest of the meat cold without a sauce. How did you like the rice pudding hot as it was tonight? You know I usually serve it cold."

"It tasted very good for a cold evening. There, all these

dishes are ready to wash, Bettina. Will you get out some tea towels for me?"

The dinner that night consisted of:

Hot Beef Loaf		Tomato Sauce
	Escalloped Potatoes	
Bread		Butter
	Rice Pudding	

BETTINA'S RECIPES

(All measurements are level)

Beef Loaf (Five portions)

1 lb. beef cut from the round	⅛ t-onion salt
¼ lb. salt pork	¼ C-cracker or bread crumbs
½ t-salt	1 egg yolk
¼ t-pepper	1 T-milk
	1 T-butter

Grind the meat well, and mix all the ingredients excepting the butter. Pat into an oblong shape and place in a well-buttered pan. Add three tablespoons of water to the pan, and place the butter in small pieces on the top of the loaf. Cover the pan and bake thirty-five minutes in a moderate oven.

Tomato Sauce (Three portions)

1 C-tomatoes, cut up	1 slice of onion or
½ C-water	⅛ T-onion salt
2 bay leaves	2 T-butter
1 t-sugar	2 T-flour
¼ t-ground cloves	1/3 t-salt

Simmer for fifteen minutes the tomatoes, water, bay leaves, sugar, cloves and onion. Strain and press out all the pulp. Melt the butter, add the flour, blend well, slowly add the strained tomato and salt. Cook one minute. Serve hot on the meat.

Escalloped Potatoes (Three portions)

4 potatoes (medium sized)	1 T-salt
2 T-flour	¼ t-pepper
2 T-butter	milk (about one cup)

Wash and peel the potatoes. Slice very thin. Mix through the sliced potatoes, the flour, salt, pepper and the butter in small pieces. Place the mixture in a well-buttered pan or baking dish, and cover with milk. Usually one cup suffices. Bake in a moderate oven forty-five to fifty minutes. (Do not fill the pan more than three-fourths full, as the pctatoes will boil over.)

Rice Pudding (Three portions)

1¼ C-milk	1 t-vanilla
1 egg	1 C-cooked rice
4 T-sugar	1 t-butter
¼ t-salt	⅛ t-grated nutmeg

Beat the egg, add the suger, salt, nutmeg, vanilla, and milk. Add the rice. Pour the mixture into a well-buttered baking dish and dot over with the butter. Bake in a moderate oven twenty-five minutes. It may be served hot or cold. Cream may be served with it if desired.

Penoche

2 C-"C" sugar	2/3 C-milk
1 C-granulated sugar	¼ t-cream of tartar
1 T-butter	¼ C-nut-meats
	1 t-vanilla

Mix the sugar, butter, milk and cream of tartar. Cook, stirring occasionally to prevent from scorching, until a soft ball is formed when a little candy is dropped in cold water. Remove from the fire, and do not stir until it is cool. Put back on the stove for one minute, stirring constantly. Remove from stove, and beat vigorously until very creamy. Add the nuts and vanilla. When hard and creamy, remove from the pan, patting into shape and kneading until soft and creamy. Place on a buttered pan, patting to the thickness of three-fourths of an inch. Cut into the desired shape.

SEPTEMBER.

Apple-tree, apple-tree, crowned with delight,
Give me your fruit for a pie if you will;——
Crusty I'll make it, and juicy and light!——
Give me your treasure to mate with my skill!

CHAPTER XLV

RUTH MAKES AN APPLE PIE

"I'LL tell you, Ruth," said Bettina, in answer to some questions, "you come home with me now, and make an apple pie for our dinner! I'll watch and direct you, and perhaps I can show you what made the crust tough on the one you made at home. Do come. I can't promise you an elaborate dinner tonight, for my funds are very low and I must be careful. But I had planned to make an apple pie myself. Bob is so fond of it that no matter what else we may have, an apple pie dinner is a feast to him."

"But goodness, Bettina! I might spoil it!"

"No, you wouldn't, and I would show you just what to do. I suspect that you handled the dough too much before and that was what made the pie seem tough."

"I suppose I did; I was so anxious to have it well mixed."

"Did you use your fingers in mixing in the shortening? I know that many good cooks do it, but it is really better to use a knife, with the blade flat. And then roll the pastry out just as lightly as possible."

"Do you make pastry with lard or butter?"

"I usually make it with an equal amount of each. Lard makes a more tender crust than butter, and a whiter crust, but I think butter gives it a better flavor."

Bettina and Ruth had reached home by this time, and Bettina brought out the materials for Ruth's pie. "I'll give you ice-water to moisten the pastry," said she; "it isn't necessary, but it is really better in the summer time. And while you're mixing in the shortening with this knife, I'll be cooking some eggs hard for eggs a la goldenrod which I am going to give you tonight."

"Eggs a la goldenrod!" exclaimed Ruth, "How good that does sound!"

"It is a very good luncheon-dish, but I find it also good for dinner when I'm not having meat. I think it looks appetizing, too."

"I must learn how to make it. You know Father comes home at noon, and it is hard to think of a variety of luncheon-dishes. I usually have eggs or cheese in some form or other, but 'eggs a la goldenrod,' are new to me."

"We also have cottage-cheese tonight," said Bettina. "I plan to make it about once a week. Ruth, I believe I hear Bob now! Well, he'll have to wait half an hour or more for his dinner!"

That night they had:

Eggs a la Goldenrod	Potato Cakes
Strained Honey	Cottage Cheese
Bread	Butter
Apple Pie	Coffee

BETTINA'S RECIPES

(All measurements are level)

Eggs a la Goldenrod (Four portions)

3 hard-cooked eggs	1½ C-milk
3 T-butter	½ t-salt
3 T-flour	⅛ t-pepper
	⅛ t-parsley

Melt the butter, add the flour, salt and pepper. Mix well. Add the milk gradually. Cook until a white sauce consistency. Add chopped egg-whites. Pour this mixture over slices of toast arranged on a platter. Force the yolks through a strainer on top of the sauce on the toast. Garnish with parsley and serve hot.

Potato Cakes (Four portions)

2 C-mashed potatoes   1 T-lard
1 T-butter

Form cold seasoned mashed potato into cakes two inches in diameter. Dip the cakes lightly into a little flour. Allow one tablespoon butter and one tablespoon lard to get very hot in a frying-pan. Put in the cakes, brown on each side, and serve.

Cottage Cheese (Four portions)

1 qt. sour milk   ¼ t-paprika
1 t-salt   1 T-cream

Place thick freshly soured milk over a pan of hot water, not boiling. When the milk is warm and the curds separate from the whey, strain off the whey in a cheese cloth. Put into a bowl, add salt, pepper and cream to taste. Stir lightly with a fork.

Some of Bettina's Pastry Rules

One—All the materials must be cold.

Two—Always roll one way and on one side of the pastry.

Three—Shortening should be handled as little as possible.

Four—Dough should be mixed with a knife and not touched with the hands.

Five—Shortening should be cut in with a knife.

Six—Cook pastry in a hot oven having the greatest heat at the bottom so that it may rise before browning. Crust is done when it slips from the pan.

CHAPTER XLVI

BETTINA MAKES APPLE JELLY

"WHAT have you been doing?" asked Bob, as he and Bettina sat down to dinner.

"Oh, Bob, I've had the nicest day! Mother 'phoned me this morning that Uncle John had brought her several big baskets of apples from the farm, and that if I cared to come over to help, we would put them up together, and I might have half. Well, we made apple jelly, plum and apple jelly, and raspberry and apple jelly. I had made all these before, and knew how good they were, but I learned something new from Mother that has made me feel happy ever since."

"And so you came home, and in your enthusiasm made this fine dandy peach cobbler for dinner!"

"Bob, that was the very way I took to express my joy!"

"Well, what is this wonderful new apple concoction?"

"Perhaps it isn't new, but it was new to me! It is an apple and mint jelly, and I know it will be just the thing to serve with meat this winter."

"How did you make it? (I hope you are noticing how interested I'm becoming in all the cooking processes!)"

"Well, I washed and cut into small pieces four pounds of greening apples. Then I washed and chopped fine one cup of fresh mint, and added it to the apples. I covered the mixture with water, and cooked it all till the apples were so tender that they were falling to pieces. I strained it then, and used three-fourths of a cup of sugar for each cup of juice. I cooked this till the mixture jellied, and then I added four teaspoons of lemon juice and enough green vegetable color paste to give it a delicate color."

"Isn't that coloring matter injurious?"

"Oh, no, Bob! It's exactly as pure as any vegetable, and it gives things such a pretty color. Why, I use it very often, and I'm sure that more people would try it if they knew how successful it is! It is such fun to experiment with. Of course, I never use anything but the vegetable coloring."

"Well, go on with the jelly. What next?"

"That's all, I think. I just poured it into glasses, and there it is, waiting for you to help me carry it home from Mother's. Now, Bob, won't that be good next winter with cold roast beef or cold roast veal? I know it will be just the thing to use with a pork roast!"

"I'm growing very enthusiastic. Sounds fine. But speaking of cooking, this is a mighty good dinner. I like peach cobbler as well as any dessert there is."

"I'm glad you like it. But I forgot to tell you, Bob, that I'm to have all the apples I can use in the fall. Uncle John has promised them to me. Then Mother says we'll make cider. Won't that be fine?"

"I should say it will! Cider and doughnuts and pumpkin pie! Makes me long for fall already! But then, I like green corn and watermelon and peaches, so I suppose I can wait."

That evening Bettina served:

Sliced Beef Loaf

Sautèd Potatoes   Creamed Corn

Cinnamon Rolls   Butter

Peach Cobbler   Cream

BETTINA'S RECIPES

(All measurements are level)

Sautèd Potatoes (Two portions)

2 large potatoes cooked ½ t-salt
2 T-lard   ¼ t-pepper

Peel cold boiled potatoes. Put two tablespoons of lard in the frying-pan. When hot, add the potatoes and season well with salt and pepper. Brown thoroughly on all sides. (They should cook about ten minutes.)

Creamed Corn (Two portions)

1 C-corn cut from the cob	1 t-butter
	1 T-milk or cream
½ C-water	½ t-sugar
¼ t-salt	

Cook the corn and water together very slowly for twenty minutes, or until the water is all cooked out. (Place on an asbestos mat to prevent burning.) Add butter, milk, sugar and salt. Serve hot.

· Cinnamon Rolls (Twelve rolls)

2 T-sugar	¼ C-lukewarm water
½ t-salt	1½ C-flour
1 C-milk (scalded and lukewarm)	3 T-butter
	4 T-sugar
1 yeast cake	¼ C-butter
½ C-sugar	

Mix sugar, salt and scalded milk. When lukewarm, add the yeast cake dissolved in one-fourth of a cup of lukewarm water. Add one and a half cups flour. Cover and set in a warm place to rise. When double in bulk, add the butter (melted), four tablespoons sugar and more flour (enough to knead). Let rise, knead and roll into a sheet half an inch thick, spread with a mixture made by adding melted butter, one and a fourth cups sugar and the cinnamon. Roll up like a jelly roll. Cut in slices three-fourths inch thick. Place in a pan one inch apart, let rise again. Bake in a moderately hot oven twenty-five minutes.

Peach Cobbler (Two portions)

1 C-flour	3 good-sized peaches
1 t-baking powder	1/3 C-sugar
⅛ t-salt	¼ t-vanilla
1 T-butter	¼ C-sugar
¼ C-milk	¼ C-water

Cut the butter into the dry ingredients (baking powder, salt and flour), and add the milk. (The resulting dough should be of biscuit dough consistency.) Peel and slice the peaches, mix well with the sugar (one-third cup) and place on the bottom of a baking dish. (not tin.) Place dough shaped to fit, on the top of the pe: .hes. Make three holes to allow the steam to escape. Bake thirty minutes in a moderate oven. Boil the sugar and water four minutes. When the cobbler has cooked for twenty minutes, pour the syrup over it and allow to cook ten minutes more. Cream may be served with the cobbler if desired.

CHAPTER XLVII

AFTER A PARK PARTY

"A BEAUTIFUL day," said Bettina at the breakfast table. "September is doing better than August."

"I was just thinking," said Bob, "that it might be fun to get Harry and Alice, and go out to Killkare park this evening. I don't believe you've been on a roller coaster this year."

"It would be fun to go," said Bettina, "although I haven't missed the roller coaster."

"Well, let's ask them to go. We can stay there awhile and then——"

"Then what?"

"Oh, nothing. Then go home."

"Bob, you meant—come here afterward and have a nice little lunch; didn't you?"

"I confess that I thought of that, and then I happened to remember that you were going out this afternoon and wouldn't want to bother with any preparations for a party."

"Going out this afternoon would not worry me at all—it is just that my funds are getting a little low, and I couldn't serve anything expensive. Let me think what I have on hand—yes, I believe I could do it by serving a salad and a dessert out of my own head."

"A Bettina salad? That's the very best kind. And what will the dessert be?"

"A Bettina dessert, too. I have some lovely apples, Bob, and I just can't afford anything very expensive. I know this will be good, too, but you mustn't complain if I have sponge cake to eat with it."

"I should say not, Bettina. Whatever you give us will tickle me, and Alice and Harry are in such a state of blindness that they won't know what they're eating."

That evening they had:

Bettina Salad	Boston Brown Bread Sandwiches
Bettina's Apples	Sponge Cake
	Coffee

BETTINA'S RECIPES

(All measurements are level)

.. **Bettina Salad** (Four portions)

1 C-chopped New York cheese	¼ C-chopped roasted peanuts
12 Pimento stuffed olives, chopped	¼ t-salt
	⅛ t-paprika
3 sweet pickles, chopped very fine	4 T-salad dressing
	4 pieces of lettuce

Put the cheese through the food chopper or grate it, add the olives chopped, the sweet pickles, peanuts, salt and paprika. Blend well, and form into balls, one inch in diameter. Arrange several on a lettuce leaf. Serve salad dressing with the salad.

Bettina's Apples (Six apples)

6 apples	8 marshmallows
1 C-"C" sugar	½ C-cocoanut shredded
1 C-water	6 cherries

Peel and core the apples. Drop into the sugar and water which has been boiled for ten minutes to form a syrup. Place a lid on the pan and cook the apples until tender. Remove from the syrup and roll in the cocoanut. Add the marshmallows to the syrup (which has been removed from the fire) and allow them to melt. Stir them in the syrup. When the marshmallows are dissolved, stir the mixture to mix the marshmallows with the syrup. Pour around the apple, and fill the hole in the center of the apple. Place a red cherry on the top of each.

Hot Water Sponge Cake (Eight portions)

2 egg-yolks	1 t-grated rind lmon
1 C-sugar	2 egg-whites
1 C-boiling water	1 C-flour
1 T-lemon juice	1 t-baking powder
¼ t-salt	

Beat the yolks until thick and lemon colored, add the sugar gradually and beat for two minutes. Add the flour, sifted with the baking powder, and salt. Add the boiling water, lemon juice, and grated rind. Beat with a Dover egg-beater, two minutes. Fold in whites of the eggs. Bake thirty-five minutes in a moderate oven in an unbuttered pan. Do not cut sponge cake, except through the crust, then break apart.

CHAPTER XLVIII

BETTINA SPILLS THE INK

"WHERE are you, Bettina?" called Bob one September evening when Bettina failed to meet him at the door. "Oh, Bettina!"

"Here I am, Bob, in the kitchen! I'm so ashamed of myself!"

"What for?"

"My carelessness. I just spilled a whole bottle of ink on this new apron of mine! I had begun to get dinner, and as it was a little early, I sat down for a minute to finish a letter to Polly. Then all at once I thought something was burning, and jumped up in such a hurry that I spilled the ink. I ought to have known better than to try to do two things at once! Luckily, the dinner was all right, but look at this apron! And it was such a pretty one!"

"Well, Bettina, I'm always getting ink and auto grease on my clothes, and you seem to keep yours spotless. So it is a surprise to me that it happened. Still, spoiling a new apron may be unfortunate, but I shouldn't call it tragic. Is it really spoiled?"

"No, I think I can fix it up so it will be almost as good as new, but it's a nuisance. See, I'm soaking it in this sour milk. I'll leave it here for four hours, and then apply some more milk for awhile. Then I believe the ink will come out when I rinse it."

"Well, Bettina, I'm glad you didn't spill ink on the dinner. Something smells mighty good!"

They had:

Beef Balls   Gravy
Mashed Potatoes
Bettina's Celery and Eggs
Cinnamon Rolls   Butter
Watermelon

BETTINA'S RECIPES

(All measurements are level)

Beef Balls (Three portions)

1 lb. round steak   ¼ t-paprika
1 t-salt   ⅛ t-celery salt
¼ t-onion salt

Grind round steak, season, shape into round cakes and broil them for seven minutes under the flame. While they are cooking, prepare the horseradish sauce.

Horseradish Sauce (Four portions)

2 T-butter   1 C-milk
2 T-flour   2 T-horseradish
½ t-salt

Melt the butter, add the flour. Mix well, add the milk and cook one minute. Add the salt and the horseradish. Serve immediately.

Mashed Potatoes (Three portions)

4 medium-sized potatoes   ½ C-milk
1½ T-butter   ½ t-salt
⅛ t-pepper

Cook the potatoes (peeled) in boiling salted water. When done, drain off the water, pass through a vegetable ricer, or mash well with a potato masher. Add butter, salt, pepper, and the milk. Beat vigorously, reheat and pile lightly in a hot dish.

Bettina's Celery and Eggs (Three portions)

1 C-cooked diced celery   2/3 C-vegetable white sauce
2 hard-cooked eggs sliced   1 T-butter
3 T-fresh bread crumbs

Add the sliced hard-cooked eggs and cooked celery to the white sauce. Mix well. Pour the mixture into a well-buttered baking dish. Cover with the crumbs which have been mixed with melted butter. Bake in a moderate oven until a delicate brown. (About twenty minutes.)

CHAPTER XLIX

BETTINA ATTENDS A PORCH PARTY

"WELL, what have you been doing today?" asked Bob, after he had finished an account of events at the office.

"I've been away all afternoon, Bob, at the loveliest little porch party at Alice's! You know her porch is beautiful, anyhow, and her party was very informal. She telephoned to five of us this morning, and asked us to come over and bring our sewing; the day was so perfect. She served a delicious little luncheon from her tea cart, very simple but so good! And the beauty of it was that she had made everything herself! She didn't tell the girls, but she whispered it to me. Of course, if she had told the others, she would have given herself away; they are a little suspicious of her now because she is seen everywhere with Harry!"

"He told me he wished they could announce it right away! He doesn't like to make a secret of it."

"It won't be very long now—you know they are to be married in October or November. But, Bob, as I was telling you, Alice did all the cooking for this party herself. Of course, it was simple, but really, I think she is quite wonderful. She has never done anything useful before, but she is so clever, and she has such a 'knack' that it will really be easier for her than for Ruth. And Ruth will work twice as hard. Alice says that she is going to give other little parties this way, and practice on her guests. She says she is determined to do things just as well as anybody else, and now that she is interested, she has a tremendous pride in being a success. You know how high-spirited Alice is. Well, she isn't to be surpassed by anyone in anything she cares to do! Oh, I forgot, Bob, she gave me some cakes to bring to you, and also some salted nuts."

"Hurray for Alice! She's some friend all right! What else did you have at the party?"

"Such good salad—she gave me the recipe—well, her menu consisted of:

<table>
<tr><td>Honolulu Salad</td><td>Graham Bread Sandwiches</td></tr>
<tr><td>Frozen Apricots</td><td>White Cake</td></tr>
<tr><td>Salted Nuts</td><td>Coffee</td></tr>
</table>

BETTINA'S RECIPES

(All measurements are level)

Honolulu Salad (Six portions)

6 slices canned pineapple	¼ t-salt
½ C-cottage cheese	6 nut-meat halves
1 T-chopped pimento	6 pieces of lettuce
1 t-chopped green pepper	6 T-salad dressing

Add the chopped pimento, green pepper and salt to the cottage cheese. Work all together well, shape into balls one inch in diameter. Place a ball in the center of each slice of pineapple, which has been arranged upon a piece of lettuce. Place a nut meat upon the top of each cheese ball. Serve one tablespoon of salad dressing upon each service.

Frozen Apricots (Six portions)

2 C-peeled and quartered apricots	2 T-lemon juice
	1 C-water
1 C-sugar	1 egg-white

Cook apricots, sugar and water until the apricots are soft. (About five minutes.) Cool, add the lemon juice and freeze. When the mixture is half frozen, add the stiffly beaten white and continue freezing until stiff. More sugar may be used if desired.

CHAPTER L

A DINNER COOKED IN THE MORNING

"WE'LL treat Uncle Eric so well that he'll have a good time in spite of himself," Bob had said when he had proposed that his gruff old uncle be invited. "I'll take Saturday afternoon off, and we'll go to the matinee, then we'll come home to dinner, and then go again to the theatre in the evening." For a great actor was to be in town, and this was the reason for Uncle Eric's possible visit. "If he'll only come," Bob had added doubtfully.

"He'll come," said Bettina confidently, for she felt that she had discovered the soft spot in Uncle Eric's heart. "We'll have a good dinner, too."

Bob remembered what she had said about the dinner and repeated it to himself as they stepped from the street car after the matinee. "It's late, Bettina," he said anxiously, "will it take you long to get dinner?"

"A very few minutes," answered Bettina. "Just long enough to warm it over."

To warm it over! But then, all of Bettina's dinners were good, so he resolved not to worry. Nevertheless, he could not help leaving Uncle Eric for a few minutes to come into the kitchen. "What can I do to help?"

"Not a thing, Bob dear. You see, I had this whole dinner ready this morning, and I have warmed it all up in the oven. I have discovered that croquettes are exactly as good when fried in the morning, and so are veal cutlets. And wait till you try the cauliflower!"

173

"I trust you, Bettina," said Bob, laughing. "It all looks mighty good to me. Here, I'll help you put it on the table." For dinner that night they had:

Veal Cutlets   Potato Croquettes
Escalloped Cauliflower
Baked Apples
Bread   Butter
Chocolate Ice Cream   White Cake

BETTINA'S RECIPES

(All measurements are level)

Veal Cutlets (Three portions)

1 lb. ½-inch slices of	¼ t-paprika
veal cut from the leg	1/3 t-salt
1 t-salt	1 egg-white or yolk
1½ pints of water	1 T-water
1 C-cracker crumbs	Hot fat for frying

Wipe the meat, place in one and one-half pints of boiling water, to which has been added one level teaspoon of salt. Boil gently until tender (about thirty minutes). Remove from the water and allow to cool until easy to handle. Remove the bone and skin, and cut into pieces for serving. Mix the paprika, salt (one-third of a teaspoon) and the cracker crumbs. Roll each piece of meat in the crumbs, then in the egg, to which the water has been added, and again in the crumbs. Pat the crumbs onto the meat. Arrange the meat on a platter and allow to stand fifteen minutes. Have sufficient fat in a pan to cover articles of food. When the fat is smoking hot, add the veal cutlets, and turn to cook each side. When a delicate brown (after about five minutes), remove and drain on paper. Keep hot in the oven. Place the veal cutlets on a platter and arrange baked apples around the edges. Serve the potato croquettes on the same platter, garnished with parsley.

Potato Croquettes (Three portions)

1 C-hot mashed or	1 egg-yolk
riced potatoes	1 T-milk
⅛ t-celery salt	1 t-salt
½ t-chopped parsley	1 T-butter
⅛ t-onion extract	⅛ t-paprika
3 T-flour	

Mix the mashed potatoes, celery salt, parsley, onion extract, egg yolk, milk, salt, butter and paprika. Beat two minutes. Shape into balls two inches in diameter. Roll in flour and allow to stand fifteen minutes. Cook in deep fat three minutes or more until a delicate brown. Drain on brown paper and keep hot in a moderate oven.

Escalloped Cauliflower (Three portions)

1 small head of cauliflower	1½ C-vegetable white sauce,
1 qt. water	seasoned
1 t-salt	¼ C-buttered crumbs

Soak the cauliflower in cold water to which a tablespoon of vinegar has been added. Cut apart and cook in a quart of water to which salt has been added. Make white sauce and add the cauliflower. Pour into a well-buttered baking dish. Cover with buttered crumbs. Bake twenty minutes in a moderate oven.

CHAPTER LI

A SUNDAY DINNER

"WE have gone 'over home' for so many Sunday dinners lately," Bettina had said to her mother, "that I want you and father to come here tomorrow."

"But, Bettina," her mother protested, "isn't it too much work for you? And won't you be going to church?"

"I can't go to church tomorrow, anyhow, for Bob's Uncle Eric is to be in town all morning; he leaves at noon, and the Dixons have offered us their car to take him for a drive. Don't worry, Mother, I'll have a simple dinner—a 'roast beef dinner,' I believe. I often think that is the very easiest kind."

Sunday morning was so beautiful that Bettina could not bear to stay indoors. Accordingly, she set the breakfast table on the porch, even though Uncle Eric protested that it was too far for her to walk back and forth with the golden brown waffles she baked for his especial delight. When he and Bob had eaten two "batches," Uncle Eric insisted that he could bake them himself for a while. He installed Bettina in her chair at the table, and forced waffles upon her till she begged for mercy.

"Gracious!" Bettina exclaimed as she heard the "honk" of the Dixons' automobile at the door. "There are the Dixons already and we have just finished breakfast! Bob, you and Uncle Eric will have to go on without me, for I must get the roast in the oven and do the morning's work."

"Well, I learned today to make waffles," said Uncle Eric.

For dinner that day Bettina served:

Roast Beef	Brown Gravy
Browned Potatoes	Baked Squash
Lettuce	French Dressing
Lemon Sherbet	Devil's Food Cake

Coffee

BETTINA'S RECIPES

(All measurements are level)

Roast Beef (Eight portions)

3½ lb. rump roast of beef	2 t-salt
4 T-flour	¼ C-hot water

Roll the roast in the flour and set on a rack in a dripping-pan. Place in a hot oven and sear over all sides. Sprinkle the salt over the meat and add the hot water. Cover the meat and cook in a moderate oven. Baste every fifteen minutes. Allow fifteen minutes a pound for a rare roast, and twenty minutes a pound for a well done roast. When properly done, the outside fat is crisp and brown.

Brown Potatoes (Six portions)

6 potatoes   2 t-salt

Wash and peel the potatoes. Sprinkle with salt. Forty minutes before the roast is to be done, add the potatoes. During the last ten minutes of cooking the lid may be removed from the meat and potatoes to allow all to brown nicely.

Browned Gravy (Six portions)

4 T-beef drippings	1 C-water
2 T-flour	¼ t-salt

Place four tablespoons of beef drippings in a pan, add the flour and allow to brown. Add the rest of the drippings, the water and the salt. Cook two minutes. Serve hot.

Baked Squash (Six portions)

1 squash	1½ t-salt
2 T-butter	¾ t-paprika

Wash and wipe the squash, and cut into halves, then quarters. Remove the seeds. Place the pieces of squash, skin down, in a baking-dish and bake in a moderate oven until tender (about one hour). Remove from the oven, mash up with a fork, and add to each portion one-half a teaspoon of butter, one-fourth a teaspoon of salt, and one-eighth a teaspoon of paprika. Reheat in the oven and serve hot.

Devil's Food Cake (Sixteen pieces)

1/3 C-butter	2/3 C-sour milk
1½ C-sugar	1 t-vanilla
1 egg	2 C-flour
2 squares of melted chocolate	

Cream the butter, add the sugar and continue to cream the mixture. Add the egg, well beaten, and the chocolate. Mix well. Add the soda and flour sifted together, and the sour milk and vanilla. Beat three minutes. Bake in two layer cake pans prepared with waxed paper for twenty-five minutes in a moderate oven.

Icing (Sixteen portions)

2 C-"C" sugar	2 egg-whites beaten stiffly
½ C-water	1 t-vanilla

Cook the sugar and water together until it clicks when a little is dropped into a cup of cold water. Pour slowly over the beaten egg whites. Beat vigorously until creamy. Add the vanilla. Pour on one layer of the cake. Place the upper layer on top, and pour the rest of the icing upon it. Spread evenly over the top and over the sides.

CHAPTER LII

BOB MAKES PEANUT FUDGE

"**I** USUALLY complain when it rains—I have that habit—but I must confess that I like a rainy evening at home once in a while," said Bob, as he and Bettina sat down at the dinner table. "Dinner on a rainy night always seems so cozy."

"Liver and bacon don't constitute a very elaborate dinner," said Bettina. "But they taste good for a change. And oh, Bob, tonight I want you to try a new recipe I heard of—peanut fudge. It sounds delicious."

"I'm there," said Bob. "I was just thinking it would be a good candy evening. Then, when the candy is done, we'll assemble under the new reading lamp and eat it."

"Yes, it'll be a good way to initiate the reading lamp! Wasn't it dear of Uncle Eric to give it to us? I kept wondering why he was so anxious to know just what I planned to do with the money I won for my nut bread at the fair. I even took him around and pointed out this particular lamp as the thing I had been saving for. And here it arrived the day after he left, as a gift to me! It was dear of Uncle Eric! But now what on earth shall I do with my fair money?"

"Don't worry about that, Bettina. Put it in the bank."

"But I'd like to get something as sort of a monument to my luck. Have you any particular needs, Bob?"

"Not a need in the world! Except for one more of those fine fruit gems over there."

That night they had for dinner:

Liver and Bacon	Creamed Turnips
Fruit Gems	Apple Sauce

Tea

BETTINA'S RECIPES

(All measurements are level)

Creamed Turnips (Two portions)

1 C-turnip cubes	1 T-flour
1/3 t-salt	¼ t-salt
1 T-butter	½ C-milk

Peel the turnips. Cut into one-half inch cubes. Soak in cold water ten minutes. Cook in boiling water in an uncovered utensil until transparent no longer. Drain and sprinkle with salt. Melt the butter, add the flour and the one-fourth teaspoon salt, blend well, add the milk gradually and cook until creamy. Add the turnips and serve.

Liver and Bacon (Two portions)

4 slices bacon	1 t-salt
2/3 lb. liver	¼ t-paprika
3 T-flour	

Cover slices of calves' liver cut one-half inch thick with boiling water. Allow to stand five minutes. Drain and cut into pieces for serving. Sprinkle with salt and pepper and roll in flour. Have a frying pan very hot. Add sliced bacon. When the bacon has cooked on each side, pile up on one side of the pan and add the liver, placing a piece of bacon on top of each portion of liver, thus preventing the bacon from getting too well done, and also seasoning the liver. Brown the liver thoroughly on both sides. (It should be cooked about ten minutes.) Serve hot.

Fruit Gems (Nine Gems)

2 C-flour	¾ C-milk
3 t-baking powder	1 egg
3 T-sugar	1 T-melted butter
¼ t-salt	1/3 C-seeded, chopped
	raisins or currants

Mix the flour, baking powder, sugar and salt. Break the egg into the milk, stir well, pour into the dry ingredients. Beat vigorously one minute. Add the melted butter and raisins or currants. Bake in nine well buttered gem pans for twenty minutes in a moderate oven.

Peanut Fudge (Six portions)

1 C-"C" sugar	2/3 C-milk
1 C-granulated sugar	1 T-butter
¼ t-cream of tartar	1 t-vanilla
2 squares of chocolate	½ C-broken peanuts

Mix the sugar, cream of tartar, chocolate, milk and butter. Cook over a moderate fire until the fudge forms a soft ball when a little is dropped into cold water. Remove from the fire, allow to stand without stirring for twenty minutes. Beat vigorously until creamy. Add the vanilla and peanuts. When very thick remove to a buttered plate. Allow to harden and cut in squares.

CHAPTER LIII

DINNER AT THE DIXONS

"IS it still as much fun to keep house as it was at first, Charlotte?" asked Bettina as she and Bob sat down to dinner with the Dixons.

"Fun?" said Charlotte. "Bettina, look at me! Or better still, look at Frank! And the funny part of it all is that Aunt Isabel thinks our keeping house is a result of her preachments against boarding and hotel living. Why, she quite approves of me now! And I'll just keep quiet and let her feel that she was the one who did it, but all the while in my heart I'll be remembering that it was the sight of your happiness that roused my ambition to make a home myself."

"I tell you," said Mr. Dixon, "we can never thank you enough, Bettina. Now shall I play 'Home Sweet Home' on the piano? And will you all join in the chorus?"

"Not if you sing, too," said Mrs. Dixon, smiling at her husband's foolishness. "I've learned a great deal from you, since I began, Bettina, and not the smallest lesson is that of having company without dreading it. I don't try to make things elaborate, just dainty and simple food such as we have every day. Why, tonight I didn't make a single change for you and Bob! And I don't believe I should dread even Aunt Isabel's sudden arrival now."

"Aunt Isabel is really a good soul, Bettina," said Frank. "Charlotte has never learned how much worse her bark is than her bite, and she takes it to heart when Aunt Isabel speaks her mind. Why, I remember so well the scoldings she used to give me when I was a boy, and the cookies she would manage to treat me with afterward! I used to anticipate those pleasant scoldings!"

"If a scolding always comes before food," said Bob, "Charlotte must have given you an extra good one before inviting us to partake of that delicious-looking chocolate pie!"

That evening they had:

Cold Sliced Ham   Creamed Potatoes
Tomatoes Stuffed with Rice
Peach Butter
Chocolate Pie
Coffee

BETTINA'S RECIPES

(All measurements are level)

Tomatoes Stuffed with Rice (Six portions)

6 tomatoes	2 T-grated cheese
½ C-rice, cooked	1 t-chopped onion
½ C-green pepper, chopped	¼ t-salt
	1 T-butter

Remove a piece one inch in diameter from the stem end of each tomato. Take out the seeds. Fill the shells with the rice, pepper, cheese, onion and salt, well mixed. Place a small dot of butter on top of each. Place in a small pan and bake twenty-five minutes in a moderate oven.

Chocolate Pie Crust (Six portions)

1 C-flour	¼ t-salt
1/3 C-lard	3 T-ice water

Mix the flour and salt, cut in the lard with a knife, add the liquid slowly, stirring with the knife. More water may be needed. Roll out thin, fit onto a tin pan, prick with holes, and bake in a hot oven until light brown (about seven minutes).

Filling (Six portions)

1 C-sugar	2 eggs
5 T-flour	1½ squares melted
⅛ t-salt	chocolate
2 C-milk	½ t-vanilla

Mix well the sugar, flour and salt. Add gradually the milk and beaten egg yolks. Cook in a double boiler fifteen minutes. Add the melted chocolate. Cook until thick (about ten minutes), and add the vanilla. Fill the baked shell, and cover with meringue. Place in a moderate oven and cook until the meringue is a delicate brown (about five minutes).

Meringue

2 egg whites   4 T-sugar

Beat the whites of eggs very stiff. Add the sugar. Pile lightly on the chocolate mixture. Brown in the oven. Chocolate pie should be served cold.

CHAPTER LIV

A GOOD-BY LUNCHEON FOR BERNADETTE

"**B**IG success!" was what Bettina's eyes telegraphed to Ruth across the purple and white asters in the center of a long porch table. Ruth was giving a farewell luncheon for Bernadette, her young cousin, who was leaving that night for a fashionable New York school. Although there was no suggestion of it in the dainty dishes the two girls served to the hungry and vivacious young guests, Ruth was "trying out" her cooking with all of the stage-fright of the beginner. The recipes and suggestions were chiefly Bettina's, and the two had been busy in Ruth's kitchen since early that morning. Bernadette was a critical young person, although light-hearted and affectionate, and Ruth felt that she could set her humble efforts before no sterner judge. Yet all the while, as she tasted each course in its turn, her mind was running on, "Will Fred like this? Some day I'll be serving this to Fred!" It was certainly a satisfaction to feel one's self able to cook a luncheon acceptable to "the younger society set!"

With each course an enormous motto, supposedly of the "Don'ts for School Girls' Series," was brought in ceremoniously on a tray and suspended from the chandelier over the table, until finally five huge, if foolish, "Don'ts" were dangling there for Bernadette's inspection.

With the last course, Ruth, in the postman's hat, coat and bag, brought in an endless supply of letters for Bernadette, to be opened at such times as "When You Meet Your Impossible Room-mate," "When You Feel the First Pangs of Home-

185

sickness," "When Reprimanded by a Horrid Old Teacher," "When Forced to Mend Your Own Stockings," etc.

Bernadette seized them all delightedly, glanced at the covers and cried out, half in laughter, half in tears, "Oh, girls, I simply can't go 'way off there! I'll die!" Her friends fell upon her with scoldings and hugs, and in the midst of the noise and clamor, Ruth and Bettina slipped out to laugh and talk over Ruth's first serious culinary effort.

The menu consisted of:

Iced Cantaloupe Balls

Chicken Croquettes   Potatoes in Cream

Green Peppers Stuffed with Corn

Rolls   Peach Pickles

Cherry Salad   Wafers

Chocolate Cream Pudding

Coffee

BETTINA'S RECIPES

(All measurements are level)

Chicken Croquettes (Eight croquettes)

1½ C-cooked chopped chicken	1 t-parsley chopped fine
¼ t-celery salt	¼ C-thick white sauce
1 t-lemon juice	½ t-salt
	2 C-crumbs
4 T-egg, beaten	

Mix the chicken, celery salt, lemon juice, parsley, salt and thick white sauce. Shape into croquettes. Roll in cracker crumbs, beaten egg and more crumbs. Deep fry. Serve hot.

Green Peppers Stuffed with Corn (Six portions)

1 C-corn-pulp, cooked	2 T-bread crumbs
½ t-salt	⅛ t-pepper
1 egg-yolk	½ t-sugar
¼ C-milk	1 T-butter
6 green peppers	

Scoop out the contents of the peppers. Mix the corn, salt, egg yolk, milk, bread crumbs, pepper and sugar. Fill the peppers. Dot with butter. Place in a pan and bake thirty minutes in a moderate oven. Cover the bottom of the pan with water. Baste the peppers frequently.

Cherry Salad (Six portions)

2 C-California   ½ C-hazelnuts
    cherries   6 lettuce leaves
       6 T-salad dressing

Remove the seeds from two cups of California white cherries, and fill with filberts or hazel nuts. Arrange on crisp lettuce leaves, and serve with salad dressing.

Chocolate Cream Pudding (Six portions)

2 C-milk   1½ squares of melted
5 T-cornstarch   chocolate
½ C-sugar   3 T-hot water
¼ t-salt   2 egg-whites
       1 t-vanilla

Mix the cornstarch, sugar and salt. Add cold milk gradually, mixing well. Melt the chocolate in the hot water, and add it to the other mixture. Cook in the double boiler ten minutes, stirring occasionally. Beat three minutes. Add the stiffly beaten white and the vanilla. Mould, chill and serve. If the chocolate does not melt in the hot water, cook over the fire a minute. Whipped cream may be served with the pudding.

CHAPTER LV

BETTINA PLANS AN ANNOUNCEMENT LUNCHEON

"AND so I thought, if you were willing, I would have the luncheon the last of this week," said Bettina to Alice one sultry afternoon which they were spending on Bettina's porch.

"That's dear of you, Bettina. Oh, how queer it will seem to have everyone know about it! You must let me help with the luncheon, of course."

"No, indeed, Alice! Ruth and I are going to do it all alone, and the guest of honor is not to lift a finger! You can advise us, of course, but you mustn't arrive that day till everything is ready. I want to tell you about a few plans I've made. I wish I could consult Harry, too."

"But he won't be at the announcement party!"

"No, but he's the leading man in the drama, and important even when off the stage. Let's telephone him to come here to dinner tonight. It is so warm that I have planned only a lunch, but we can set the porch table and have a jolly informal time. Do call him up, Alice."

"I'd love to, of course, if you really want us."

"Indeed I do, but we'll have to hurry, for it's after five now."

"I'll help you," said Alice, after Harry had given his hearty acceptance. "Let me fix the salad."

"All right, and I'll stir up some little tea cakes. It's better not to cut those beets too small, Alice; it makes them soft.

I never add them till just before I serve the salad. There, that's fine! Do you want to fix the parsley to garnish the ham? Ham looks so much better with parsley that I never fail to garnish it. I have nasturtiums for the center of the table, and we'll garnish the salad with them, too."

"It will be a festive little meal. What else can I do while you're baking the tea cakes?"

"You can make the iced tea, Alice. You do everything so easily and deftly that I love to watch you. And you have never cooked at all until lately, have you?"

"No, but I really like it. Wouldn't it be a joke if I should become very domestic?"

"Well, your fate is pointing in that direction! Time is swiftly passing, and in a few short weeks—Alice, shall I call off the announcement luncheon?"

"Oh, no, no, Bettina! Let fate do her worst! I'm resigned."

Supper that night consisted of:

Cold Sliced Ham	Beet Salad
Bread	Butter
Tea Cakes	Apple Sauce
Iced Tea	

BETTINA'S RECIPES

(All measurements are level)

Beet Salad (Four portions)

1 C-cold boiled beets cut in ½-inch cubes
1/3 C-cold boiled potatoes, cubed
1/3 C-diced celery
1 hard-cooked egg, diced
1/3 C-diced cucumber
½ t-salt
Salad dressing

Mix the beets, potatoes, celery, egg, cucumber and salt very lightly together with a fork. Mix with salad dressing. Serve in a bowl garnished with nasturtium leaves and flowers.

"Lightning" Tea Cakes (Twelve cakes)

1½ C-flour
¾ C-granulated or powdered sugar
2 t-baking powder
½ t-vanilla
1/3 t-salt
3 T-butter (melted)
1 egg
½ C-milk

Sift and mix together the flour, sugar, baking powder and salt. Make a "well" in the center of the mixture and pour in the melted butter, egg, milk and vanilla. Stir all together and beat vigorously for two minutes. Fill well buttered muffin pans half full of the mixture and bake fifteen minutes in a moderate oven.

CHAPTER LVI

RUTH AND BETTINA MAKE PREPARATIONS

"OH, Bettina, aren't the butterflies darling?" exclaimed Ruth, looking once more at the table display of her work. "And with everything ready to begin in the morning, won't things be easy for us both? What shall I do next?"

"Not a thing, Ruth dear. You've worked too hard all this afternoon, I'm afraid. Now we're going to sit down to a good hot dinner, and tell Bob all about our preparations."

"M—m! Something smells good!" said Ruth. "I've been so busy with all these cunning things that I haven't even thought of eating. But now that you mention it, I'll admit that I have a fine healthy appetite."

"Well, dinner is almost ready, and Bob will be here any minute. It's all in the oven except the corn: meat loaf, sweet potatoes and apricot cobbler."

"Oh, how good it sounds! More sensible than all our fluffy dishes for the announcement luncheon. But then, I do love fluffy things. I'm sure Alice will like it, and all the others, too. Makes me 'most wish I'd kept my engagement a secret, and announced it with ceremony as Alice is doing. But I couldn't, somehow."

"No, you couldn't, Ruth, and neither could Fred. He'd give it away if you didn't. So I guess there's no use wishing you had kept it. Anyhow, you just suit me as you are. You've been such a dear to help with the luncheon! Goodness, there's Bob now!"

The dinner consisted of:

Beef Loaf   Sweet Potatoes
                    Corn on the Cob
Bread   Butter
                    Apricot Cobbler

BETTINA'S RECIPES

(All measurements are level)

Beef Loaf (Three portions)

1 lb. beef ground	½ t-salt
¼ lb. salt pork, ground	⅛ t-pepper
¼ t-onion salt	⅛ C-tomato
1/3 C-fresh bread crumbs	¼ C-water
1 egg	1 T-fat drippings

Mix the ground beef and salt pork, add the onion salt, fresh crumbs, egg, salt, pepper and tomato. Mix thoroughly. Shape into a loaf which will fit into a small buttered pan. Add the water and pour fat drippings over the top. (Bacon fat is good.) Cover the pan, and allow to cook in the oven one-half hour. Uncover the loaf, basting frequently, and brown it. This will take fifteen or twenty minutes. Serve hot. More water may be added while cooking if necessary.

Sweet Potatoes (Three portions)

3 potatoes   ¾ t-salt

Peel the potatoes, salt them with one-fourth a teaspoon of salt in each potato, and place them in the pan with the meat. This gives the potatoes a good flavor.

Bettina's Apricot Cobbler (Three portions)

1 C-cooked and sweetened apricots	1/3 t-salt
	2 T-butter
1 T-flour	1/3 C-milk
½ t-cinnamon	1/3 C-sugar
1 C-flour	½ C-water
2 t-baking powder	½ t-vanilla

Mix the apricots, one tablespoon flour and cinnamon. Mix and sift together flour, baking powder and salt. Cut in the butter with a knife. Add the milk until a soft dough is formed. Place the apricot mixture in a baking-dish and the dough on top of the apricots. Cook the water and sugar together for three minutes. Add the vanilla. When the cobbler has baked fifteen minutes pour syrup over it. Bake ten minutes more in a moderate oven.

CHAPTER LVII

A RAINBOW ANNOUNCEMENT LUNCHEON

"OH, Bettina, how lovely!" cried the ten guests in a chorus, as Ruth and Bettina ushered them into the softly lighted dining-room. Not one had had even a glimpse of the luncheon table before, for Ruth had been entertaining them on the porch while Bettina put on the finishing touches. It all seemed a burst of soft rainbow colors. "What is it?" cried someone. "How did you ever get the rainbow effect?"

"Let's not examine it too closely," said Bettina. "You know a rainbow after all is nothing but drops of water with the sun shining through, and maybe my rainbow table has a prosy explanation, too."

From the low mass of variegated garden flowers in the center—pink, yellow, lavender, orange, blue, and as many others as the girls could find—ran strips of soft tulle in rainbow colors. The strips were attached at the outer end to the dainty butterflies which perched lightly on the tulle covered candy cups. These candy cups held pink, lavender and green Jordan almond candies. More butterflies in all sizes and colors hovered among the flowers. Upon the plain white name cards, little butterflies had been outlined in black and decorated in butterfly colors. Ruth and Bettina had cut with the scissors around this outline and then, when it had been cut almost away, had folded back the butterfly so that it stood up on the card, as ready for flight as its brothers and sisters.

"Aren't they cunning?" exclaimed Barbara, taking her butterfly from her favor cup. "Goodness, it's attached to something!" Pulling gently by the rainbow tulle to which the butterfly had been pasted, she drew forth from the greenery in the center a little golden bag. It was in reality a little fat bag of soft yellow silk tied with gold cord and holding something that, seen through the mesh, appeared to be—gold?

The other girls, in great excitement, drew forth their little bags.

"Rice!" declared Mary, "though it looks yellow!"

"It's the bag of gold at the foot of the rainbow!" exclaimed Ruth, with flushed cheeks. "Discovered by——"

"Harry Harrison and Alice!" cried the girls, laughing almost hysterically. For one small card which read, "Discovered by" and the two names, in gold letters, was tied to the little bag by the gold cord.

"Alice, how did you ever manage to keep it a secret?" asked someone.

"Well, it would have been harder if you had all known Harry, but you see, we haven't been with the crowd much lately, have we? Now admit it! You haven't even missed me!"

."But you're more of a butterfly than any of the rest of us. And the limits of the old crowd don't always bound your flutterings."

"I'm not a butterfly any more," said Alice. "I suppose I'll have a butterfly wedding (Harry will detest it, but he'll have to give in that once), but after that I expect to be as domestic as Bettina here, though not such a success at it, probably. Aren't these orange baskets the prettiest things?"

The girls, in their excitement, had almost forgotten to eat, but now they looked down at their plates. Fruit cups in orange baskets, with handles of millinery wire twisted with pink, green, yellow and violet tulle, added to the rainbow effect. The baskets were placed on paper doilies on tea plates, and were artistically lined with mint leaves.

"It looks too pretty to eat," said Dorothy.

"Ruth will feel hurt if you don't like it, but I know you will," said Bettina. "She prepared this course, and made most of the table decorations, too."

"And didn't you wish that you were announcing something yourself, Ruth?" asked Mary. "Although I don't believe the crowd could stand two such surprises! We've known Fred and you so long that your engagement seems the natural thing, but when a perfectly strange man like Mr. Harrison happens by, and helps himself to one of our number—well, it certainly takes my breath away! Where did you first meet him, Alice? Was it love at first sight?"

"Love at first sight? Bob introduced us—here, in this very house, and I thought—well—I thought Harry the most disagreeably serious man I'd ever had the misfortune to meet! And he thought me the most disagreeably frivolous girl he had ever seen! So our feud began, and of course we had to see each other to fight it out!"

"And then comes Bettina's rainbow luncheon to show us how serious the feud proved to be," laughed Barbara. "What? More courses, Bettina? This is a beautiful luncheon! I wonder who'll be the next to discover the treasure at the foot of the rainbow?"

The menu consisted of:

Fruit Cups in Orange Baskets
_____

Cream of Celery Soup   Whipped Cream
Salt Wafers
_____

Tuna Moulds   Egg Sauce
Potatoes a la Bettina
Green Peppers Stuffed with Creamed Cauliflower
Rolls   Butter
_____

Head Lettuce, Russian Dressing
Thin Sandwiches in Fancy Shapes
_____

Marshmallow Cream
Coffee

BETTINA'S RECIPES

(All measurements are level)

Tuna Loaf (Eight portions)

1½ C-tuna	1 t-lemon juice
1 C-fresh bread crumbs	1 t-chopped green pepper
2 eggs (just the yolks may be used)	1 t-salt
	¼ t-paprika

Mix all the ingredients together thoroughly, picking the fish apart with a silver fork. Mould firmly in a loaf. Roll in flour, and place in a buttered bread pan. Dot with butter, and bake thirty minutes in a moderate oven. This same recipe may be distributed among fancy individual moulds, filled half full. Arrange a star-shaped piece of pimento, green pepper, beet or egg in the bottom of a fancy aluminum mould. An attractive design may be made by putting the star cut from any vegetable with radiating pieces of any other kind of vegetable of a different color. Place the design firmly on the fish. Set the moulds in a pan of hot water and bake until the mixture is firmly set. (About thirty minutes.) Remove from the oven, let moulds stand three minutes, and then, with the assistance of a knife, slip them from the pan, unmould all the moulds in one flat pan, and keep them hot until needed. Do not forget that the mould must be thoroughly buttered before using. When ready to serve, make a regular vegetable white sauce (two T-butter, 2 T-flour, 1 C-milk, ¼ t-salt). When ready to serve and while steaming hot, add one beaten egg yolk. The hot sauce will cook the egg. Pour around the mould.

CHAPTER LVIII

AN EARLY CALLER

BOB had scarcely left the house the next morning when Bettina was called to the door. "I couldn't resist coming!" said Alice. "The announcement party was lovely, and I must thank you for doing it. Aren't you tired to pieces?"

"No, Ruth helped me a great deal, and by the time Bob came home to dinner, the luncheon dishes were washed and put away and the house was in apple-pie order."

"Everything tasted delicious, Bettina. Maybe it sounds altogether too practical for my own announcement party, but I'm armed with a pencil and a notebook, and I do want to get some of those recipes of yours!"

"You're welcome to them all, Alice, of course. They are all recipes that I have used over and over again, and I'm sure of them."

"What kind of soup was it? Celery? I thought so. Wasn't it hard to prepare?"

"Why, Alice, it was canned celery soup, diluted with hot milk. Then I added a teaspoonful of chopped parsley and a teaspoonful of chopped red pepper."

"But surely it had whipped cream in it, Bettina!"

"Yes, I put a teaspoonful of whipped cream in the bottom of the bouillon cup and poured the hot soup on it, so that it would be well mixed."

"Well, that accounts for it; I thought it must be made with whipped cream. Oh, Bettina, everything was so pretty! The tulle bows on the baskets holding the wafers and the rolls—

and the butterflies perched on them! How did you ever think of it?"

"Well, butterflies are a happy choice for decorations! They can be put anywhere, and they are easy to make—at least Ruth says so."

"You use paper doilies a great deal, don't you? Aren't they expensive?"

"Expensive? Well, I wish you'd price them! They are so inexpensive that I like to use them even for a very informal meal; they add such a dainty touch, I think."

"I must write down the recipes for your tuna loaf, and green peppers stuffed with cauliflower, and Russian dressing—and oh, that wonderful kind of rainbow dessert! Bettina, what was that dessert?"

"Marshmallow cream made with gelatine and cream and marshmallows and whites of eggs. I puzzled a long time over a real 'rainbow' dessert, and finally decided on marshmallow cream with a few variations. Come into the kitchen, where I keep my card index, and I'll get all the recipes for you."

BETTINA'S RECIPES

(All measurements are level)

Potato Balls (Four portions)

4 potatoes	1 t-salt
1 C-crumbs	2 T-egg

Boil potatoes of uniform size with the skins on. When cold, peel, roll in crumbs, to which salt has been added and then the beaten egg and crumbs. Deep fry in very hot fat.

Green Peppers Stuffed with Cauliflower (Four portions)

4 green peppers	1 C-vegetable sauce
1 C-cooked cauliflower	2 T-crumbs
1 T-butter, melted	

Cut a thin slice from the stem end of each large green pepper and remove the seeds. Parboil ten minutes, and fill with creamed cauliflower and buttered crumbs. Bake until the skins are tender, basting occasionally with butter and water.

Marshmallow Cream (Four portions)

2 t-granulated gelatin	1 t-lemon extract
4 T-cold milk	¼ lb. marshmallows, **cut in**
2/3 C-sugar	one-fourth cubes
1 1/3 C-double cream	4 toasted marshmallows
1 t-vanilla extract	4 pecans
1 **egg** white well beaten	4 almonds

Soften the gelatin in milk for five minutes, and dissolve by setting the dish in boiling water. Add the sugar. Allow the mixture to cool. When it begins to congeal, add the flavorings. Beat in the whipped cream, and continue beating until it is firm. Fold in the egg-white and the marshmallows cut in cubes. When the mixture begins to set, pile lightly in sherbet cups. Place one-half of a toasted marshmallow on the top, and arrange pecan meats and candied cherries in a conventional design. Set aside one hour to cool and harden.

Bettina colored the mixture with vegetable coloring of a very delicate green. Then on the top she placed a teaspoonful of white whipped cream, then the toasted marshmallow and the different fruits. Bettina browned the marshmallows quickly in the oven, after she had cut them the desired shape. She used cups with handles, and decorated them with fluffy bows of variegated tulles. To make these bows, she took strips of each color desired, one inch wide, tied them together, and "fluffed them out." She might have gained a real rainbow effect by dividing the marshmallow cream (when mixed, but not yet firm) into three bowls, and coloring them green, lavender and pink, with delicate vegetable colors. Then, having beaten in the whipped cream, she might have placed in each sherbet cup three layers, pink, lavender and green. Then, on the top, she might have placed the whipped cream.

CHAPTER LIX

RUTH COMES TO LUNCHEON

"AND here we are, busily planning Alice's affairs," said Bettina, "when we might be talking of yours, Ruth. Are you sure, sure, sure, that you don't want any parties, or showers, or affairs of any sort?"

"Sure, sure, sure!" said Ruth, emphatically. "I may be silly, Bettina, but to me such a fuss beforehand takes something away from the beauty of the wedding! And then there are other reasons. We've had to postpone building till next summer, and may not be married till the house is done—you know that. So we'll have been engaged a long time. It seems to me that after a long engagement like ours, it is better to have a simple wedding and no parties. Alice's is happening just as I always expected that it would—a surprising announcement, a short engagement, and many parties, with an elaborate wedding as the climax! Sometimes I think that sort would be the kind to have—but you see, Bettina, when you're expecting to be married only once, you want to have just the kind that seems best to you."

"And yours will be just right for you, Ruth," said Bettina, warmly. "You are you, and Fred is Fred, and I can't imagine either of you caring for much excitement. And when you are in your new house——"

"I'm going to have you over at least once a week to just such a dear little luncheon as this! Or rather—as much like it as I can devise. Bettina, how did you have time to cook such good things?"

"Well," said Bettina, "Bob will have these same things for

dinner tonight, with the addition of some cold sliced meat. So now, Ruth, we have a long afternoon before us—to sew and talk!"

Bettina's luncheon consisted of:

Bettina's Mexican Salad   Brown Bread
Apricot Preserves
Orange Cake   Hot Chocolate

BETTINA'S RECIPES

(All measurements are level)

Bettina's Mexican Salad (Four portions)

1 cucumber diced	2 T-green pepper, cut fine
2 tomatoes cut in one-inch cubes	1/3 C-cottage cheese
1 C-cut celery	1 t-salt
¼ C-cooked beets	2/3 C-salad dressing
1 T-chopped parsley	4 lettuce leaves

Mix all the ingredients in order given and serve on lettuce leaves.

Brown Bread (Baked) (Two loaves)

2 C-graham flour	1 t-salt
2 C-white flour	1 C-molasses
2 t-soda	2 C-sour milk

Mix well the graham flour, white flour, soda and salt. Add the molasses and sour milk; mix thoroughly. Pour into two well-buttered bread tins, and bake forty minutes in a moderate oven.

Orange Cake (Sixteen pieces)

1/3 C-butter	¼ t-salt
1 C-sugar	¼ C-orange juice
2 eggs beaten separately	¼ C-milk
Grated rind of one orange	1 2/3 C-flour
3 t-baking powder	½ t-lemon extract

Cream the butter, add the sugar and egg-yolks; mix thoroughly. Add the orange rind. Add the baking powder, salt and flour sifted together and then the orange juice and milk. Mix, and beat one minute. Add the egg-whites beaten stiffly, and the lemon extract. Bake in two square cake tins fitted with waxed paper for twenty-five minutes in a moderate oven.

Orange Filling for the Cake (Sixteen portions)

½ C-sugar	Grated rind of ½ an
3 T-flour	orange
⅛ t-salt	¼ C-water
1 egg yolk	¼ C-orange juice
½ t-lemon juice	

Mix the flour, sugar and salt well; add slowly the egg-yolk and the grated rind, the orange juice and water. Cook slowly over hot water for ten minutes, or until thick enough to spread. Add the lemon juice or lemon extract. Spread on one layer of cake. Place the other layer carefully on the top and spread Quick Cake Icing over the top and sides of the cake.

OCTOBER.

Oh, hazy month of glowing trees,——
And colors rich to charm our eyes!
Yet—not less fair than all of these
Are Mother's fragrant pumpkin pies!

CHAPTER LX

A KITCHEN SHOWER FOR ALICE

"DID you want me for something, Mary?" asked Alice at the door. "Mother said you had telephoned."

"Come in! Come in!" cried ten girls at once, while Bettina whispered to Ruth: "Thank goodness, she's come! The muffins are all but done!"

"What in the world!" said Alice.

"A party for you!"

"And I'm wearing my old suit!"

"We caught you this time, but never mind. Come in, and take off your things."

As soon as Alice reappeared in the living room, a small table was drawn up before the open fire. Two girls appeared, wearing gingham aprons and carrying overflowing market baskets.

"This is a kitchen shower for you, Alice," Ruth explained somewhat ceremoniously. "But if you are willing, we will use the utensils in serving the luncheon and afterwards present them to you. May we unpack the baskets?"

"Do," said Alice, laughing.

From the larger basket, Ruth removed twelve white enamelled plates of different sizes (suitable for holding supplies in the refrigerator), and twelve cross-barred tea-towels. The latter she passed around to be used as napkins, and Mary distributed the plates. On the small serving table before the fire, a white muslin table cover was placed. As she unfolded it, Ruth read from the attached card:

> "If breakfast you should chance to eat
> Upon the kitchen table—
> I'll make it dainty, fair and neat
> So far as I am able."

When the steel forks and spoons of various sizes were taken out and passed around, two glass measuring cups were found to hold loaf sugar wrapped in frilled paper. Upon one of these Ruth read:

> "Please eat us all, but let your sweet
> Sweet hours be duly treasured,
> For we belie the worldly eye—
> True sweetness can't be measured."

A glass rolling-pin filled with stick candy came next, and its sentiments read, and meanwhile the girls had begun to read aloud the advice pinned upon the tea-towels, such as:

> "No matter what his whims and wishes—
> Just tell him he must wipe the dishes!"

and

> "But if he breaks a cup or plate,
> Just throw the pieces at him straight."

"What vindictive dish-towels!" said Alice. "They're not a bit sentimental!"

When the contents had been removed and all the verses read, the large basket was presented to Alice, who read from its handle:

"To market, to market, to buy your supplies!
You'll go there in person, if careful and wise."

"I will, Mr. Basket, with you over my arm!" answered Alice.

Meanwhile the girls had carried in the salad in an earthenware mixing-bowl, the muffins heaped high in a small basket with a dainty dustcloth over them, the coffee in a large enamelled pitcher, and the "molasses puffs" wrapped in frilled paper in a basket suitable for holding supplies. "Bettina's apples" were arranged in two flat enamelled pans. All the food was served informally from the small table, and the merriment grew as the luncheon progressed.

"I wish that all the meals Harry and I have together might be as jolly as this one! I'm sure I should be glad to eat always from kitchen dishes, if that is what makes the fun," said Alice.

At the kitchen shower, the luncheon was as follows:

Bettina's Potato Salad	Bettina's Spiced Beets
Twin Mountain Muffins	Currant Jelly
Molasses Puffs	Bettina's Apples
Coffee	Stick Candy

BETTINA'S RECIPES

(All measurements are level)

Bettina's Potato Salad (Twelve portions)

3 C-cold boiled potatoes, diced	3 T-diced pimento
1 C-diced celery	2 t-salt
½ C-diced hard-cooked egg	1 T-chopped onion
¼ C-diced sweet pickles	1 C-salad dressing
12 lettuce leaves	

Mix all the ingredients in the order named. Serve the salad very cold on crisp lettuce leaves.

Bettina's Spiced Beets (Twelve portions)

5 large, cooked beets,	1 T-"C" sugar
sliced	6 cloves
½ C-vinegar	1 t-salt
⅛ t-pepper	

Heat the vinegar, add the cloves, sugar, salt and pepper.

Pour over the beets, cut in one-third inch slices. Allow to stand one hour before serving.

Molasses Puffs (Twelve portions)

¾ C-molasses	1 egg, well beaten
¾ C-sugar	2 t-ginger
½ C-hot water	1 t-cinnamon
1/3 C-butter and lard	2 t-soda
(melted)	3 C-flour

Mix the molasses and sugar. Add the hot water and fat. Beat well, add the egg and mix thoroughly. Sift the ginger, cinnamon, flour and soda together, and add to the rest of the ingredients, mixing well. Fill well-buttered muffin pans three-fourths full. Bake in a moderate oven for twenty-five minutes. Ice with "C" sugar icing.

Icing

2 egg-whites beaten	2 C-"C" sugar
stiffly	½ C-water
	½ t-vanilla

Cook the sugar and water together until it "clicks" when a little is dropped into cold water. Pour the syrup slowly over the stiffly beaten egg whites. Beat vigorously until cool and creamy. Add the vanilla and spread on the cakes. If the icing gets hard before it is cool, add two tablespoons of water and continue beating. The secret of good icing is steady, constant beating.

Bettina's Apples (Twelve portions)

12 apples	¼ t-cinnamon
3 C-"C" sugar	½ t-vanilla
2 C-water	18 marshmallows
	1 T-butter

Wash, peel and core the apples. Place in a broad flat pan in which the sugar and water have been thoroughly mixed. Cook the apples, turning often until tender, remove from the syrup and place in a serving dish. Fill the center with one-half a marshmallow. Add the cinnamon and butter to the syrup and cook five minutes or until it thickens. Pour over and around the apples. Decorate with a marshmallow cut into fourths. Serve warm.

CHAPTER LXI

A RAINY NIGHT MEAL

"WHY, Bob, I thought you'd be miles away by this time!" cried Bettina, as Bob came into the house at the usual time one evening.

"They called off our trip on account of the weather. And I supposed you'd be at your mother's!"

"It was raining so that I decided to build a cozy little fire in the fireplace and stay at home."

"Well, I'm glad you're here! I was expecting to come home to a cold, dark house, and this is much more cheerful."

"And I expected not to see you till midnight, so I'm well suited too! But, Bobby, you mustn't complain if I give you a 'pick-up meal.' I expected to eat only a lunch myself."

"I don't care what you give me, just so it's hot. My walk through the rain has given me an appetite. I'll help you get supper and wash the dishes, Bettina, and then afterward we'll pop corn and toast marshmallows by the fire. What do you say?"

"Fine, Bob! I cooked some celery today—just a little— and I think I'll fix 'celery au gratin' for you. The cooky-jar is full of rocks——"

"A full cooky-jar! Bettina, that ought to be the symbol of our happy home. May it always be full!"

"You're altogether too oratorical for a staid married man, Bob. Well, as I was saying, here is apple sauce, and I'll soon have some emergency biscuit stirred up. Then with scrambled eggs——"

"Hurry, Bettina! My appetite grows with every dish you mention!"

They had a meal of:

Scrambled Eggs	Celery au Gratin
Emergency Biscuit	Fresh Apple Sauce
Rocks	Coffee

BETTINA'S RECIPES

(All measurements are level)

Scrambled Eggs (Two portions)

3 eggs   ¼ t-salt
5 T-milk   ⅛ t-paprika
        1 T-butter

Beat the eggs slightly; add milk, salt and paprika. Melt the butter in a frying pan or omelet pan. When hot, add the egg mixture, and cook slowly, scraping from bottom and sides of the pan when mixture first sets. Cook until creamy, or longer if preferred. If desired, the egg may be constantly "scrambled" with a fork while cooking. Turn into a hot dish and serve at once.

Celery au Gratin (Two portions)

1 C-cooked diced celery   ½ C-milk and celery stock
1 T-butter   3 T-grated cheese
1 T-flour   ⅛ t-paprika
            ¼ t-salt

Cook the celery in a small amount of water at a low temperature, as too fast boiling makes it tough. Simmer until tender.

Melt the butter, add the flour and blend well. Add the milk and stock, pepper and salt. Add the cheese. Allow to cook until it is the consistency of a thin vegetable white sauce. Add the celery. Place in a hot oven for fifteen minutes.

(Bettina uses a part of the water in which the celery is simmered to make up the cup of combined milk and celery stock. The remainder of the celery stock she saves for soup.)

Rocks (Two dozen)

1½ C-brown sugar	¼ t-salt
2/3 C-butter	2½ C-flour
2 eggs	1 t-soda
1 t-cinnamon	1½ C-chopped nut meats
¼ t-ground cloves	and raisins
	1 t-vanilla

Cream the butter, add the sugar, and cream the mixture. Add the eggs, well beaten, and the remaining dry ingredients (except nuts and raisins) sifted together. Mix well. Add the nut meats and chopped raisins, and vanilla. The mixture should be very stiff. Drop from a spoon onto flat buttered pans or preferably onto a buttered baking sheet. Bake about twelve minutes in a moderate oven.

(Bettina keeps rocks in a stone jar, and finds that they keep well, and are really better when a day old.)

CHAPTER LXII

ALICE GIVES A LUNCHEON

"THESE are the first baking powder biscuits I have ever made for company," said Alice, "but I knew that I must begin some time. Mother has gone out to spend the day; I persuaded her that my efforts to serve a luncheon would upset her nervous system completely. Just think, girls! You are at my mercy—for I have prepared this humble repast with my own useless hands!"

"Shame on you, Alice! Don't pretend to be so humble. You do everything so easily that I'll not be surprised to see you papering your own house and acting as your own plumber and doing every other hard thing. A useless butterfly like you who turns out to be so competent after all is the despair of all us plodders who have always plodded and always will!" And Ruth sighed.

"Never mind, Ruthie," said Bettina. "I've eaten a mighty fine luncheon that you cooked yourself—four or five courses, if I haven't forgotten!"

"Yes, and I worried every minute during that day!"

"We all do at first, except maybe Alice!"

"Why worry?" said Alice. "(Seems to me I've heard that expression before.) You girls won't die if the biscuits do fail—I'll give you bread. Harry and I are going to laugh at our own mistakes—and enjoy them. Isn't that a good philosophy? But, girls, to get down to biscuits. I want to ask you—one and all—collectively and individually, to be in my wedding party. With the addition of Sister, who isn't here. She and Bettina will be the matrons of honor. Will you?"

"Will we!" they all cried with enthusiasm.

The luncheon menu was as follows:

Salmon Salad

Green Beans   Butter Sauce

Baking-powder Biscuits

Watermelon Pickles

Cream Puffs   Coffee

BETTINA'S RECIPES

(All measurements are level)

Salmon Salad (Six portions)

1 C-salmon	1 t-salt
1 C-diced celery	3 hard-cooked eggs, cut fine
¼ C-sweet pickles, cut fine	1 C-salad dressing

Break the salmon apart carefully with a silver fork, add the diced celery, sweet pickles, salt and hard-cooked eggs. Mix together well, and add the salad dressing. Arrange on lettuce leaves in a salad bowl, garnish with hard-cooked eggs to represent daisies, and pickles cut in strips. Serve very cold. (To represent daisies, cut the whites of each hard-cooked egg in six long petals. Arrange these on the salad. Cut the yolks in half, and place in the center—round side out. Arrange the pickle to represent stem and leaves.)

Green Beans, Butter Sauce (Six portions)

2 C-green beans	1 t-salt
(canned)	¼ t-paprika ·
1 T-water	3 T-butter

Remove beans from the can and rinse with cold water. Add water, salt, paprika and butter. Cook over a moderate fire for three minutes. Serve.

Cream Puffs (Twelve Puffs)

1 C-boiling	¼ t-salt
water	1 C-flour
½ C-butter	3 eggs

Place the water and butter in a sauce pan. Heat to the boiling point, then add the flour, all at once, and stir till smooth. Cook till the paste comes away from the sides of the pan. (A very short time.) Remove from fire, and when cold, add the unbeaten eggs, one at a time, beating thoroughly after each egg is added. (The mixture should be stiff enough to hold its shape without spreading.) Chill the paste by placing in the ice-box and then drop by tablespoonsful on a buttered sheet. Bake thirty-five minutes in a hot oven. When cold, make an opening in the side of each and fill with cream filling.

Cream Filling (Twelve portions)

1 C-milk	1 T-flour
½ C-sugar	1 egg
¼ t-salt	1 t-butter
4 T-cornstarch	½ t-vanilla

Mix the sugar, salt, cornstarch and flour. Gradually add the milk and egg. Cook until very thick, in a double boiler. Add the butter and vanilla. Beat one minute. Cool before using.

CHAPTER LXIII

MOTORING WITH THE DIXONS

"NOT through dinner yet?" exclaimed the Dixons at the door. "May we sit down and wait? It's a beautiful evening, and we've come to get you to take a long drive with us."

"Fine," said Bob. "Come out to the dining-room and talk till we're through."

"And then I'll help Bettina clear off the table," said Charlotte. "Well, people, it looks like a good dinner, and Sherlock Holmes deduces, moreover, that you had roast lamb yesterday for your Sunday dinner."

"You might also deduce that we had baked potatoes, from which these creamed ones are made," laughed Bettina. "Nothing else to guess at, except that part of a cabbage made cold slaw yesterday and escalloped cabbage today. And my dessert, while simple, has no secret past," she added as she removed the first course. "A plain and simple custard, that's all."

"Suits me," said Bob, heartily, "especially when it's cold like this."

"By the way, Bettina," said Charlotte, "did you ever get rid of those black ants you were telling me about?"

"Yes, I've never seen one since."

"Well, you know how worried I was about the little red ones that bothered me. Aunt Isabel, in a letter, gave me a remedy that has worked like magic."

"Aunt Isabel has her uses, after all," teased Frank.

"I should say she has! She knows all about housekeeping, from A to Z! Her remedy sounds queer, but I can vouch for its efficacy, so if anyone ever asks you what to do for red ants, you tell them this, Bettina. I took some covers from baking powder cans, and some Mason jar covers, and some pie tins, and chalked the sides well with common school crayon. Then I set them on the pantry shelves to hold dishes of whatever kinds of food the ants liked. The ants never climbed over those chalked covers and soon they had all disappeared. I don't have to use the chalked tins any more, but if I ever see a red ant in my pantry again, I'll get out the chalk."

"Couldn't you make a heavy chalk mark on the shelf paper around the dish of food?" asked Bob.

"I tried that, but it didn't do any good. But the other way worked beautifully."

"I'm glad to know about it," said Bettina. "Well, Bob, are you ready? It will take only a few minutes to carry out the dishes and pile them up. I'm sorry we've kept you people waiting."

For dinner that night they had:

Cold Sliced Lamb	Creamed Potatoes
Chili Sauce	Escalloped Cabbage
Bread	Butter
Baked Custard	

BETTINA'S RECIPES

(All measurements are level)

Escalloped Cabbage (Two portions)

1 C-cooked cabbage	¼ t-salt
1 T-butter	½ C-milk
1 T-flour	2 T-fresh bread crumbs
1 T-melted butter	

Melt the butter, add the flour and salt, and mix well. Slowly pour over the milk and cook until creamy. Add the cabbage. Pour into a buttered baking dish. Add bread crumbs to melted butter, and place the buttered crumbs on the cabbage. Bake in a moderate oven for fifteen minutes, or until the crumbs are browned.

Chili Sauce (One and one-half pints)

12 large, ripe tomatoes	2 T-salt
3 green peppers	2 T-sugar
2 onions	1 T-ground cinnamon
3 C-vinegar	

Peel the tomatoes and onions, and chop separately very fine. Chop the pepper also, and add the salt, sugar and cinnamon. Mix all the ingredients together and add the vinegar. Cook one and one-half hours over a moderate fire, stirring sufficiently to prevent sticking. Bottle, and when cool, seal with paraffin.

Cup Custard (Three portions)

2 eggs	⅛ t-salt
2 C-milk	A few gratings of
4 T-sugar	nutmeg
¼ t-vanilla	

Beat the eggs slightly, add the sugar and milk slowly. Add salt and flavoring. Stir well. Pour into well-buttered cups. Sprinkle the nutmeg gratings on the top. Set the cups in a pan of hot water and bake in a moderate oven until a knife comes out clean upon piercing the custard (about thirty-five minutes). Do not allow the water in the pan to boil. Serve the custard cold, removing from the cups just before ready to serve. The custards may be served in cups.

CHAPTER LXIV

RUTH MAKES BAKING POWDER BISCUITS

"OH, Ruth!" called Bettina from her door to Ruth, who was walking past. "Come in and stay to dinner!"

"My dear, I'd love to, but——"

"I'm going to have baking powder biscuits, and I remember that you were longing to learn how to make them."

"Oh, Bettina! Would you really show me? I'll simply have to come, then. I hesitated because Aunt Martha is here, but I know she'll excuse me for one evening. What time is it? Five? I'll take these packages home and be back in fifteen minutes!"

When Ruth returned she found Bettina in her kitchen with all of the ingredients for the biscuits set out on the table.

"Perhaps two cups of flour will make too many for three people," she said, "but Bob has a good-sized appetite these crisp fall days, and he's fond of biscuits with jelly. Now, Ruth, you can get to work! Sift the flour, baking powder and salt together, and then cut the lard in this way with this knife. . . . Fine! Now add the milk very slowly—perhaps it will take a little more than two-thirds of a cup, it all depends on the flour. There! Now pat the dough into shape on this floured board, and then you can cut the biscuits out with this little cutter. Yes, about three-fourths of an inch thick. Ruth, those look fine! We'll wait a little while to bake them, they're better perfectly fresh. Set them out in the cold, there, until I have fixed the macaroni, and they can pop into the oven at the same time."

"That was so easy, Bettina. I do hope those biscuits will be good!"

The dinner consisted of :

Lamb Chops	Macaroni and Cheese

Sliced Tomatoes
Baking Powder Biscuits   Jelly
Apple Tapioca Pudding   Cream

BETTINA'S RECIPES

(All measurements are level)

Macaroni and Cheese (Three portions)

½ C-macaroni, broken in pieces	4 T-cheese, cut in small pieces
1 qt. water	1½ C-milk
1 t-salt	½ t-salt
2 T-butter	¼ t-paprika
	3 T-flour

Cook the macaroni in the boiling salted water until tender. (About fifteen minutes.) Drain and rinse thoroughly with cold water. Melt the butter, add the flour, salt and pepper. Gradually add the milk and cheese. Cook three minutes. Add the macaroni. Mix well, and pour into a well-buttered baking dish. Place in a moderate oven and cook twenty minutes.

Baking-powder Biscuits (Fifteen biscuits)

2 C-flour	½ t-salt
4 t-baking powder	3 T-lard
	2/3 C-milk

Mix the flour, baking powder and salt, and cut in the fat with a knife. Slowly add the milk. (More or less may be required, as it depends on the flour.) Pat into shape three-fourths of an inch thick. Cut with a cutter, place side by side on a tin pan. Bake in a hot oven twelve to fifteen minutes.

Apple Tapioca (Three portions)

6 T-pearl tapioca	3 T-sugar
¼ C-cold water	1 C-sweetened apple
1½ C-boiling water	sauce
1/3 t-salt	½ t-vanilla

Soak the pearl tapioca in the cold water for ten minutes in the upper part of the double boiler. Add the boiling water, salt and sugar. Cook in the double boiler until transparent. Add one cup of apple sauce and the vanilla. Mix well. Serve either hot or cold.

CHAPTER LXV

PLANS FOR THE WEDDING

"OH, Bob, I can hardly wait to tell you all of Alice's wonderful plans," said Bettina.

"Don't wait, then. (Say, these are my favorite potatoes, all right!) Well, what about the wedding? All the gowns are being made, I suppose?"

"Yes, indeed. You know the four bridesmaids are to wear lavender maline over lavender taffeta, very fluffy and short,—can you picture them in your mind, Bob?'

"Not exactly, but then, go on."

"Well, they're nearly finished. I saw them today, and they're lovely. The girls are to carry lavender maline muffs, too—the round kind with fluffy bows at each end, and little pink rosebuds around the hand, you know. Then a corsage bouquet of violets with a pink rose in the center will be pinned on each muff. The bridesmaids will also wear lavender maline hats, with fluffy tam o' shanter crowns and pink rosebuds around them."

"Is that what you'll wear?"

"No, Lillian and I are the matrons of honor, and we will be all in white, with white muffs, and corsage bouquets of pink roses on them. Won't that be lovely? I don't know yet whether Lillian's little Elizabeth, who will scatter rose petals from a fluffy long-handled basket, is to wear pink or white. Oh, I wish you might have seen the girls this afternoon! We tried on our dresses and planned the hats and muffs. I shall

220

begin my muff this evening; won't that be exciting?"
For dinner that night they had:

Pork Chops   Bettina's Potatoes
Date Bread   Butter
Head Lettuce   French Dressing
Chocolate Sponge Cake
Coffee

BETTINA'S RECIPES

(All measurements are level)

Bettina's Potatoes (Two portions)

1 C-cold cooked potatoes diced   1 T-pimento, cut up
1 T-butter   1 piece of soft cheese—a 1-inch
1½ T-flour   cube
½ t-salt

Melt the butter, add the flour, cheese and salt. Mix well, and add the milk gradually. Cook until thick and creamy. Add the pimento and potatoes. Serve hot. (Bob considers this dish superfine.)

Date Nut Bread (Twelve pieces)

1 C-graham flour   4 T-nut meats
1 C-white flour   3 T-chopped dates
½ C-"C" sugar   3 t-baking powder
1 t-salt   1 C-milk

Mix the ingredients in the order given. Place in a well-buttered bread pan, and bake in a moderate oven for thirty-five minutes.

Chocolate Sponge Cake (Fourteen cakes)

5 T-butter   ¼ t-cloves
4 T-cocoa   1 C-flour
1 egg   3 t-baking powder
⅛ C-sugar   ½ C-cold water
1 t-cinnamon   ½ t-vanilla

Cream the butter, add the sugar. Stir in the egg and beat well. Add the cinnamon, cloves, baking powder, cocoa, flour, vanilla and water. Beat vigorously for two minutes. Bake in well-buttered gem pans for eighteen minutes. Serve warm if desired.

CHAPTER LXVI

A GUEST TO A DINNER OF LEFT-OVERS

"AHA, I've found you out!" Bettina heard a laughing voice shout as she hurried up the steps.

"Why, Jack, when did you come to town?"

"This afternoon. Went to Bob's office the very first thing, and he insisted on bringing me home with him to dinner. I told him it might 'put you out,' but he spent the time it took to come home assuring me that you were always waiting for company—kept a light ever burning in the window for them and all that. He said that I'd see,—that you'd be on the doorstep waiting for us!"

"And after all that—you weren't here!" said Bob reproachfully.

"I'm just as sorry as I can be not to live up to Bob's picture of me," said Bettina. "I generally am waiting for Bob,—almost on the doorstep if not quite. But this afternoon I've been to a shower for Alice,—do you remember Alice, Jack?"

"Very well. The gay, dark-eyed one. You don't mean to say that she's found a man who's lively enough to suit her?"

"Well, she seems to be suited, all right. But I must fly into an apron if you boys are to get any dinner within a half-hour. Jack, you'll have to pardon me if after all of Bob's eloquence I give you a meal of left-overs——"

"Don't apologize to a bachelor, Bettina. He probably won't know left-overs from the real thing," said Bob.

"Bachelors are said to be the most critical of all," she answered. "But I'll do my little best to please."

That night Bettina served:

Roast Beef Pie
Bread   Butter
Sliced Tomatoes with Salad Dressing
Marble Cake   Coffee

BETTINA'S RECIPES

(All measurements are level)

Roast Beef Pie (Three portions)

2 C-chopped cold roast beef	1 C-flour
1 C-gravy	2 t-baking powder
1 C-cold diced potatoes (cooked)	2 t-lard
2 T-chopped onion	⅛ t-salt
	6 T-milk

Mix the beef, gravy, potato and onion. Place in a shallow buttered baking dish. Make a biscuit dough by cutting the lard into the flour, which has been sifted with the baking powder, and salt, and gradually adding the milk. Pat the dough into shape and arrange carefully on top of the meat. Make holes in the top to allow the steam to escape. Bake in a moderate oven twenty minutes.

Marble Cake (Fourteen slices)
1 C-sugar ½ C-butter

Cream together and divide into two parts, half for light and half for dark.

Dark Part
To one half add:

¼ C-molasses	1 t-baking powder
½ C-milk	1 t-powdered cinnamon
2 egg-yolks	½ t-powdered cloves
1 C-flour	¼ t-grated nutmeg
	½ t-vanilla

Mix this together thoroughly and set aside while the light part is being mixed.

Light Part

To the other half of the butter and sugar add:

½ C-milk	½ t-vanilla
1 C-flour	Whites of two **eggs**
1 t-baking powder	beaten stiff

Put large spoonfuls of light and dark batter, alternating, in a loaf cake pan well fitted with waxed paper, until the pan is two-thirds full. Bake thirty-five minutes in a moderate oven.

CHAPTER LXVII

A HANDKERCHIEF SHOWER

"WHAT a cunning table!" exclaimed four girls in various words and ways. Ruth and Bettina smiled happily to each other, for they, too, had admired the low bowl of purple and yellow pansies in the center, and the tiny individual vases for a few pansies at each place. The dainty doilies were also attractive, and Ruth had darkened the room and lit the small yellow candles on the table.

"But Bettina helped with the soufflè and the gold hearts," she said gallantly. "Did you see her disappear a short time ago? She was baking the cakes. When she suggested refreshments that should be made just before they were served, I was frightened. But when she offered to bake the things, you may be sure I was delighted."

At this moment a small figure appeared in the doorway. "Weady, Cousin Wuth?"

"Yes, dear."

In popped little Marjorie, Ruth's cousin, carrying a huge bouquet of handkerchiefs folded like white roses, fastened somehow to long stems with green leaves attached, tied with streaming yellow satin ribbon. Making a low bow to Alice, she recited in a baby voice:

"A handkerchief posie to carry each day.
    We trust they will not come amiss,
  In fact, we are sure that no other bouquet
    Was ever so useful as this!"

"Thank you, you darling!" said Alice, receiving the gift with delight.

Ruth served:

Apricot Souffle   Whipped Cream
Gold Hearts
Salted Peanuts   Coffee

BETTINA'S RECIPES

(All measurements are level)

Apricot Souffle (Soo-Flay) "Lightened with Air" (Six portions)

¼ lb. dried apricots	⅛ t-salt
½ C-sugar	3 eggs
1 t-lemon extract or 1	1 t-baking powder
˙ t-lemon juice	¼ t-vanilla
6 candied cherries	

Wash the dried apricots and soak for three hours in sufficient water to cover them. Cook slowly until tender (about ten minutes) in the same water in which they were soaked. Press through a colander, add the sugar and cook until very thick, stirring constantly to prevent burning. Add salt and extract. Allow to cool. Beat the egg whites until very stiff, add the baking-powder, apricots and vanilla. Stir just enough to mix. Pour into well buttered individual tin or aluminum moulds until two-thirds full. Place the moulds in a pan of hot water and bake thirty-five minutes in a slow oven. Turn off the fire and allow the pans to remain in a warm place so that they will not fall. When slightly cool, remove carefully and serve as quickly as possible. Place whipped cream and a candied cherry on the top.

Whipped Cream (Six portions)

½ C-heavy cream	¼ t-vanilla
1 t-sugar	3 drops of lemon extract

Beat the cream until thick, add the sugar, vanilla and lemon extract. Place in a cool place until used.

Gold Hearts (Twelve Hearts)

4 T-butter	¼ C-milk
½ C-sugar	⅞ C-flour
3 egg-yolks	1 t-lemon extract
1 T-water	1 t-baking-powder
⅛ t-salt	

Cream the butter, add the sugar, and mix well. Add the egg yolks, beaten well, and the water, milk, flour, baking-powder, lemon extract and salt. Beat for two minutes. Pour into a large flat pan prepared with waxed paper. The batter should be three-fourths of an inch thick in the pan. Bake twelve minutes in a moderate oven. Remove the paper, and cut when cool with a heart-shaped cooky cutter. Wet the cutter with water before using, as this assures even edges. Keep in a moist place until ready to serve.

Salted Almonds (Six portions)

¼ lb. almonds (shelled) 1 t-salt
1 qt. boiling water   3 T-olive oil

Allow the almonds to stand in boiling water in a covered utensil for fifteen minutes. Rinse off with hot water and place in a colander. Remove the skins. Place oil in a frying-pan when hot, add nuts. Stir constantly over a moderate fire for fifteen minutes. Pour into a clean cloth. Rub off any oil which has remained on the almonds. Sprinkle salt over the nuts while warm. When thoroughly cooled, place the almonds in a covered tin can until ready to serve.

CHAPTER LXVIII

JUST THE TWO OF THEM

"**I**T seems good to be alone this evening, doesn't it, Bettina?" said Bob, as they sat down to dinner. "Or are you growing so accustomed to gaiety lately that a dinner for two is a bore?"

"Bob!" said Bettina reproachfully. "If I thought you really believed that I was ever bored by a dinner for the two of us,—well, I'd never be in a wedding party again! Alice likes excitement, and I suppose that next week will be very gay, but after the wedding I hope that you and I can have a quiet winter, with just invitations enough to keep us from becoming too stupid."

"But tell me what the wedding will be like. Is it all planned down to the last detail? I suppose it is, although Harry doesn't seem to have any idea what it is to be."

"Poor Harry, he seems to be left out of most of the showers and parties so far."

"Don't pity him; he wouldn't go if he could. I'm just wondering what they'll do after the wedding. Will Alice go and Harry stay at home? Or, will he be obliging and force himself to go, too?"

"I don't know, I'm sure. Alice is so full of life that I don't see how she can settle down and never go anywhere, as Harry would have her. But time will tell. Perhaps they'll compromise. Meanwhile, we must plan some sort of a shower or prenuptial party that Harry can enjoy, too. One with the men included, I mean. Of course, I know he hates parties, but I think he would really like a very jolly informal one with just a few friends!"

The dinner for two consisted of:

Cold Sliced Lamb   Baked Potatoes
Creamed Carrots and Peas
Bread   Butter
Apple Dumplings

BETTINA'S RECIPES

(All measurements are level)

Creamed Carrots and Peas (Three portions)

½ C-cooked, diced   ½ t-salt
carrots   1 T-butter
½ C-peas   1 T-flour
½ C-milk

Melt the butter, add the flour and salt, gradually add the milk. Cook two minutes. Add the peas and carrots. Serve very hot.

Apple Dumpling (Three portions)

½ C-flour   1 T-lard
1 t-baking powder   2 T-milk
⅛ t-salt   2 apples
4 T-sugar   ½ t-cinnamon

Mix the flour, baking-powder and salt, cut in the lard with a knife. Add the liquid, mixing to a soft dough. Roll on a well floured board to one-fourth of an inch in thickness. Wash, pare and quarter the apples. Sprinkle with sugar and cinnamon. Cut the dough in five inch squares; place two quarters of apple in the center of a square; moisten the edges of the dough with water and bring the four corners together around the apple. Place in a tin pan and bake in a moderate oven until the apples are soft. (About thirty minutes.) Serve warm with cream.

CHAPTER LXIX

A LUNCHEON IN THE COUNTRY

"OH, Charlotte, I've just come from the loveliest luncheon," said Bettina, coming face to face with Mrs. Dixon in front of her own home.

"You have? Another for Alice?"

"No, this was in the country—on the interurban, at Cousin Kate's. Frances, her daughter, who was married last spring, has come home on a visit, and Cousin Kate was entertaining for her."

"Tell me about it!"

"Oh, it was just an informal luncheon, but I couldn't help thinking how delicious everything was, and at the same time inexpensive. In fact, I wrote down several of Cousin Kate's recipes after the guests had gone, and I'm sure that there aren't many such inexpensive luncheons that are also so good."

"You must let me have some of the recipes."

"Of course I will. Come in now, and copy them."

"I can't possibly, Bettina. As it is, I'm afraid that Frank will be home before I am. It's almost six o'clock now."

"Is it? Then I must hurry in and start dinner; I want to make some muffins. I hate to have Bob eat a cold dinner just because I've been out in the afternoon; in fact, I usually spend more time than usual in the morning fixing some dessert that he especially likes, if I'm to be out in the afternoon. Good-bye, Charlotte!"

"Good-bye, dear!"

The luncheon menu was as follows:

Oyster Cocktail in Pepper Cases
Cream of Celery Soup   Croutons
Cheese Timbales   Creamed Peas
Baked Apples
Baking-Powder Biscuit
Green Bean Salad   Salted Wafers
Lemon Sherbet   Devil's Food White Icing
Coffee

BETTINA'S RECIPES

(All measurements are level)

Oyster Cocktail in Pepper Cases (Six portions)

6 green peppers   1 T-lemon juice
1 pint oysters   1 T-horseradish
5 T-tomato catsup   ½ t-salt
½ t-tobasco sauce

Cút the stem end from the sweet green peppers. Remove the seeds and allow to stand in iced water. Pick over the oysters to remove any shells, and surround with chipped ice until ready to serve. Mix the catsup, lemon juice, horse radish, salt and tobasco sauce. Fill each pepper with four oysters, and put on tablespoon of the mixture on the top. Serve very cold.

Cheese Timbales (Six portions)

1 T-butter   ¼ t-paprika
1 T-flour   ¼ C-fresh, soft bread crumbs
½ C-milk   ¼ C-grated American cheese
½ t-salt   1 egg

Melt the butter, add the flour, salt and paprika. Mix well, gradually add the milk, cheese and bread crumbs. Cook three minutes, and then stir in the egg, well beaten. Butter six timbale moulds well. Place the cups in a pan of hot water and cook fifteen minutes in a moderate oven. Allow to stand three minutes, and remove from the moulds. Serve hot with creamed peas.

Bettina's Green String Bean Salad (Six portions)

1 C-cooked green beans   1 t-salt
¼ C-cut celery   ¼ t-paprika
¼ C-pimento, cut fine   ½ C-salad dressing
1 hard-cooked egg, diced   6 pieces of lettuce

Mix thoroughly the beans, celery, pimento, egg, salt and paprika. Add the salad dressing and serve on a piece of crisp lettuce.

Devil's Food Cake (Twenty-four pieces)

2 C-brown sugar	3 squares chocolate
1 C-milk	2 C-flour
2/3 C-butter	1 t-soda
2 eggs	1 t-vanilla

Cream the butter, add one cup sugar. Mix egg yolks, the other cup sugar, one-half cup milk and chocolate; cook two minutes, stirring constantly. When cool, add this to the first mixture. Add the rest of the milk, vanilla, the flour and soda sifted together. Beat two minutes. Add stiffly beaten egg whites. Fill two tin pans prepared with waxed paper, bake in a moderate oven twenty-five minutes. When cool, ice with white icing.

CHAPTER LXX

A "PAIR SHOWER" FOR ALICE

WHEN Bettina called the girls into the dining-room after several hours spent in hemming dish towels for Alice, they exclaimed that the time had passed so quickly. The table was set for twelve, and the chair at the right of the hostess was gaily decorated with white ribbon and white paper flowers.

"Oh, for me?" cried Alice. "How important I feel!"

As soon as the girls were seated, Ruth rose and placed before the guest of honor a large wicker basket heaped high with packages of all shapes and sizes, each wrapped in white tissue paper and tied with white ribbon. A card hung from the handle of the basket. "I'll read it aloud!" laughed Alice.

> "Dear Alice, we have tried to choose
> Some gifts for you that come by twos.
> A few, perhaps, you'll often use,
> While some may comfort and amuse,
> If you should chance to get the blues,
> When household cares your mind confuse.
>
> "This basket, which our blessing bears,
> Besides the gifts that come in pairs,
> Our friendship and our love declares.
> 'Twill share your troubles and your cares
> And hold the hose that Harry wears.
> So keep them free from holes and tears."

"Goodness!" cried Alice. "The thought of my future cares

frightens me! But now I must open all the packages!"
She discovered a salt and pepper shaker, a pair of guest
towels, a pair of hose, a sugar bowl and a creamer, and many
other gifts in pairs. It was a long time before the girls could
calm down sufficiently to eat the luncheon that Bettina, with
Ruth's assistance, set before them.

Bettina served:

Bettina's Tuna Salad
Date Bread Sandwiches   Salted Peanuts
Maple Ice Cream   White Cake with Maple Icing
Coffee

BETTINA'S RECIPES

(All measurements are level)

Tuna Salad (Twelve portions)

2 C-tuna fish	4 T-pimento, cut **fine**
2 C-diced celery	2 t-salt
3 hard-cooked eggs, diced	½ t-paprika
3 T-green pepper, chopped fine	1 T-lemon juice
4 T-sweet pickle, chopped fine	1 C-salad dressing

Mix the tuna, celery, eggs, sweet pickle, pepper, salt and
paprika with a silver fork. (Care should always be taken not
to mash salads.) Add the salad dressing; more than a cup
may be necessary. Keep very cold, and serve attractively on
a lettuce leaf.

Salad Dressing (Twelve portions)

4 egg-yolks	1 t-mustard
½ C-vinegar	4 T-sugar
½ C-water	¼ t-paprika
1 t-salt	2 T-flour

Beat the egg yolks, add the vinegar. Mix the salt, mustard,
sugar, paprika and flour thoroughly. Slowly add the water,
taking care not to let the mixture get lumpy. Pour into the
yolks and vinegar. Cook slowly, stirring constantly until thick
and creamy. Thin with sour cream or whipped cream.

Date Bread (Eighteen Sandwiches)

1 C-graham flour	2 t-salt
2 C-white flour	1/3 pound of dates, cut fine
3 t-baking powder	1½ C-milk
1/3 C-"C" sugar	1 egg

Mix the flour, baking-powder, sugar, salt and dates ground fine. Beat the egg with a fork, and add the milk. Pour slowly into the dry ingredients. Mix thoroughly and pour into two well-buttered bread pans. Allow to stand fifteen minutes and bake forty minutes in a moderate oven. When cold, cut very thin and spread with butter for sandwiches. Date bread is better for sandwiches when one day old.

Maple Icing

1½ C-maple sugar   2/3 C-milk
1½ C-granulated sugar   1 t-butter
⅛ t-cream of tartar

Cook all the ingredients together until a soft ball is formed when a little is dropped into cold water. Beat until creamy enough to pour on the cake.

Salted Peanuts (Twelve portions)

2/3 lb. peanuts (shelled)   4 T-olive oil
2 t-salt

Cover the peanuts with boiling water; allow to stand for fifteen minutes. Place one-third of the amount in a strainer (allowing remainder to stay in water) and remove the skins. Prepare all the peanuts the same way. Place two tablespoons of oil in the frying pan, when hot add the peanuts; stir constantly with a fork and cook over a moderate fire fifteen minutes. When brown remove the nuts, add another tablespoon of oil and another third of the peanuts, continue until all the nuts are cooked. Add the salt. Lard may be used in place of oil, but the latter makes the nuts taste and brown better.

CHAPTER LXXI

BOB MAKES POPCORN BALLS

"OH, I forgot to tell you, Bettina," said Bob at the dinner table, "the Dixons are coming over this evening. Frank asked me if we would be at home."

"I'm so glad they're coming," said Bettina. "I haven't seen Charlotte for several weeks; I have been so busy with the affairs we girls have been giving for Alice. But I wish I had known this afternoon that they were coming. I'd like to celebrate with a little supper, but I haven't a single thing in the house that is suitable."

"There's the cider that Uncle John brought us," suggested Bob.

"Yes," said Bettina, "we might have cider. But what else?"

"I'll tell you," said Bob, "I'll make some popcorn balls. I've made them before, and I know exactly how."

"I'll help," said Bettina.

"No, I won't need you at all; I'm the chef."

"Well, Bobbie, at least you'll let me look on. May I be washing the dishes at the same time?"

"Yes, I'll permit that. These are going to be champion popcorn balls, I can tell you, Bettina—as big as pumpkins!"

"We'll serve them in that large flat wicker basket, and I'm sure they'll look and taste delicious. But we must hurry, Bob; it's after seven now!"

For dinner that night they had:

<table>
<tr><td>Broiled Ham</td><td></td><td>Mashed Potatoes</td></tr>
<tr><td>Chili Sauce</td><td>Creamed Onions</td><td>Hot Scones</td></tr>
<tr><td colspan="3">Prune Blanc Mange with Cream</td></tr>
</table>

235

BETTINA'S RECIPES

(All measurements are level)

Broiled Ham (Four portions)

1 lb. ham   2 C-milk

Soak a one-half inch slice of ham in one cup of lukewarm milk for half an hour. Drain and wipe dry. Place in a hot tin pan and cook for five minutes directly under the flame, turning frequently to prevent burning.

Scones (Fourteen scones)

2 C-flour	1 egg
4 t-baking powder	2/3 C-milk
1/3 t-salt	1 T-"C" sugar
2 T-lard	½ t-cinnamon

Mix the flour, baking-powder and salt. Cut in the lard with a knife, add all but one teaspoonful of the beaten egg, then add the milk gradually. Mix with a knife into a soft dough. Pat into a square shape one-half inch thick. Brush over the top with one teaspoonful of egg and sprinkle with the sugar and cinnamon (mixed thoroughly). Cut into one and one-half inch squares. Place in a tin pan and bake twelve minutes in a hot oven.

Prune Blanc Mange (Four portions)

2 T-cornstarch	¼ t-salt
2 T-sugar	½ C-cooked, cut prunes
4 T-cold milk	½ t-lemon extract
2/3 C-hot milk	½ t-vanilla

Mix the cornstarch, sugar and salt, and add the cold milk slowly. Gradually add the hot milk. Cook in a double boiler for twenty minutes. Add the prunes, lemon extract and vanilla. Beat well, and serve cold with cream.

CHAPTER LXXII

AND WHERE WAS THE DINNER?

"HELLO!" called Bob at the door one evening.
No answer.

"Hello, Bettina!" he called again. Again the dark house gave forth no reply.

Feeling, it must be admitted, a little out of harmony with a world that allowed weary and hungry husbands to come home to dark and empty houses when the clock said plainly that it was a quarter after six, Bob made his way to the kitchen. Perhaps Bettina had left his dinner there for him; perhaps she had been called away, or perhaps, even, she had rushed out on some errand after dinner preparations were begun. The kitchen, however, was so immaculate as to seem distinctly forbidding to a hungry man whose appetite was growing keener every minute. And he had been thinking all the way home that a hot dinner would taste so good!

At that moment a clamor of voices at the door aroused him.

"You poor old Bob!" cried Bettina, kissing him twice before Fred and Ruth without the least embarrassment. "Have you waited long?"

"It seemed hours," admitted Bob.

"Ruth and I have been to a tea for Alice. Fred came for her there, and I persuaded them to come home to dinner with me. I'll give you each something to do while I stir up a little cottage pudding. Then dinner will be ready in half an hour."

"Half an hour?" cried Bob. "But Bettina, where is the dinner? I didn't see any!"

"In the fireless cooker, you crazy boy! Are you 'most starved?"

"Well," said Bob, "that cooker was the neatest, stiffest-looking thing in the kitchen! I didn't dream that it was busily cooking a dinner. Say, I'll be glad to see a hot meal again!"

The dinner consisted of:

Round Steak with Vegetables

Dutch Cheese

Bread   Plum Butter

Cottage Pudding Vanilla Sauce

BETTINA'S RECIPES

(All measurements are level)

Round Steak with Vegetables (Six portions)

2 lbs. round steak	2 T-flour
6 potatoes	2 T-lard
6 carrots	2 t-salt
6 onions	¼ t-paprika
	¼ C-water

Pound the flour into the round steak with the edge of a small plate. This breaks the fibers of the meat, making it more tender. Wash and peel the potatoes, slicing in half lengthwise. Scrape the carrots, and cut into one-half inch slices lengthwise. Wash the onions and remove their outside skins. Sprinkle the vegetables with one and a half level teaspoons of salt, and the paprika. Add the water, and place in the bottom of the large fireless cooker utensil. Place the lard in a frying pan, and when hot, add the meat. Brown thoroughly on each side. Salt the meat with one-half level teaspoon of salt, and place in the kettle on top of the vegetables. Place the heated disks of the fireless cooker over and under the utensil, and cook at least one hour in the cooker.

Cottage Pudding (Six portions)

1½ C-flour	1 egg
3 t-baking powder	½ C-milk
¼ t-salt	½ t-vanilla
½ C-sugar	3 T-melted butter

Mix the flour, baking powder, salt and sugar. Add the egg, milk and vanilla, and beat one minute. Add the melted butter, and pour into a well buttered tin pan. Bake twenty minutes in a moderate oven. Serve warm with vanilla sauce.

Vanilla Sauce (Six portions)

2/3 C-sugar	½ t-lemon extract
3 T-flour	¼ t-salt
1 t-vanilla	1½ C-water
	1 t-butter

Mix the sugar, flour and salt thoroughly. Add the water slowly. Boil two minutes. Add the vanilla, lemon extract, and butter. Beat one minute and serve. If too thick, more water may be added.

CHAPTER LXXIII

ALICE TELLS HER TROUBLES

"AND the minute I caught a glimpse of you, Bettina, at the tea this afternoon, I thought, 'Oh, if Betty would only ask me to go home with her to a sensible homelike dinner, with no one there but herself and Bob——' "

"Not even Harry, Alice?"

"No, not even Harry! I'm so sick and tired of teas and dressmakers and wedding gowns and bridesmaids that I'm tired even of Harry, too! Almost."

"But, Alice, then why do it all? Why have all this fuss and feathers?" And Bettina's knife, with which she was cutting bread, came down with a click of vehemence. "It has always seemed silly to me—all the worry and bother——"

"But what can I do now, Bettina? I've started, and I'll have to go through with it! Why, even now, I ought to be home for dinner—mother has several guests—but I phoned her that I had a headache and was coming here, where I could be quiet. And I do have a headache—and no appetite, and——"

"Just wait till you taste this nice brown meat that I have in the oven, Alice! The trouble with you is that you've been eating silly party food for such a long time. And tonight you are to have a sensible dinner with plain people."

"Plain people? Who calls me plain?" interrupted Bob, coming in like a tornado. "Hello, Alice! How can you spare any time from all these festivities I hear about?"

For dinner that night they had:

Rolled Flank of Beef with Bread Dressing
Browned Potatoes   Hot Slaw
Prune Pudding   Cream
                    Coffee

BETTINA'S RECIPES

(All measurements are level)

Rolled Flank of Beef (Four portions)

1 lb. round steak one inch thick	1 t-salt
2 T-flour	2 one-inch cubes of suet

Wipe the meat, trim the edges, pound on both sides with the edge of a plate to break the tendon. Place the dressing (given below) on the steak, roll, and tie with a cord. Roll in the flour and salt. Place in a small dripping pan, put the suet on the top of the meat, add enough water to cover the bottom of the pan, and bake in a moderate oven for fifty minutes. Baste frequently.

Bread Dressing

1 C-soft bread crumbs	⅛ t-celery salt
1 T-melted butter	½ t-salt
1 t-chopped parsley	⅛ t-pepper
½ t-chopped onion	2 T-water

Mix all the ingredients in the order named, stirring lightly with a fork. Place in shape on the meat. Care should be taken not to have the dressing soggy or heavy.

Prune Pudding (Four portions)

1 C-cooked, seeded and chopped prunes	1 t-vanilla
	½ t-lemon extract
¾ C-sugar	½ C-cracker crumbs
¼ C-nut meats, cut fine	1 t-baking powder
½ C-milk	⅛ t-salt

Mix all the ingredients in the order named. Pour into a well-buttered shallow earthenware dish. Place the dish in a pan of hot water and bake twenty-five minutes in a moderate oven, or until the mixture is firm. Serve warm. Individual amounts may be made in moulds.

CHAPTER LXXIV

THE DIXONS COME TO DINNER

"CHARLOTTE, you must have Bettina tell you how to cook fish this way," said Frank.

"It's the Bechamel sauce on it that you like, I suspect," said Bettina. "And it isn't at all hard to make. I serve it with so many things. We like it with carrots——"

"Oh, is it the very same sauce that you serve with carrots?" said Charlotte. "I can make it, Frank. I'll have it for dinner one of these days, with halibut, just as Bettina has served it tonight."

"There is only one thing to think about especially in making it," said Bettina. "After you have beaten the egg slightly, add a very little of the hot liquid to it, and then pour the mixture into the rest. Then cook it a short time, not long, as a sauce made with egg sometimes separates."

"I'll remember," said Charlotte. "You do have such good meals, Bettina. How do you manage it? Sometimes I can think of the best things to cook, and other days I don't seem to have a bit of imagination!"

"I plan my menu all out a week, and sometimes two weeks, ahead," said Bettina. "It is really quite a complicated process, as I want to have a variety, as well as inexpensive things that are on the market. Of course, I may change my plans in many details, but I keep to the general outline. Planning the meals seems simple, but it really requires a lot of thinking sometimes. Excuse me while I bring in the dessert. Bob, will you please help me take the plates?"

The menu that night consisted of:

Sautèd Halibut Steak Bechamel Sauce
Potato Cubes Butter Sauce
Sliced Cucumbers and Onions with Vinegar
Rolls Butter
Prune Whip Whipped Cream
Coffee

BETTINA'S RECIPES

(All measurements are level)

Bechamel Sauce (Four portions)

2 T-butter	1/3 t-salt
2 T-flour	⅛ t-paprika
1½ C-milk	1 egg-yolk

Melt the butter, add the flour, salt and pepper, mix well, and gradually add the milk. Cook until it thickens. (Not as thick as white sauce for vegetables.) Add the egg yolk. Serve immediately.

To add egg yolk to the hot liquid, beat the egg slightly, add a small portion of the hot liquid slowly and pour it all into the remainder of the hot liquid. Cook only a short time, as the mixture may separate if cooked longer.

Potato Cubes (Four portions)

2 C-raw potatoes cut in ¾-inch cubes	½ t-salt
	4 C-boiling water

Add the salt to the boiling water, add the potatoes and boil till tender. (About ten minutes.) Drain and shake over the fire for a moment. Add the sauce, and serve.

Butter Sauce (Four portions)

2 T-butter	1 t-chopped green pepper
1 T-chopped parsley,	¼ t-paprika

Mix together, heat and add to the potatoes.

Prune Whip (Four portions)

1/3 lb. prunes	1 T-lemon juice
3 egg-whites	½ C-sugar

Pick over and wash the prunes, then soak for several hours in cold water, enough to cover. Cook slowly until soft, about fifteen minutes. Rub through a strainer. Add sugar and lemon juice and cook five minutes; the mixture should be the consistency of marmalade.

Beat the whites until stiff, add the prunes when cold, pile lightly into a buttered baking dish and bake twenty minutes in a slow oven. Serve with cream.

CHAPTER LXXV

THE WEDDING INVITATIONS

BOB and Bettina had scarcely sat down to dinner one crisp cold evening, when they heard laughing voices at the door. "It sounds like Alice," said Bettina. "What can she be up to now? And Harry, too!"

Bob had already thrown open the door, and there, as Bettina had guessed, were Alice and Harry, each carrying a large box.

"We've come to deliver your invitation to the wedding," said Alice. "It may be unconventional, but it's fun. The rest we are going down to mail—that is, if we don't get frightened at the idea, and pitch the boxes in the river instead."

"If that's the way you feel," said Harry firmly, "I'll carry your box myself."

"Please don't, Harry! Just think, I may never have another opportunity of mailing the invitations to my own wedding, so don't deprive me of the privilege."

"Stay to dinner won't you?" said Bettina. "We had really planned on having Uncle John and Aunt Mary this evening, but they didn't come to town after all. So I am sure we have plenty, even to apple dumplings for dessert."

"Harry had asked me to take dinner with him down town," said Alice, "by way of celebrating when these invitations were mailed. But perhaps we might stay here instead, since this was the very place in which we met first! Harry, I believe sentiment demands that we accept Bettina's invitation."

"I must broil another steak," said Bettina, "but that will take only a few minutes. I'm so glad you can stay."

"But we'll have to leave immediately after dinner," said

Alice, "for these invitations simply must be mailed this evening."

That night for dinner, Bettina served:

Beefsteak   Mashed Potatoes
                    Turnips
Lettuce   Bettina's Russian Salad Dressing
          Apple Dumplings and Cream

BETTINA'S RECIPES

(All measurements are level)

Turnips (Four portions)

4 turnips   ¼ t-salt
1 T-butter   ⅛ t-pepper

Wash, pare and cut the turnips in small pieces. Cook until transparent and tender. Drain, mash, add the butter, salt and pepper, mix thoroughly and return to the fire to dry out the superfluous water. Serve hot with vinegar. (Never cook turnips until brown.)

Head Lettuce (Four portions)

1 head lettuce

Remove the outer leaves and core of the lettuce. Clean thoroughly. Place very wet in a towel, wrap well and lay directly on the ice. Allow to stand one hour before serving to allow the lettuce to get very cold and crisp.

Bettina's Russian Dressing (Four portions)

½ C-salad dressing   2 T-chili sauce
      1 T-chopped green pepper

Mix the ingredients in the order named. Shake thoroughly in a glass jar. Serve cold.

Apple Dumplings (Four portions)

1 C-flour   1/3 C-water
2 t-baking powder   4 apples
¼ t-salt   ½ C-sugar
2 T-lard   1 t-cinnamon

Mix thoroughly the flour, baking powder and salt. Cut in the lard with a knife, and then add the water, mixing to a soft dough. Roll on a well-floured board to one-fourth of an inch in thickness. Wipe and pare the apples, and cut them in quarters.

Cut the dough in four square pieces. Place four quarters of apple in the center of each piece of dough. Sprinkle with sugar and cinnamon. Moisten the edges of the dough with water. Bring the four corners of each piece up around the apple, pressing tightly together. Pierce with a fork to allow the escape of steam. Place each dumpling upside down on a floured tin, and bake thirty-five minutes in a moderate oven. Serve warm with cream.

CHAPTER LXXVI

HALLOWE'EN PREPARATIONS

"THERE it is again!" said Bob to Ruth, who was dining with them. "And now it's gone!"

"I feel the same old Hallowe'en thrill that I used to, years ago," said Bettina, "when I turn around suddenly and see a jack-o'-lantern grinning in at the window! Don't you love them?"

"Those are the Stewart children," said Bob. "They're just hoping that I'll come out and chase them away! There's no fun for them in having us like it too well! You girls ought to give at least an imitation of a shriek apiece. You don't have ladylike nerves at all!"

"Bob, that jack-o'-lantern reminds me that we have a piece of work laid out for you—making the jack-o'-lanterns for a Hallowe'en party we have planned. Will you do it?"

"Will I?" said Bob. "Indeed I will! I haven't made one for years and years! Not since I was a boy!"

"Years and years and years and years!" said Ruth, laughing. "Well, this party is in honor of Harry, so you mustn't tell him anything about it—not even that we're giving it. And Bob, I believe Fred would help make the jack-o'-lanterns."

"See here, Ruth," said Bob, "you want Fred to get half the credit for the artistic job I'm going to do. Well, for your sake, I may let him help a little, but I'm bossing the work, I can tell you. Why, I'm particular."

That evening's menu consisted of:

Breaded Lamb Chops   Baked Potatoes
Creamed Peas
Sliced Tomatoes   Salad Dressing
Steamed Date Pudding   Lemon Sauce
Coffee

BETTINA'S RECIPES

(All measurements are level)

Breaded Lamb Chops (Four portions)

4 chops	½ C-bread crumbs
1 egg-yolk	½ t-salt
1 T-water	1 T-butter

Wash and look over the chops carefully to remove any particles of bone. Beat the egg yolk and water. Dip each chop into the egg mixture, and then roll in the crumbs, to which the salt has been added. Place in a buttered pan, dot well with butter, and bake twenty-five minutes in a hot oven.

Steamed Date Pudding

2/3 C-soft, fresh bread crumbs	1 egg
2/3 C-flour	2/3 C-dates, chopped fine
2 t-baking powder	½ t-salt
2/3 C-fine chopped suet	1 t-vanilla
2/3 C-sugar	2/3 C-milk

Mix all the ingredients in the order given. Stir well for two minutes, and place in a buttered mould. Steam two hours on the stove or in the fireless cooker. Serve hot with lemon-sauce.

Lemon Sauce

½ C-sugar	The juice of one lemon
1 T-flour	⅛ t-salt
1 C-water	1 t-butter

Mix well the flour, sugar and salt, add the water and cook for one minute. Add the lemon juice and butter. Beat vigorously, and serve with the date pudding.

CHAPTER LXXVII

HALLOWE'EN REVELS

"Come, on mystic Hallowe'en,
Let us seek the dreadful scene,
Where the witches, imps and devils,
Elves and ghosts will hold their revels!
1107 Carberry Avenue.
Seven o'clock."

THIS was the invitation received by Harry, Alice, Fred
and even Bob, who had an inkling of what was about to
happen, inasmuch as 1107 Carberry Avenue happened to be his
own address. At seven o'clock that evening Bob was no-
where to be found. However, when four horribly disguised
figures were ushered into the house, the witch who pointed
the way up the stairs seemed satisfied. A few minutes later,
the ghosts and demons having removed such garments as were
needed only in the outer air, assembled in the weirdly lighted
living-room. All of the electric lights were covered with yellow crêpe paper shades, with faces cut in them. Jack-o'-
lanterns stood in every conceivable place, and a fire burned
brightly in the open fireplace.

The two witches, who were evidently the hostesses, com-
menced a weird chant in a minor key. The male ghosts, three
in number, immediately took up the music, if it could be so
called, howling in loud and uncanny tones. Thereupon the
witches beckoned the whole company with all speed to the
dining-room.

The table was a mass of color and light. Potatoes, carrots
and beets, with sticks for legs, held the lighted candles. At
each place were individual favors, witches holding the place
cards, and small Jack-o'-lanterns standing beside them. The

center of the table was a miniature field of pumpkins and corn-stalks.

The place cards were read and the places were found. The guest of honor, he who sat at the right of her who was evidently "witch-in-charge," discovered the following on his card, and the others were equally descriptive and illuminating:

> This place is laid for one who soon
> Will marry!
> O youth bewitched by maid and moon,
> Be wary!
> But if you can't, then make it soon,
> Dear Harry!

The supper, decorative as well as delicious, was all upon the table. Little individual pumpkin pies on paper doilies stood beside each place. The salad caused much delight among the guests, who at the invitation of the witches, had now removed their masks. A large red apple with a face cut on the outside, had been hollowed out, and the salad was within. On the top of the apple was a round wafer with a marshmallow upon it to represent a hat. The hat was further decorated with a "stick-up" of stick candy on one side. The apple stood on a leaf of lettuce, with a yellow salad dressing necktie. The favor boxes, which were under the witches, were filled with candy corn, while the popcorn balls, placed on a platter, had features of chocolate fudge, and bonnets of frilled paper.

The supper menu was as follows:

Oyster Patties		Bettina's Surprise Salad	
	Hallowe'en Sandwiches		Pickles
	Pumpkin Pie		
Cider		Doughnuts	
Jumbles		Popcorn Balls	

"Have another jumble, Harry," urged Ruth. "See, this one has unusual eyes and a particularly soulful expression."

"I have already eaten so many that I fear my memory of this party will be a jumble of faces! I'll see them in my sleep—all with that soulful expression!"

"Another toasted marshmallow, Bettina?" asked Fred,

thrusting it toward her on the end of a hat-pin. "This candle is nearly burned out, so I'm afraid I can't offer you any more."

"It is really time to bob for apples," said Bettina. "Who ever heard of a Hallowe'en party without that! And we must each try to bite the swinging doughnut, and then we must blindfold each other and try to pin the tail on the unfortunate black cat. Bob, will you carry this tub into the living-room? And Ruth, will you remove the popcorn balls to the piano bench? Perhaps someone will grow hungry from the exertion of these games. And I know that later in the evening Alice, though a guest, will tell our fortunes."

"Alice can tell my fortune by looking at her own hand," said Harry. "Because she holds my happiness there."

"What a sentimental sentence, Harry!" said Fred, looking amazed. "See, you've embarrassed us all!"

"Well, I'm always being called cold and reserved, and I've decided to turn over a new leaf."

"Oh, Harry, don't be so foolish!" said Alice, who had grown as red as the apples on the table. "It's time for games!"

BETTINA'S RECIPES

(All measurements are level)

Oyster Patties (Six portions)

3 T-butter	½ t-salt
4 T-flour	⅛ t-paprika
1 C-milk	½ pint of oysters

Clean the oysters by removing any shells, and drain off the liquor. Melt the butter, add the flour and salt, and mix thoroughly. Gradually add the milk, stirring constantly. Cook until very thick. Place the oysters in a pan and heat one minute. This "plumps" them. Do not cook too long. Add the oysters to the white sauce, and serve immediately in patty shells which have been freshened in a hot oven.

Bettina's Surprise Salad (Six portions)

6 apples	½ C-sliced diced pineapple
1 green pepper, chopped fine	2 T-chopped nut meats
½ C-diced celery	1 C-salad dressing
½ C-seeded white grapes	½ t-salt
½ C-diced marshmallows	

Remove the insides of the apples, add the green pepper, celery, grapes, marshmallows, pineapple and nut ·meats mixed thoroughly with the salad dressing. Serve very cold.

To Make the Hallowe'en Sandwiches

When the bread is a day old, cut in slices one-third inch thick. Match in pairs. Cream the butter and spread one side. Place the other side on top. Press firmly. With a thimble cut out circles on one piece of the bread, cut nose and mouth with a knife. The butter showing through gives the resemblance to features.

Pumpkin Pie (Eight pies)
Crusts

1 C-flour	3 T-water
5 T-lard	½ t-salt

Cut the lard into the flour and salt. Add sufficient water to make a stiff dough on a floured board. Roll into shape one-fourth inch thick. Place in tin muffin pans making individual pies, filling with the following mixture and baking 30 minutes in a moderate oven.

Pumpkin Filling

1½ C-canned pumpkin	½ t-ginger
2/3 C-brown sugar	½ t-salt
1 t-cinnamon	2 eggs
	2 C-milk

Mix the ingredients in the order given, and fill the pie-crusts two-thirds full.

Jumbles (Twenty-four jumbles)

½ C-butter	½ C-sour milk
1 C-sugar	¼ t-salt
1 egg	About 2 C-flour
½ t-soda	Grape jelly.

Cream the butter, add the sugar, and gradually add the egg, the sugar mixed with the sour milk, the salt, and the flour to make a soft dough. (One which will roll easily.) Cut into shape with a round cooky cutter. On the centers of one-half the pieces, place a spoonful of grape jelly. Make features on the rest, using a thimble to cut out the eyes. Press the two together, and bake 12 minutes in a moderate oven.

NOVEMBER.

Cosy fire a-burning bright,——
Cosy tables robed in white,——
Dainty dishes smoking hot,-——
Home! And cold and snow forgot!

CHAPTER LXXVIII

A FORETASTE OF WINTER

"SAY, but it's cold today!" called Bob at the door. "Frost tonight all right! I was glad I took my overcoat this morning. Have you had a fire all day?"

"Yes, indeed," said Bettina, "and I've spent most of the afternoon cleaning my furs with corn meal, and fixing those new comforters for the sleeping porch, and putting away some of the summer clothing."

"I believe we will need those new comforters tonight. How were you fixing them?"

"I was basting a white cheese-cloth edge, about twelve inches wide, along the width that goes at the head of the bed, you know. It's so easy to rip off and wash, and I like to have all the comforters fixed that way. I was cleaning my old furs, too, to cut them up. I'm planning to have a fur edge on my suit this winter. I don't believe you'll know the furs, the suit, or Bettina when you see the combination we will make together! Fur is the thing this year, you know."

"Couldn't you spare me a little to transform my overcoat? I'd like to look different, too!"

"Silly! Come along to the kitchen! There's beefsteak tonight (won't it taste good?) and I want you to cook it, while I'm getting the other things on the table. I didn't expect you quite so soon."

That night for dinner they had:

Beefsteak	Creamed Potatoes
Devilled Tomatoes	
Rolls	Butter
Plum Sauce	
Bettina's Drop Cookies	

BETTINA'S RECIPES

(All measurements are level)

Creamed Potatoes (Two portions)

1 C-diced cooked potatoes	1 T-flour
1 T-green pepper, chopped fine	½ C-milk
1 T-butter	¼ t-salt

Melt the butter, add the flour and salt, mix well, and add the milk slowly. Cook until creamy, and add the potatoes and the chopped green pepper. Serve very hot.

Devilled Tomatoes (Two portions)

2 tomatoes	½ t-mustard
2 T-flour	⅛ t-salt
1 T-lard	A pinch of paprika
⅛ t-salt	1 hard-cooked egg
1 T-butter	½ t-flour
1 T-sugar	2 T-vinegar
1 T-water	

Peel the tomatoes, cut in half and sprinkle with flour. Place the lard in a frying-pan, and when hot, add the tomatoes. Brown nicely on both sides, and sprinkle with salt. When brown, place on a hot platter and pour over them the following sauce: Sauce—Place the butter in a pan, add the sugar, mustard, salt and paprika, the egg cut fine, and the flour. Mix well, add the vinegar and water. Heat, allow to boil one minute, and then pour over the tomatoes. (If the sauce seems too thick when it has boiled one minute, add a little more water.)

Drop Cookies (Twenty-four cookies)

1/3 C-butter	¼ t-salt
1 C-sugar	1 t-vanilla
1 egg	¼ C-chopped raisins
½ C-sour milk	2½ C-flour
½ t-soda	½ t-baking powder

Cream the butter, add the sugar, then the whole egg. Mix well. Add the sour milk and the vanilla. Mix the baking powder, soda and flour well, add the raisins and add to the first mixture. Beat well. Drop from a spoon onto a buttered and floured pan, leaving three inches between the cookies. Bake fifteen minutes in a moderate oven.

CHAPTER LXXIX

SURPRISING ALICE AND HARRY

"WE knew you'd be here, and we've come to surprise you!" shouted Bob, Fred, Bettina and Ruth, as they opened the door of the new apartment which was to be the home of Harry and Alice. "We've brought the party with us!" and they held out several bulging baskets.

"Welcome!" smiled Alice, delightedly, as she stepped down from the box on which she was standing to hang a soft, silky curtain. Harry, tall and silent, rose, hammer in hand from the crate he was opening, and welcomed each one in turn.

"Bob and I came to be chaperones if you needed us," said Bettina, putting on a prim and disapproving look, as different as possible from her usual happy expression.

"Oh, my dear!" exclaimed Alice's mother, in a shocked tone. "Surely you didn't imagine—but then, of course you didn't—because you would naturally know that I would be here."

Alice laughed her ringing laugh. "Mother is too literal for any use, Bettina!" And Alice's absent-minded father looked up from the newspaper he was reading to ask what the joke was.

"The joke, Father dear," said Alice, "is that your foolish daughter should be about to marry this solemn and serious youth!" And she turned Harry around by the shoulders till he faced her father. "But perhaps you hadn't heard about the wedding, Father. Now don't tell me you had forgotten!"

"Forgotten? Forgotten your wedding, Alice?" said her mother, astonished. "Of course your father hasn't forgotten. Why, only yesterday he was saying that the cost of a trousseau apparently hadn't lessened since Lillian was married. Weren't you, Father? It was when your new green corduroy came home, Alice, and I was saying——" but Alice had led the girls off to show them over the apartment.

Father had retired behind his newspaper and Harry was showing Fred and Bob his own private den whither he might retire from the worries of domestic life. "Only," observed Fred sagaciously, "since it opens off the living room, you can't retire very far. I predict that married life will make you rather a sociable person, Harry."

Harry shrugged his shoulders, and said nothing. "Old bear!" cried Alice, entering the room at this point. "You don't need to be a sociable person! I like you just as you are!" And she turned to the others. "Come to the party, please. It's all in the kitchen! We've made coffee, too, and everything is bee-youtiful! I love surprises!"

The "party" consisted of:

Apples   Popcorn Balls

Nut Cookies

Maple Fudge   Coffee

BETTINA'S RECIPES

(All measurements are level)

Popcorn Balls (Eight balls)

¾ C-light brown or "C" sugar	2 T-butter
¾ C-white sugar	¼ t-soda
½ C-molasses	2 qts. freshly popped corn
½ C-water,	2 t-salt
1 T-vinegar	

Place in a sauce pan, the sugar, molasses, water, vinegar and butter. Cook without stirring until the candy forms a hard ball which clicks against the side of the glass when dropped into cold water. Add the soda, stir well and pour over the corn, which has been salted and placed in a large pan. Mix the syrup thoroughly with the corn, and when partially cool, moisten the hands and press the corn into balls of uniform size. Popcorn balls should be kept in a cool place.

Nut Cookies (Three dozen cookies)

1/3 C-butter and lard mixed	1/3 C-chopped nut-meats
2/3 C-"C" sugar	(preferably black walnuts)
1 egg	1 t-powdered cinnamon
4 T-milk	¼ t-powdered cloves
2 C-flour	¼ t-mace
2 t-baking powder	¼ t-nutmeg

Cream the butter, add the sugar and mix well. Add the egg and milk and then the flour, nuts, cinnamon, cloves, mace, nutmeg and baking powder. Place the dough on a floured board. Roll it out one-fourth of an inch thick and cut with a cooky cutter. Place on a well-buttered and floured baking sheet. Bake twelve minutes in a moderate oven.

Maple Fudge (Eight portions)

¼ lb. maple sugar	¼ t-cream of tartar
2 C-granulated sugar	2 T-butter
	2/3 C-milk

Mix all the ingredients in the order named. Cook until the candy forms a soft ball when a little is dropped in a glass of cold water. Remove from the fire and let it cool. When cool, beat until it becomes creamy. Pour into a buttered plate.

CHAPTER LXXX

A DINNER FOR THE BRIDAL PARTY

THE bridal dinner, given for the wedding party by Alice's parents, was truly an elaborate affair. As the young people, who knew each other so well, and had spent so many merry hours together, glanced across the softly lighted table, a little feeling of shyness and constraint came over them because of the formality of the occasion. Even Alice, usually the ring-leader in all their fun, was a little silent.

"Shucks!" thought boyish Fred. "None of this in mine! I'd elope first! Wonder if Harry likes it! (Bet he doesn't.)"

Ruth was thinking, "Oh, how lovely! How perfectly lovely! I believe after all—as a time to remember through all the years——" But Fred could not read her thoughts, and saw only the particularly happy smile that she gave him.

"How do you like the nut cups?" Alice asked. "Bettina made these yellow 'mum' nut cups as a Christmas gift to me, and gave them to me now for this dinner! See, they just match the real chrysanthemums! I'm sure I don't know which I like best!"

The girls exclaimed so heartily over the nut cups that Bettina declared to herself that she would make sets for each of them, of different colors and kinds. These of Alice's were really charming. Their wire handles were wound with green maline and tied with a green bow. They were filled with pecans, and pink and yellow bon-bons, which were grapes covered with colored creams.

The place cards were tied with narrow green ribbon to little china slippers, cupids, doves and hearts. Besides the yellow chrysanthemums, which were the table decorations, there was for each of the girls a corsage bouquet of pink roses, and for each of the men a boutonniere of pink rosebuds in a tinfoil case. Flower pins were tucked in the maline bows of the bouquets as favors for the girls, while scarf pins were favors for the men.

When the dinner was over, and the guests were passing into the living room for dancing and music, Alice slipped her arm through Bettina's. "The dinner was lovely; wasn't it?" she said. "I did think I was too tired to enjoy it, but my heart is as light as a feather now! I am going to dance all evening till my last guest goes!"

The menu was as follows:

Grapefruit Cocktail

Cream of Asparagus Soup   Croutons

Sautèd Halibut   Potato Rosettes

Cabbage Relish in Green Pepper Cases

Peas in Timbale Cases

Celery

Hot Rolls   Currant Jelly

Vegetable Salad   Cheese Wafers

Brick Ice Cream   Individual Cakes

Coffee

Pecans   Bon-Bons

BETTINA'S RECIPES

(All measurements are level)

RECIPES OF THE BRIDAL DINNER

Grapefruit Cocktail (Twelve portions)

6 grapefruit 12 T-powdered sugar

12 cherries

Cut the grapefruit in halves crosswise. Half a grapefruit is one service. Remove all the seeds. Insert a sharp-pointed knife between the outside skin or shell and the pulp, and cut out around the inside. Cut the skin away from each section of the pulp. Insert the knife under the core and cut free from the shell, lift out the core and membranes in one piece, leaving the pulp. Sprinkle each grapefruit half with one tablespoon of powdered sugar. Garnish with a maraschino cherry in the center and a mint leaf on each side. Serve very cold on a paper doily with some green rose leaves under the grapefruit.

Cream of Asparagus Soup (Twelve portions)

4 C-strained asparagus pulp	9 T-flour
5 C-milk	2 t-salt
7 T-butter	¼ t-paprika

Melt the butter, add the flour, salt and paprika. Mix well, and gradually add the milk and asparagus. Cook until slightly thick. (About two minutes.) Serve hot.

Croutons (Twelve portions)

8 slices of bread   2 T-butter

Cut the bread into one-third inch cubes, add the butter melted, and salt. Mix well and brown in a moderate oven, stirring occasionally to permit the bread to brown evenly.

CHAPTER LXXXI

REHEARSING THE CEREMONY

ALICE'S wedding day dawned clear and cold, and Bettina realized with a start all that was before her. She had as house guests two school friends of Alice's, gay and charming girls who were, nevertheless, somewhat difficult visitors, as the little bungalow was soon strewn with their belongings and as they were completely indifferent to such a thing as punctuality.

"S'pose Geraldine'll be in to borrow my mirror in a minute," grumbled Bob. "How long'll they stay?"

" 'Till tomorrow morning, dear. Hurry! You know we have to rehearse at ten o'clock."

"Ushers and all?"

"Of course. You wouldn't know what to do without a rehearsal, would you?"

"I suppose not. But what if I can't get away from the office?"

"You'll have to, Bob, for Harry's sake. Surely you can manage it for once."

Bob went on grumbling about the foolishness of "these fancy weddings" until Bettina consoled him with the promise of waffles for breakfast.

"And we'll simply have to call Geraldine and Lenore," said she. "They are going to the rehearsal with me, and I must have my morning's work done before we start. You see I shall have them here for luncheon, and we won't be back 'till noon."

Bettina, with some effort, managed to reach the church with

her guests shortly after ten o'clock. The nervous and excited wedding party stood about in chattering groups, and when summoned, went through their parts with many mistakes and giggles.

"How can it ever seem beautiful and solemn," thought Bettina in despair, "when we all do it so stupidly? I'm afraid we are going to spoil the wedding!"

BETTINA'S RECIPES

(All measurements are level)

MORE BRIDAL DINNER RECIPES

Sautèd Halibut (Twelve portions)

2½ lb. halibut steak	4 T-egg-yolks
¼ t-pepper	1 T-water
1 t-salt	1½ C-cracker crumbs
1 T-lemon juice	4 T-fat
⅛ t-onion juice	2 T-melted butter

Mix the pepper, lemon juice, onion juice, salt, butter, egg and water. Wipe the halibut with a damp cloth and then cut into strips two and a half by four inches. Dip each strip into the above mixture and roll in cracker crumbs. Place the fat in a frying-pan, and when hot add the halibut. Brown thoroughly on each side and garnish with lemon and parsley.

Potato Rosettes (Twelve portions)

3 C-mashed potatoes	1 t-salt
3 T-milk	¼ t-paprika
2 T-butter	

Mix potatoes, milk, salt, paprika and butter. Beat one minute. Place the hot potato mixture in a pastry bag and press rosettes on a flat buttered tin pan three inches apart. Set in a moderate oven twenty minutes to brown. Remove from the pan with a spatula.

Cabbage Relish in Green Pepper Cases (Twelve portions)

12 green peppers	2/3 C-vinegar
3 C-finely chopped cabbage	2 T-"C" sugar
3 T-pimento, cut fine	1 t-salt
1 green pepper, cut fine	1 t-mustard
1 T-olive oil	

Mix the mustard, oil, salt, sugar and vinegar. Add the green pepper, pimento and cabbage. Fill the peppers with this mixture. The peppers are prepared by cutting off the stem end, removing the seeds and washing thoroughly.

Glazed Sweet Potatoes (Twelve portions)

6 sweet potatoes	½ C-water
1 C-brown sugar	3 T-butter

Wash, pare and boil the sweet potatoes. When tender, drain, cut in lengthwise slices one-half inch thick, and lay in a buttered pan. Cover with a syrup made by cooking the brown sugar, water and butter for two minutes. Baste frequently. Bake twenty minutes in a moderate oven.

CHAPTER LXXXII

AFTER THE WEDDING

THE stately wedding ceremony had taken place in the big church, and Bettina, climbing into the automobile for the drive to the reception, had, for all her own part in the affair, only a confused memory of music, lights and faces, soft lavender and soft pink, and Alice and Harry murmuring their vows.

"Wasn't it lovely, Bob? Wasn't it stately and impressive?"

"Say, aren't you cold?" was his prosy reply. "That church was too warm; take my coat!"

"No, indeed; I don't need it! Oh, wasn't it a beautiful wedding! Did Lillian and I walk slowly enough?" And she chattered on about all of the details until the house was reached.

The bride and groom were already there, and gay congratulations followed from the many guests. The dining-room, where the dainty wedding supper was served, was elaborate with palms and high baskets of roses. Tables about the room held six, and in the center, a large round table, decorated with a broad, low mound of violets and roses, was arranged for the bridal party. Here also was the bride's cake, and the small boxes of wedding cake which the guests received upon leaving the room.

When Alice cut the bride's cake, the thimble fell to Ruth, which occasioned much merriment, while the dime was discovered by Harry in his own piece. The ring went to Mary, who emphatically denied that the omen spoke truly. But when Mary also caught Alice's bouquet of lilies-of-the-valley, the young people refused to listen to her protests.

"Dear Alice," said Bettina, as she helped the bride into her traveling suit, "may your whole life be as beautiful as your wedding !"

The wedding supper consisted of :

Chicken and Mushroom Patties   Fruit Jelly
Hot Rolls
Olives   Pickles
Ice Cream in Individual Slipper Moulds
Violet Decorated Cake   Salted Pecans
Fancy Candy in Tiny Baskets
Coffee

BETTINA'S RECIPES

(All measurements are level)

THE WEDDING RECIPES

Chicken and Mushroom Filling for Patty Shells (Fifteen portions)

2 C-cooked chicken, diced	¼ t-paprika
1 C-button mushrooms, diced	2/3 C-flour
3 T-pimentoes, cut fine	2/3 C-chicken fat
1 t-salt	3 C-milk

Melt the fat, add the flour and salt; mix thoroughly. Add one-half a cup of milk. Cook until thick, remove from the fire and heat one minute. Add one cup of milk and reheat. When it thickens, beat vigorously until creamy. Add the rest of the milk, and cook until thicker than vegetable white sauce. Add the chicken, mushrooms and pimentoes. Serve hot in patty cases.

To prepare the cases for serving, heat until hot in a moderate oven.

To obtain the chicken fat, cook a fat chicken slowly for a long time. Remove the chicken from the stock and allow the stock to cool. The fat will rise to the top. Use this instead of butter. It has a better flavor and is cheaper.

Fruit Jelly (Fifteen portions)

4 T-granulated gelatin	2 C-sugar
2/3 C-cold water	1 C-white grapes, seeded
4 C-boiling water	½ C-diced pineapple
2/3 C-lemon juice	½ C-maraschino cherries, halved

Soak the gelatin twenty minutes in the cold water, and dissolve in the boiling water, stirring till all is thoroughly dissolved. Strain through a moistened cheese-cloth and add the sugar and the lemon juice. Place in moistened individual moulds or one large pan. When the mixture is slightly thick and cool, add the fruit, well-mixed. Set in a cold place for one hour. Cut in squares when desired for use.

CHAPTER LXXXIII

A "HAPPEN-IN" LUNCHEON

BETTINA had finished her morning's work and was busy with her mending when the telephone rang.

"Why, hello, Bob!" she answered, surprised to hear his voice at this time of day.

"Bettina," said he, "could you possibly arrange to let me bring Carl Edwards and his wife home to luncheon? They blew in a few minutes ago and leave at two-thirty. We haven't much time, you see, and they are especially anxious to see the house. They are planning to build for themselves soon."

"Why, of course, Bob," said Bettina, hesitating for the briefest possible second. "It's after eleven now, but I'll be glad to have you bring them. Let's see—I'll give them the salad I had planned for tonight, but I don't know what else—but, then, I'll manage somehow."

"All right, dear; that's fine. We'll be there early—a little after twelve."

Bettina's "emergency shelf" was always well stocked, and before her conversation with Bob was over her mind had hastily reviewed its contents. In a very short time, her oven held escalloped salmon, graham gems and "quick pudding," and she was setting the dainty porch table. "I'm glad the weather is so beautiful," she said to herself, "for it is so much fun to have a hurry-up luncheon like this out-of-doors. Well, whatever the guests think, I'm sure that Bob will like my menu, for "quick pudding" is a favorite dessert of his, and he can always eat several graham gems!"

For luncheon they had:

Escalloped Salmon   Graham Gems
             Apricot Sauce
        Bettina's Vegetable Salad
Chocolate   Marshmallows
        Bettina's "Quick Pudding"

BETTINA'S RECIPES

(All measurements are level)

Escalloped Salmon (Four portions)

1½ C-salmon	¼ t-paprika
3 T-sweet pickles, chopped fine	½ t-salt
1 T-lemon juice	¼ C-milk
½ C-cracker crumbs	2 T-fresh bread crumbs
1 egg	1 T-melted butter

Pick the salmon apart with a fork and add the pickles, lemon juice, cracker crumbs, egg, paprika, salt and milk, using a fork for mixing. Place in a well-buttered baking dish. Melt the butter, add the fresh crumbs and spread evenly over the top. Bake twenty minutes in a moderate oven.

Graham Gems (Ten gems)

1 C-graham flour	¼ C-sugar
1 C-white flour	¾ t-soda
1 t-salt	¾ C-sour milk
1 egg	

Mix the graham and white flour, the salt, sugar and soda, add the milk and egg. Beat two minutes. Fill well-buttered muffin pans one-half full. Bake twenty minutes in a moderate oven.

Apricot Sauce (Four portions)

¼ lb. dried apricots   2 C-water
           ½ C-sugar

Wash the dried apricots well. Add the water and allow them to soak for three hours or longer. Cook very slowly in the same water until tender. Add the sugar, and cook three minutes.

Bettina's Vegetable Salad (Four portions)

½ C-cooked peas	1 T-chopped onion
½ C-diced celery	2 hard-cooked eggs, diced
¼ C-green pepper, chopped	2 t-salt
½ C-diced cooked potatoes	2/3 C-salad dressing

Mix the peas, celery, green pepper, potatoes, onion, egg and salt thoroughly. Add the salad dressing, and serve cold on lettuce leaves. Garnish with rings of green pepper and egg slices.

Bettina's "Quick Pudding" (Four portions)

2 egg-whites, stiffly beaten	3 T-nuts, cut fine
4 T-powdered sugar	½ t-vanilla
10 dates, cut fine	⅛ t-salt
¼ t-baking powder	

Beat the eggs stiffly, add the nut meats, dates, vanilla, salt, sugar and baking powder. Place in a well-buttered tin mould or a pan and bake in a moderate oven for twenty-five minutes. Allow the mould to stand in a pan of hot water while in the oven. Serve hot.

CHAPTER LXXXIV

UNCLE JOHN A GUEST AT DINNER

"WELL, well! In time for dinner; am I?" said Uncle John, letting in a gust of snow-filled air as he opened the front door.

"Why, Uncle John, I should say you are!" answered Bettina with delight as she removed her kitchen apron. "Do you smell my date buns? I believe you'll like them!"

"Date buns? Never heard of anything so absurd in my whole life! What are they?" And then, without waiting for an answer, he went on, "A regular blizzard tonight, I do believe! I telephoned your Aunt Lucy that I wouldn't be back to the farm till morning, then I found a place to leave my car, and came up here to see if I couldn't get a bite to eat. But date buns! I don't know about that! I'm not used to anything so fancy."

"Well, Uncle John, there's a salmon loaf baking in the oven, and also some lemon rice pudding, so I believe there'll be something you'll like."

"Maybe!" said Uncle John, doubtfully, but with a twinkle in his eye that belied his words. "But let me see! Aunt Lucy sent you something; what was it? Oh, yes, some cream!" And he took a glass jar from its wrappings.

"Oh, Uncle John, how lovely!" said Bettina. "Won't we just revel in cream! There comes Bob now! Get behind the door, Uncle John, and say 'boo'! the way you used to do with me when I was a little girl!"

That night for dinner Bettina served:

Salmon Loaf	Creamed Potatoes
Date Buns	Butter
Cranberry Sauce	
Lemon Rice Pudding	
Coffee	

BETTINA'S RECIPES

(All measurements are level)

Salmon Loaf (Three portions)

1 C-flaked salmon	½ t-salt
½ C-fresh bread crumbs	¼ t-paprika
2/3 C-milk	1 t-melted butter
1 egg-yolk	1 t-flour

Mix the salmon, bread crumbs, milk egg-yolk, salt and paprika. Pack down in a well-buttered pan. Pour one teaspoon of melted butter over the top. Dredge with flour. Bake thirty-five minutes in a moderate oven. Serve hot or cold.

Date Buns (Twelve Buns)

3 C-flour	1/3 T-butter
½ t-salt	¾ C-milk
1 yeast cake	1 egg
2 T-sugar	2/3 C-dates

Mix and sift the flour and the salt. Add the dates, which have been pitted and cut into small pieces. Mix with sugar the yeast cake (broken up). Heat the milk and add the butter. When the butter is melted, cool the milk mixture slightly, and add it to the yeast mixture, stirring carefully until the yeast is dissolved.

Add the egg well-beaten to the milk mixture, and add this to the flour. Mix thoroughly and toss onto a well-floured board. Knead two minutes. Place in a warm place and allow to rise one hour. Divide into twelve pieces by cutting with a knife. Allow to rise ten minutes. Brush the tops with one tablespoon of egg to which has been added one tablespoon of milk. Bake twenty minutes in a hot oven.

Lemon Rice Pudding (Three portions)

2/3 C-cooked rice	1 T-lemon juice
¼ t-salt	¼ C-sugar
1 C-milk	1 T-powdered sugar
1 egg	1 t-lemon juice

Beat the egg-yolk, add the sugar, salt and lemon juice. Add the milk and the rice. Cook one minute, stirring constantly to prevent scorching. Pour into a well-buttered pudding dish. Beat the egg-white very stiff. Add the powdered sugar and the lemon juice. (One teaspoon.) Pile lightly on top of the pudding. Bake thirty minutes in a slow oven.

CHAPTER LXXXV

DURING THE TEACHERS' CONVENTION

"SO you'll not be back until dinner time?" Bettina had said at the breakfast table to Bob's cousin, Edna, and her friend, Catherine. "A whole day of it! How tired you'll be!"

Edna laughed her ripply laugh thât always made everyone else laugh, too. "Tired getting me a hat and a suit? Oh, Bettina! That makes me feel livelier than ever!"

Catherine looked troubled. "Now, Edna," she said, "you positively mustn't miss that afternoon meeting. I know it will be so inspiring! Remember what Professor Macy said!"

Edna laughed again. "Catherine always quotes Professor Macy as if he were an oracle or a sphinx or something instead of a nice solemn young high school teacher who's getting a little bald!"

"He isn't bald and he isn't solemn," declared Catherine with some spirit.

"Forgive me, Catherine dear! He is a lamb and a darling and everything else you want me to say!"

"I want you to say? Why, Edna, aren't you ashamed!" said Catherine, growing very red. "Who ever heard of such nonsense?"

"I love to tease you, Catherine. It's so easy! So you won't help me get my hat? I want a beautiful purple one—or else a perky little black one. I haven't decided whether to be stately and gracious, or frivolous and cunning. But I do know that I will not look as if I were about to cram the multiplication table into the head of some poor little innocent!"

"Don't worry, Edna," said Bob. "You won't look that way at all. In fact, I wonder that you can be serious long enough to impress the members of the school board when they come visiting."

"She doesn't try to impress them; she just smiles at them instead, and that does just as well," said Catherine. "But she's not so utterly frivolous as her conversation sounds. She wants to hear the convention addresses just as much as I do— and I know she'll be there this afternoon. In fact, I intend to save a seat for her."

"Between you and Professor Macy?" asked Edna, innocently. "Or on his left?"

"Shame on you, Edna," said Bettina. "Now you girls tell me just what you'd like for dinner! Aren't there some special dishes you're hungry for?"

"Pork tenderloin and sweet potatoes!" said Edna. "Our landlady never has them, and I often dream of the joy of ordering such delicacies!"

And so that evening for dinner Bettina had:

Pork Tenderloin and Sweet Potatoes
Baked Apples
Bread   Butter
Cottage Pudding with Chocolate Sauce
Coffee

BETTINA'S RECIPES

(All measurements are level)

Pork Tenderloin and Sweet Potatoes (Four portions)

1½ lbs. pork tenderloin   ¼ t-pepper
1 t-salt   4 large sweet potatoes

Wipe the tenderloins which have been prepared by cutting into small pieces (by the butcher). Place in a small roaster and put in a hot oven. When brown on each side, season with salt and pepper. Pare the potatoes and place in the pan with the meat. Baste every ten minutes with one-fourth cup of water if there are not sufficient drippings to baste both the potatoes and meat. Cook until the potatoes are done (about forty-five minutes).

Baked Apples (Four portions)

4 Jonathan apples 2 t-cinnamon
8 T-"C" sugar   1 C-water
½ t-vanilla

Wash and core the apples. Fill each with one tablespoon of sugar and one-half teaspoon of cinnamon. Place in a small tin pan just large enough to hold them. Add the water and the rest of the sugar, and bake forty-five minutes in a moderate oven. Baste frequently with the syrup. After the apples have cooked thirty minutes, add the vanilla to the syrup.

Bettina's Cottage Pudding (Four portions)

½ C-sugar   3 T-chopped nuts
¼ t-salt   ½ t-vanilla
1 C-flour   1 egg
2 t-baking powder ½ C-milk
3 T-melted butter

Mix the sugar, salt, flour, baking powder and nuts. Add the egg and milk and mix well. Add the vanilla. Beat vigorously for two minutes, and then add the melted butter. Pour into well-buttered gem pans, filling each half full. Bake fifteen minutes in a moderate oven. Serve with chocolate sauce.

Chocolate Sauce (Four portions)

½ C-sugar ⅛ t-salt
2 T-flour   1 square of chocolate
1 C-water ¼ t-vanilla

Mix thoroughly the sugar, flour and salt. Add the water and the chocolate. Cook slowly until the chocolate is melted (about two minutes). Add the vanilla and serve hot. If too thick, add more water until the desired consistency is reached.

CHAPTER LXXXVI

A LUNCHEON FOR THE TEACHERS

"I 'LL stay at home and help you this morning; may I, Bettina?" asked Edna, looking wistfully around at Bettina's white kitchen.

"No, indeed, my dear. It is such a simple little luncheon that I have planned that I can easily do it all alone. And you must go to the meeting. All I ask is that you won't forget to come home at noon."

"Edna would much rather fuss around with you in this dear little kitchen than to go to the meetings," said Catherine, "but I won't let her. She is always crazy to cook and do housework and things like that, but she came to this convention with me, and I intend to have her get the benefit of it. Do you hear me, you bad girl? It's almost time for us to be there. Go and get your things!"

"This is the way I'm managed all the time!" complained Edna to Bettina. "Do you wonder that I look thin and pale?"

"Poor Edna!" said Bettina, smiling at her round figure and rosy cheeks. "Now do run along with Catherine. But don't forget we'll have three other guests at noon! So wear your prettiest smile!"

"And I'll help you serve!" Edna smiled back.

That day for luncheon, Bettina had:

Creamed Oysters on Toast
Pear Salad   Brown Bread Sandwiches
Pecan Ice Cream   Sponge Cake
Mints   Coffee

BETTINA'S RECIPES

(All measurements are level)

Creamed Oysters on Toast (Six portions)

6 pieces of toast,	¼ t-paprika
cut circular	1 t-salt
3 T-butter	1½ C-milk
4 T-flour	2 C-oysters

Pick over the oysters, and drain off the liquor. Melt the butter, add the flour, salt and paprika, and mix thoroughly. Gradually add the milk, cook until thick and creamy (about three minutes), and add the oysters. Serve very hot on toast. Garnish with parsley.

Pear Salad (Six portions)

6 halves of pear	6 halves of walnuts
½ C-cottage cheese	⅛ t-paprika
1 T-chopped pimento	6 T-salad dressing
1 T-chopped green pepper	6 pieces of lettuce

Arrange the pears on the lettuce leaves. Mix the cheese, pimento, green pepper and paprika thoroughly. Fill the half of the pear with the mixture. Place salad dressing over the mixture and lay one nut meat on top of each portion. Serve cold.

Pecan Ice Cream (Ten portions)

1 qt. of cream	1½ T-vanilla
¾ C-sugar	½ C-pecan meats, cut fine

Mix the cream, sugar and vanilla. Fill a freezer half full of the mixture. When half frozen add the pecan meats. Continue freezing until stiff. Pack and allow to stand two hours to "ripen" before serving.

Sponge Cake (Ten portions)

6 egg-yolks	6 egg-whites
1 C-sugar	1 C-flour
1 t-lemon extract	¼ t-salt

Beat the egg-yolks until thick and lemon colored. Add the sugar gradually and continue beating, using a Dover egg-beater. Add the extract and whites of the eggs very stiffly beaten. Remove the egg beater and cut and fold the flour which has been sifted four times, the salt having been added to the last sifting. Bake one hour in an unbuttered, narrow pan in a slow oven.

Genuine sponge cake has no baking powder or soda in it. The eggs must be vigorously beaten so that the cake will rise. A very slow oven is necessary. Increase the heat slightly every fifteen minutes.

Do not cut sponge cake; it should be broken apart with a fork.

CHAPTER LXXXVII

RUTH COMES TO LUNCHEON

"**B**ETTINA, what makes the gas stove pop like that when I light it? I've often wondered."

"Why, Ruth, that's because you apply the match too soon. You ought to allow the gas to flow for about four seconds; that fills all the little holes with gas and blows out the air. Then light it, and it won't pop or go out. The flame ought to burn blue; if it burns yellow, turn it off, and adjust it again."

"Well, I'm glad to know that. Sometimes it has been all right and sometimes it hasn't, and I never realized that it was because I applied the match too soon. I'm glad I came today."

"I'm glad, too, but not because of instructing you, I'm not competent to do that in very many things, goodness knows! When I called up and asked you to lunch, it was because I had such a longing to see what lovely things you'd be making today. You will have the daintiest, prettiest trousseau, Ruth!"

"I love to embroider, so I'm getting great fun out of it. I tell Fred it's a treat to make pretty things and keep them all! They were usually for gifts before! Oh, lobster salad?"

"No, creamed lobster on toast. There, Mister Lobster, you're out of your can. I always hurry him out in double-quick time onto a plate, or into an earthen-ware dish, because I'm so afraid something might interrupt me, and I'd be careless enough to leave him in the opened can! Though I know I never could be so careless. Then I never leave a metal fork standing in lobster or canned fish. It's a bad thing."

"I knew about the can, but not about the fork, though I don't believe I ever do leave a fork or a spoon in anything like that."

"Would you prefer tea, coffee, or chocolate with these cookies for dessert?"

"Coffee, I believe, Bettina. Aren't they cunning cookies! What are they?"

"Peanut cookies. I think they are good, and they are so simple to make. They are nice with afternoon tea; mother often serves them. There—lunch is all ready but the coffee, and we'll have that last."

Luncheon consisted of:

Creamed Lobster on Toast
Head Lettuce   French Dressing with Green Peppers
Bread   Butter
Peanut Cookies
Coffee

BETTINA'S RECIPES

(All measurements are level)

Creamed Lobster on Toast (Two portions)

2/3 C-lobster	2 T-flour
2 T-butter	1 C-milk
A few grains of	½ t-lemon juice
cayenne pepper	1 egg-yolk
1/3 t-salt	3 slices of toast

Melt the butter, add the salt, cayenne and flour. Gradually add the milk, cook until thick, stirring constantly unless in double boiler. Add the egg-yolk. Add the lobster, separated with a fork, and the lemon juice. Serve very hot on toast, garnished with parsley.

Head Lettuce (Two portions)

1 head lettuce

Remove the outside leaves and the core. Soak in cold water with one-half teaspoon salt in it, with the head of the lettuce down. Cut into quarters. Serve a quarter as a portion.

French Dressing with Green Peppers (Two portions)

½ t-salt	4 T-olive oil
¼ t-pepper	2 T-chopped green
2 T-vinegar	peppers

Bettina's

With Bettina's Best Recipes

With Bettina's Best Recipes

Mix the salt, pepper, and green pepper. Add the vinegar. Beat well and add the olive oil slowly. Beat with a silver fork until the dressing thickens.

Peanut Cookies (Two dozen)

½ C-sugar	¼ t-salt
3 T-butter	1 C-flour
1 egg	½ C-chopped peanuts
1 t-baking powder	½ t-lemon juice

Cream the butter, add the sugar, mix well, and add well-beaten egg. Add the baking-powder, salt, flour, chopped peanuts, and lemon juice. Mix thoroughly, and drop two inches apart on a greased baking-tin or in pans. Bake fifteen minutes in a moderate oven.

CHAPTER LXXXVIII

THE HICKORY LOG

"SAY, this feels good!" said Bob, as he warmed his hands by the cheerful blaze.

"Doesn't it!" said Bettina, enthusiastically. "And see, I've set the dinner table here by the fireplace. It's such fun when just the two of us are here. Isn't the log burning well?"

"I wondered if we could use one of our new logs tonight— thought about it all the way home. And here you had already tried it! November has turned so much colder that I believe winter is coming."

"So do I, but I don't mind, I don't want a warm Thanksgiving."

"Dinner ready? M—m, what's that? Lamb chops? Escalloped potatoes? Smells good!"

"Come on, dear! After dinner, we'll try those nuts we left so long out at Uncle John's. Do you think they're dry enough by this time? Charlotte phoned me that they had tried theirs, and found them fine. By the way, she and Frank may come over this evening."

"Hope they do. Listen—I hear a car outside now."

"Sure enough, that's Frank and Charlotte. Go to the door, Bob! We'll persuade them to eat dessert with us. . . Hello, people! Come in; you're just in time to have some tea and a ginger drop-cake apiece."

"That's what we came for, Bettina!" shouted Frank, laughing. "And then you must come out in the car with us. It's a beautiful, clear, cold night, and you'll enjoy it—if you take plenty of wraps!"

For dinner that night Bettina served:

Lamb Chops   Escalloped Potatoes
                    Egg Plant
        Bread   Butter
                Ginger Drop-Cakes
                    Tea

BETTINA'S RECIPES

(All measurements are level)

Broiled Lamb Chops (Two portions)

2 lamb chops   1 t-salt
¼ t-paprika

Wipe the chops and place in a red-hot pan over the flame.
When the under surface is seared, turn and sear the other side.
Turn often for twelve minutes. When nearly cooked, sprinkle
with salt and paprika.

Escalloped Potatoes (Two portions)

1½ C-raw potatoes, sliced   ½ C-milk
 ½ t-salt   1 T-butter
 1 T-flour   ⅛ t-paprika
        1 T-chopped green pepper

Mix the potatoes, salt, flour, paprika and green pepper.
Place in a buttered baking dish or casserole. Pour the milk
over the mixture and dot with butter. Put a cover on the dish
and allow to cook for half an hour. Remove the cover and
allow to cook twenty minutes more. More milk may be added
if the mixture is too dry.

Egg Plant (Three portions)

1 egg plant   1 T-water
1 t-salt   ½ C-cracker crumbs
1 T-egg-yolk   2 T-lard

Peel and slice the egg plant in slices one-half an inch thick.
Sprinkle each slice with salt. Place the slices on top and allow
to stand for two hours. This drains out the liquid. Wipe each
piece with a cloth and dip in the beaten egg-yolk, to which the
water has been added. Dip in the cracker crumbs. Place the
lard in a frying-pan, and when very hot, add the slices of egg
plant. Brown thoroughly on both sides, lower the fire and

cook five minutes. Serve on a hot platter with the slices over-lapping each other.

Ginger Drop-Cakes (Fifteen cakes)

1 C-molasses	2 t-ginger
½ C-boiling water	½ t-salt
2¼ C-flour	½ C-chopped raisins
1 t-soda	4 T-melted butter

Put the molasses in a bowl, add the boiling water and the dry ingredients, sifted. Then add the raisins and the melted butter. Beat well for two minutes. Pour into buttered muffin pans, filling the pans one-half full. Bake twenty minutes in a moderate oven.

CHAPTER LXXXIX

SOME CHRISTMAS PLANS

"CHRISTMAS is in the air today, I believe," said Charlotte as she took off her hat and warmed her cold hands at Bettina's open fire. "You ought to see the children around the toys downtown—swarming like flies at the molasses! Still, we ought to think about Thanksgiving before we begin our Christmas plans, I suppose."

"I try to get all my Christmas packages ready by Thanksgiving," said Bettina. "Of course, I don't always succeed, but it is a splendid aim to have! There is always so much to do at the last minute—baking and company and candy making! This year we plan to give very few gifts—but to send a card at least to each of our friends. We're racking our brains now to think of something that will be individual—really ours, you know. I think a tiny snapshot of yourself or your home, or your baby or your dog—or even a sprig of holly or a bit of evergreen on a card with a few written words of greeting means more to a friend than all the lovely engraved cards in the world! Of course, some people can draw or paint and make their own—Alice will, I'm sure. One girl I know makes wonderful fruit cake, and she always sends a piece of it, in a little box tied with holly ribbon, to each of her friends. Aren't the little gifts that aren't too hard on one's purse the best after all—especially when they really come straight from the giver, and not merely from the store?"

"Bettina, I'll be afraid to send you anything after such an eloquent sermon as this!"

"Oh, Charlotte, how you talk! I'm telling you my idea of

287

what a Christmas gift should be, but I'll probably fall far below it myself! Luncheon is ready, dear."

For luncheon Bettina and Mrs. Dixon had:

<table>
<tr><td>Mutton in Ramekins</td><td>Rice</td></tr>
<tr><td>Peanut Bread</td><td>Butter</td></tr>
<tr><td colspan="2" align="center">Apple Sauce</td></tr>
<tr><td>Tokay Grapes</td><td>Coffee</td></tr>
</table>

BETTINA'S RECIPES

(All measurements are level)

Mutton in Ramekins (Three portions)

1½ C-cold mutton	1 t-chopped mint
2/3 C-brown gravy	1 egg-yolk
½ t-salt	1 egg-white, beaten stiff

Mix the mutton, gravy, salt, mint and egg-yolk thoroughly. Add the egg-white. Turn into well-buttered ramekins or china baking dishes. Bake in a moderate oven in a pan of hot water for twenty-five minutes. Serve in the ramekins.

Rice (Three portions)

½ C-rice	1 t-salt
2 qts. boiling water	1 T-butter

Wash the rice, add slowly to the boiling salted water. Boil twenty minutes. Pour the rice in a strainer and rinse with cold water. Place in the oven for five minutes to dry. Serve warm, dotted with butter.

Peanut Bread (Twelve slices)

2 C-flour	4 T-"C" sugar
4 t-baking powder	1 egg
½ t-salt	½ C-chopped peanuts
	¾ C-milk

Mix thoroughly the flour, baking powder, salt, sugar and peanuts. Add the egg and milk. Stir vigorously two minutes. Place in a well-buttered bread pan, and bake thirty-five minutes in a moderate oven.

XC

AFTER THE FOOTBALL GAME

"THERE are the men now," said Mrs. Dixon, rolling up the hose she had been darning. "Good!" said Bettina. "The dinner is just ready for them, and I'm glad they didn't keep us waiting."

"Hello! Hello!" shouted Frank and Bob, letting in a gust of cold air as they opened the door. "Whew! It's cold!"

"How was the game?"

"Fine! 39 to 0 in favor of Blake!"

"Not very exciting, I should think."

"Still, Frank here wanted to bet me that Blake would be badly beaten!"

"Frank!" said Charlotte in exasperation. "Is that the way you show your loyalty to your home college?"

"Shame on you, Frank!" grinned Bob. "Well, dinner ready? I'm about starving!"

"Bettina has a regular 'after-the-game' dinner tonight," said Charlotte. "Just the kind to make a man's heart rejoice!"

"Hurray!" said Bob, stirring up the grate fire. "And afterward we'll have our coffee in here, and toast marshmallows. Shall we?"

"Suits me!" said Frank. "Anything you suggest suits me, if it's something to eat."

"Dinner's ready," said Bettina. "Come into the dining-room, people, and tell us about the game. Charlotte and I have mended all your hose this afternoon, and we deserve a royal entertainment now."

"Bettina," said Frank, "do you expect us to talk when you set a dinner like this before us?"

The menu consisted of:

Flank Steak, Braized with Vegetables
Cabbage Salad
Bread   Butter
Brown Betty with Hard Sauce
Coffee

BETTINA'S RECIPES

(All measurements are level)

Flank Steak Braized with Vegetables (Four portions)

1½ lbs. flank steak, 1¼ inches thick	1 T-butter
	1½ C-sliced, raw potatoes
2 T-flour	½ C-thinly sliced onions
2 t-salt	1 green pepper, sliced thin
1 C-tomato pulp	

Cut with a knife across the grain of the flank steak, to prevent it from curling up. Sprinkle the flour and one teaspoonful of salt on both sides of the meat. Dot with butter, and place in an oblong baking pan. Over the meat place a thick layer of sliced raw potatoes. Add the green pepper, and season with one-half a teasponful of salt. Place the onions next and the rest of the salt. (One-half a teaspoonful.) Pour one cup of stewed or raw tomato pulp over all the mixture, and cover the baking pan tightly. Cook slowly in the oven for two hours. One-half hour before the meat is done, remove the cover to allow it to brown. Water may need to be added to prevent burning. In serving, very carefully transfer the steak to a hot platter, preserving the various layers of vegetables. To serve, slice down through the layers as through a loaf.

Cabbage Salad (Four portions)

2 C-chopped cabbage   ½ t-salt
2 pieces of celery   ¼ t-paprika
½ C-salad dressing or enough to moisten

Chop the cabbage and the celery fine. Add salt, paprika and salad dressing. Serve cold.

Brown Betty (Four portions)

2 C-bread crumbs	1 t-cinnamon
2 C-sliced apples, pared and	½ C-water
cored	1 T-lemon juice
¼ C-sugar	1 T-butter
	⅛ t-salt

Mix the crumbs, apples, sugar, salt and cinnamon well. Pour water and lemon juice over the mixture. Place in a buttered baking-dish. Place the butter over the top in small pieces. Cover the pan with a lid and bake in a moderate oven forty-five to sixty minutes. Remove the lid after the Brown Betty has been cooking twenty-five minutes More water may be needed if the apples are not very juicy.

Hard Sauce (Four portions)

3 T-butter	¼ t-lemon extract
1 t-boiling water	¼ t-vanilla extract
	¾ C-powdered sugar

Cream the butter, add the water and slowly add the sugar. Continue mixing until very creamy. Add the lemon and vanilla extract. Form into a cube and place in the ice box. Allow to stand half an hour, then cut into slices and serve on top of the Brown Betty.

CHAPTER XCI

A THANKSGIVING DINNER IN THE COUNTRY

AFTER all the excitement of Alice's wedding, Bettina was more than delighted when she and Bob were invited to a family dinner at Aunt Lucy's on Thanksgiving day. "It always seems to me the most comfortable and restful place in the world," said she to Bob. "And Aunt Lucy is such a wonderful cook, too! We're very lucky this year, I can tell you!"

"Who's to be there?"

"Father and mother—we are to drive out with them—and Aunt Lucy's sister and her big family. Thanksgiving seems more natural with children at the table, I think. And those are the liveliest, rosiest children!"

Bob had slept late that morning, and consequently had eaten no breakfast, but he did not regret his keen appetite when Uncle John was carving the great brown turkey.

"The children first, John," said kind Aunt Lucy. "The grown folks can wait."

Little Dick and Sarah had exclaimed with delight at the place cards of proud turkeys standing beside each plate. In the center of the table was a great wicker basket heaped with oranges, nuts and raisins.

"It doesn't seem natural without pumpkin pie," said Aunt Lucy, "but John was all for plum pudding instead."

"We can have pie any day," said Uncle John, "but this is a special occasion. What with Dick here—and Sarah—and Bettina—who's some cook herself, I can tell you!—I was determined that mother should show her skill! And she did; didn't she?"

The menu was as follows:

Turkey with Giblet Gravy   Oyster Dressing
Mashed Potatoes   Creamed Onions
Cranberry Frappé
Bread   Celery   Butter
Plum Pudding   Hard Sauce
Nuts   Raisins
Coffee

BETTINA'S RECIPES

(All measurements are level)

THE THANKSGIVING DINNER RECIPES

Roast Turkey (Fourteen portions)

1 12-lb. turkey

The turkey should be thoroughly cleaned and washed in a pan of water to which one teaspoon of soda has been added to each two quarts of water. Wash the inside with a cloth, rinsing thoroughly, allowing plenty of water to run through the turkey. Dry well and stuff. Season all over with salt, pepper and butter. When baking, lay the fowl first on one side, then on the other until one-half hour before taking from the oven. Then it should be turned on its back, allowing the breast to brown. A twelve pound turkey should be cooked three hours in a moderate oven, basting frequently.

Oyster Dressing (Fourteen portions)

6 C-stale bread crumbs   2 t-salt
½ C-melted butter   ½ t-pepper
1 pt. oysters

Mix the ingredients in the order given, adding the oysters cleaned and drained from the liquor. Fill the turkey and sew up with needle and thread.

Preparing the Giblets

Wash thoroughly the heart, liver and gizzard. Cut through the thick muscle of the gizzard and peel it slowly without breaking through the inside lining. Cut the heart open, and remove carefully the gall bladder from the liver. Wash carefully again, and soak ten minutes in salted water. Cook slowly until tender, in one cup of water. More water may be needed. Cut fine, and add to the gravy. Save the stock.

The Gravy

1 C-stock	1 T-cold water
2 T-flour	¼ t-salt

For each cup of liquor, which is left in the roasting pan, add one tablespoon of flour. Mix the flour with two tablespoons of cold water, add the liquid slowly, and cook two minutes. Add one-fourth of a teaspoon of salt, and the giblets. Serve hot.

Creamed Onions (Six portions)

2 C-cooked onions   1 C-white sauce

Cook the onions in one quart of water in an uncovered utensil until tender. (About fifteen minutes.) Drain and add one cup of white sauce. Serve hot.

Plum Pudding (Six portions)

2 C-soft bread crumbs	½ C-molasses
¼ t-soda	4 T-"C" sugar
¼ t-cloves	1 egg
1 t-cinnamon	¾ C-milk
¼ t-salt	½ C-currants
½ C-suet	½ C-raisins
	1 t-vanilla

Chop the suet, and sprinkle with one tablespoon of flour to prevent sticking. Add the raisins, currants, "C" sugar, salt, cinnamon, cloves and bread crumbs. Add the egg and milk beaten together, add the vanilla, mix the soda in the molasses and add to the first mixture. Fill a well-buttered pudding mould one-half full. Steam two hours. Serve with hard sauce.

Hard Sauce

1/3 C-butter	¾ C-brown sugar
2 T-hot water	½ t-vanilla
½ t-lemon extract	

Cream the butter, add water and gradually add the sugar. Continue mixing until very creamy. Add the vanilla and lemon extract. Chill and serve over the hot pudding.

CHAPTER XCII

PLANNING THE CHRISTMAS CARDS

"AND what is in this dish, Bettina?" asked Bob, as he lifted the hot cover.

"Candied sweet potatoes, dear, and I'm almost sure that you'll like them. I made them in the fireless cooker, and they're really more candy than potatoes."

"They'll suit me, then," said Bob. "The sweeter the better! My mother used to cook up candied sweet potatoes with a lot of brown sugar syrup—say, but they tasted good about this time of year when I would come in from skating! Well, I believe these are exactly like hers!"

"Only hers weren't made in a fireless cooker," said Bettina. "Now, Bob, as soon as you have allayed your hunger a little we must put our heads together long enough to get an idea for Christmas cards. If we have something made, it may take several weeks, and you know it is no small task to address several hundred of them. As soon as we have ordered them, we'd better make out our Christmas list. But first, what shall the cards be? Think, Bob!"

"Goodness gracious sakes alive, but thinking is hot work! Well, how's this? Suppose we don't have cards engraved— they're expensive, and besides, 'twould take too long! We'll find some plain white correspondence cards—or perhaps white cards with a red edge—and envelopes to go with them, and in the corner of the card we'll stick a tiny round snapshot of the house. Then we'll write this verse very neatly and sign it 'Bettina and Bob.' Perhaps you can improve on this, however:

"We enclose our Christmas greetings
And the hope that we may know
Many happy future meetings
In this little bungalow!"

"Bob, that's the very thing!" cried Bettina.
For dinner that night they had:

Beefsteak   Fireless Sweet Potatoes
Creamed Carrots
Pineapple Charlotte   Custard Sauce

BETTINA'S RECIPES

(All measurements are level)

Fireless Sweet Potatoes (Candied) (Six Portions)

6 large sweet potatoes	1 t-salt
1 C-brown sugar	¼ t-pepper
¼ C-water	1 T-butter

Wash and peel the sweet potatoes. Slice them lengthwise in one-half inch slices. Make a syrup by boiling for five minutes the brown sugar and water. Add the butter. Arrange the potatoes in a fireless cooker utensil. Sprinkle with salt and pepper, and pour the syrup over them. Place the heated disks under and over the pan of potatoes, and cook in the fireless an hour and a half.

Pineapple Charlotte (Four portions)

2 T-corn starch	2 egg-whites
4 T-cold water	1 t-vanilla
¼ t-salt	½ t-lemon extract
¼ C-sugar	2 slices of pineapple cut
1 C-boiling water	in slices lengthwise

Mix the corn starch, salt and sugar; gradually add the cold water, stirring well, and then add the hot water. Cook about five minutes, stirring constantly. Then add the vanilla, and the egg-whites stiffly beaten. Pour into a moistened mould in which the slices of pineapple have been arranged. Set in a cool place for two hours. Serve with custard sauce.

Custard Sauce (Four portions)

1½ C-milk   ½ t-vanilla
2 egg-yolks   ⅛ t-salt
¼ C-sugar   1 T-flour
      ¼ t-lemon extract

Mix well the sugar, salt and flour, gradually add the beaten egg-yolks, and the milk. Cook in a double boiler until the mixture coats a silver spoon yellow. Add the vanilla and lemon extract. Beat one minute. Serve very cold.

DECEMBER.

Roasting turkeys! Rich mince pies!
Cakes of every shape and size!
Santa, though they're fond of you,
Christmas needs us housewives, too!

HARRY AND ALICE RETURN

"WHO can that be?" said Bettina, laying down her napkin. "Someone is at the door, Bob, I think. I wonder why he doesn't ring?"

"Hello!" said Bob, throwing open the door. "Why, Bettina! It's Alice and Harry! When did you get home?"

"We're on our way home now," said Harry, as he set down the suitcases he was holding. "Say, these are heavy! We thought we'd stop in for a minute to rest."

"Welcome home!" said Bettina. "Just think, we don't even know yet where you went for your wedding trip, though we suspected California."

"California it was," said Alice, "along with all the other recent brides and grooms. We escaped any particular notice; there were so many of us. It was rather a relief, though."

"Have you had your dinner?" asked Bettina, a little embarrassed at the thought of the "dinner for two" that she and Bob were just finishing. There was certainly not enough left for another person, not to suggest two. But then, of course there was her ample emergency shelf.

"We had our dinner on the diner," said Harry, "or we shouldn't have dared to stop at this hour."

"Do come on out to the kitchen," said Bettina. "Bob is

about to make some delicious sour cream candy, aren't you, Bob? Surely that is a splendid way to entertain a newly returned bride and groom."

"Fine!" said Harry, "though we can't stay long. We must hie to our own apartment and get rid of the dust of travel. We're looking forward to the time when we can return some of your hospitality. I shall learn to make even better candy than Bob's!"

For dinner that night Bettina had:

Pork Chops with Sweet Potatoes
Apple Sauce

Bread   Butter
Perfection Salad   Salad Dressing

BETTINA'S RECIPES

(All measurements are level)

Pork Chops with Sweet Potatoes (Two portions)

2 sweet potatoes   ¼ t-paprika
1 t-salt   2 chops
1/3 C-boiling water

Pare sweet potatoes, add salt and place in the bottom of a small roasting pan. Wipe pork chops and place on top of the potatoes. Place the pan, uncovered, on the top shelf of a hot oven in order to brown the chops. Brown on one side and then turn gently and brown on the other. Sprinkle with a little salt and paprika, and add one-third of a cup of boiling water. Cover, and bake one hour, or until the potatoes are done. Baste frequently.

Perfection Salad (Three portions)

1 T-granulated gelatin   4 T-sugar
4 T-cold water   ½ t-salt
4 T-vinegar   2/3 C-diced celery
1 T-lemon juice   ½ C-shredded cabbage
1 C-boiling water   1 green pepper, chopped
2 T-pimento, cut fine

Add the cold water to the gelatin, and let it stand for five minutes. Add the boiling water. When thoroughly dissolved add the vinegar, salt, lemon juice and sugar. Mix well. Add the celery, cabbage, green pepper and pimento when the jelly begins to set. Pour into a mould which has been dipped in cold water. Allow to set in a very cold place for one hour. Serve with salad dressing.

Sour Cream Candy (Six portions)

2 C-brown sugar   1 t-vanilla
½ C-sour cream or ½ C-sour milk plus 1 T-butter
¼ t-cream of tartar

Mix the sugar, cream of tartar and the sour cream or milk. Cook until a soft ball is formed when dropped in cold water. Remove from the fire and allow to cool. Beat until creamy and place in a well-buttered pan.

CHAPTER XCIV

THE FIRELIGHT SOCIAL

"AND what have you been doing all day?" asked Bob after he had related his own experiences at the office. "Just my usual work this morning, and this afternoon I went to a meeting of the social committee of our Young People's League; you know I've promised to help this winter. They plan a social to be given in about two weeks to raise money for the orphanage fund, and I do think their idea is a clever one. You see, it's a 'firelight social'; admission ten cents. Mrs. Lewis has offered her house for it. Invitations are to be sent to all members of the church, Sunday school and league, inviting people to 'come and read pictures in the fire.' The cards are to be decorated with little pen and ink sketches of hearthstones with burning logs on them. Of course there will be a huge log in her big fireplace. Then as soon as the guests are gathered around, someone is to read aloud that passage from 'Our Mutual Friend,' where Lizzie Hexam reads the pictures in the firelight for her brother. Then pencils and paper will be passed among the guests and each one writes a short description of the pictures he sees in the fire. In ten minutes these are collected and read aloud, with a prize for the best one. Then corn will be popped and marshmallows toasted, and weird ghost stories told. (Of course certain clever people have been asked beforehand to be prepared.) Then supper will be served by candlelight; it will consist of things like sandwiches, cider, coffee, nuts and cookies. Don't you thin'. a firelight social will be fun?"

"Sure it will! But I'm glad to-night we can be alone by our own firelight, Bettina!"

That evening for dinner Bettina served:

Fried Oysters   Baked Potatoes
Bettina's Relish   Asparagus on Toast
Apple Tapioca   Cream
Coffee

BETTINA'S RECIPES

(All measurements are level)

Fried Oysters (Two portions)

12 oysters	1 T-water
½ C-cracker crumbs	¼ t-salt
1 T-egg	⅛ t-paprika
2 T-fat	

Look over the selected large oysters to remove the shells. Mix the egg, water, salt and paprika. Dip the oyster in the egg mixture and in the crumbs. Place the fat in the frying-pan, and when hot add the oysters. Brown nicely on each side, three minutes. Serve very hot on a hot platter. Garnish with parsley.

Bettina's Fried-Oyster Relish (Two portions)

1 C-cabbage, cut fine	⅛ t-mustard
1 green pepper, cut fine	¼ t-salt
1 pimento, cut fine	1 T-"C" sugar
¼ t-celery salt	2 T-vinegar

Mix the celery salt, mustard, salt and sugar, add the vinegar. Pour over the pimento, green pepper and cabbage. Serve as a relish with oysters and meats. This relish should be served within one-half hour after it is made.

Asparagus on Toast (Two portions)

½ can asparagus tips	¼ t-salt
1 C-vegetable white sauce	⅛ t-pepper
2 slices of toast	

Heat the asparagus tips in the liquid in the can. When hot, remove from can upon slices of toast, sprinkle salt and pepper over each portion. Pour one serving of white sauce over each portion.

Apple Tapioca (Two portions)

4 T-pearl tapioca	⅛ t-salt
3 T-cold water	4 T-sugar
1 C-boiling water	¼ t-vanilla
2 sour apples	

Soak the tapioca in the cold water for ten minutes in the upper part of the double boiler. Add the boiling water and salt. Cook until transparent. (About twenty minutes.) Cut the apples fine, mix thoroughly with the sugar, place in the bottom of a small baking dish, pour the tapioca mixture on them, and bake in a moderate oven until the apples are soft. (About twenty-five minutes. The time depends upon the variety of apple.)

CHAPTER XCV

ALICE'S TROUBLES

"WHY, Alice, come in! Are you going out to dinner, or just on your way home from some afternoon party?"

"I'm going down town to dinner with Harry; I'll meet him there. And afterward we are going to the theatre."

"What fun!"

"Yes, fun for me," said Alice slowly. "I persuaded him to go. Just think, Bettina, we haven't been to the theatre one single time since we've been married!"

"And that is—let's see—about six weeks?" said Bettina, laughing. "Come into the kitchen, Alice. I'm making a cranberry pie for dinner."

"A cranberry pie? One of those darling criss-crossy ones?" said Alice joyfully, throwing off her evening cloak. "Do let me help. I used to make little cranberry pies in a saucer when I was little! I had forgotten that they existed! Harry shall have one to-morrow!" And she rolled out the crust with deft fingers.

"How easily and quickly you do everything, Alice."

"Yes, too easily. Getting breakfast is fun, and getting dinner is fun, but it's over too soon. What do you do in the evening, Bettina?"

"Oh, stay at home and read and mend mostly. What do you do?"

"That's the trouble. Don't you get dreadfully bored just sitting around? Harry likes it—but I don't see how he can."

"But aren't you tired in the evening? I suppose he is."

"Tired? Mercy no! Not with the care of that little apartment! I like fun and excitement and something to do in the evening! I've been studying household economy, as you suggested, and I've learned a lot, but I can't be doing that all the time! Well, I must run on, Bettina! Let me know how the pie turns out!"

That night Bettina served:

Bettina's Pork Chops and Dressing
Baked Potatoes   Apple Sauce
Bread   Butter
Cranberry Pie   Coffee

BETTINA'S RECIPES

(All measurements are level)

Pork Chops Bettina (Two portions)

2 pork chops	½ t-salt.
½ t-chopped onion	1 T-melted butter
1 T-chopped green pepper	1 egg-yolk
1½ C-fresh bread crumbs	¼ t-celery salt
¼ t-chopped parsley	1 T-water

Add the onion, green peppers, parsley, salt and celery salt to the crumbs. Add the egg-yolk, butter and water, and mix thoroughly. Wipe the chops, and place one in a small pan (to serve as a roasting pan), place the dressing on top. Place the other chop on top of the dressing. Press together and bake in a moderate oven one hour. Turn the chops so that the under one will brown. Baste occasionally with one-fourth of a cup of hot water to which has been added one teaspoon of butter. Put a lid on the pan so that the steam will cause the chops to cook. Place one tablespoon of water in the pan to prevent burning or drying out. Replenish when necessary.

Apple Sauce (Two portions)

6 Jonathan apples	⅛ t-cinnamon
½ C-sugar	Enough water to cover

Wash, pare, core and quarter the apples. Cover with water and cook until tender when pierced with a knitting needle. Add the sugar and cook five minutes more. Sprinkle cinnamon over the top when serving.

Cranberry Pie (Four portions)

2 C-cranberries	1 T-water
1 C-boiling water	1 T-flour
1½ C-sugar	½ t-butter
1 egg-yolk	½ t-almond extract

Cook the cranberries and water until the cranberries are soft. Add the sugar and cook five minutes.

Mix flour and water, add the egg-yolk, butter and extract. Mix thoroughly. Add to the cranberry mixture. Pour into the uncooked pie-crust. Place pastry bars lattice fashion across the top, and bake thirty-five minutes in a moderate oven.

Pie Crust (Four portions)

1 C-flour	¼ t-salt
5 T-lard	3 T-water

Mix the flour and salt. Cut in the lard with a knife, and add the water very carefully, to form a stiff dough. Roll into shape, and reserve a small part of the dough for the bars. Fit the crust carefully into a deep tin pie-pan. Fill the crust with the cranberry filling, being careful not to let any juice run out. Cut the bars two-thirds of an inch wide. Moisten the ends, and arrange in criss-cross fashion across the pie.

CHAPTER XCVI

SOME OF BETTINA'S CHRISTMAS PLANS

"TO-NIGHT," said Bettina at the dinner table, "I expect to finish three Christmas gifts—one for Alice, one for Mary and one for Eleanor. Now aren't you curious to know what I've been making?"

"Curiosity is no name for it," said Bob, "but I'm even more curious to know what particular thing it is that makes this ham so tender. Is it baked? Anyhow, it's the best I have ever eaten."

"Thank you," said Bettina, "but you always say that about sliced ham, no matter how it is cooked. But this is a little different. It is baked in milk."

"Great, anyhow," said Bob. "Now tell me about your conspiracy with Santa Claus."

"Well, I am making for Alice an indexed set of recipes—a card index. All the recipes are just for two, and they are all tried and true."

> "Just for two,
> Tried and true—
> Sent, with Betty's love, to you."

echoed Bob. "You can write that on the card that goes with it."

"I shall have you think what to say on all the gifts, Bob. I must show you the box of cards. It is only a correspondence-card box, with the white cards to fit, but I'm sure that Alice will like her new cook book. Then for Mary and Eleanor I have made card-table covers. Mary's is of white Indian head —just a square of it, bound with white tap and with white tape at the corners for tying it to the table. It is to have a white monogram. Eleanor's is linen-colored and is bound in green with a green monogram. Hers is finished and I shall finish Mary's this evening—that is, if you will read to me while I work!"

"Hurray!" said Bob. "What shall I read? Mark Twain?"

For dinner that night they had:

Baked Ham   Baked Potatoes
Corn Bread   Butter
Cranberry Sauce

BETTINA'S RECIPES

(All measurements are level)

Baked Ham (Three portions)

2/3 lb. slice of ham	1 C-milk
one inch thick	1 T-flour
	1 T-water

Cover the ham with boiling water and let it stand ten minutes. Remove from the pan, and place the ham in a pan just large enough to hold it. Cover with the milk. Place in a moderate oven and bake thirty minutes. More milk may be added if necessary. When the ham is done, add more liquid (enough to make one-half a cup). Mix flour with water. Add the hot milk to this slowly. Heat and cook one minute. Serve with the ham.

Corn Bread (Three portions)

½ C-corn meal	½ t-salt
2/3 C-flour	1 egg-yolk
3 T-sugar	2/3 C-milk
2 t-baking powder	1 T-melted butter

Mix the corn meal, flour, sugar, baking powder and salt thoroughly. Add the egg-yolk and milk, and beat two minutes. Add the melted butter. Mix well. Pour into a well buttered square cake pan. Bake in a moderate oven twenty minutes.

Cranberry Sauce (Four portions)

1 qt. cranberries   2 C-sugar
2 C-water

Look over and wash the cranberries. Cook them in the water until they are soft and the skins are broken. Remove from the fire, add the sugar and stir well. Cook three minutes. Pour into a mould which has been dipped in cold water.

CHAPTER XCVII

MORE OF BETTINA'S CHRISTMAS SHOPPING

"BOB, said Bettina, as she served the plum pudding, "Christmas is in the very air these days!"

"Did the Christmas spirit inspire this plum pudding?" said he. "Blessings on the head of Santa Claus! But why your outburst?"

"Because today I went shopping in earnest! I bought the very things that seem most Christmassy: tissue paper, white and green, gold cord, a ball of red twine, Santa Claus and holly stickers, and the cards to tie to the packages. I love to wrap up Christmas things!"

"And are most of your gifts ready to be wrapped?"

"No, not all, for some of them can't be made till the last minute. For instance, I thought and thought about Uncle Eric's gift! I want so much to please him, but he has everything that money can buy except perhaps a cook that suits him. Finally I decided to send him a box containing a jar of spiced peaches, a jar of Russian dressing, a little round fruit cake, and a box of fudge. The things will all be wrapped with tissue paper, and gold cord and holly——"

"Lucky Uncle Eric!" sighed Bob. "I wish Santa Claus would bring me a Christmas box like that—fruit cake and spiced peaches and Russian dressing——"

"Maybe he will if you're very good!" laughed Bettina. "If you eat everything your cook sets before you."

"Tell me something hard to do!" said Bob, with enthusiasm. For dinner that night they had:

Escalloped Eggs and Cheese
Baked Potatoes   Current Jelly
Rolls
Plum Pudding with Yellow Sauce
Coffee

BETTINA'S RECIPES

(All measurements are level)

Escalloped Eggs with Cheese (Three portions)

3 hard-cooked eggs	1 C-soft bread crumbs
2 T-butter	½ C-cheese, cut fine
2 T-flour	1 t-salt
1 C-milk	1 t-parsley

Melt the butter, add the flour and mix well. Gradually add the milk. Cook one minute, add the cheese and the eggs cut in slices. Add the parsley and the salt. Place one-half the crumbs in the bottom of a well-buttered baking dish, add the egg mixture and cover with the remaining crumbs. Dot with butter, and brown in a moderate oven.

Bettina's Plum Pudding (Four portions)

1 C-fresh bread crumbs	1 t-baking powder
¼ C-suet, chopped fine	¼ C-molasses
½ t-soda	1 egg
⅛ t-ground cloves	1/3 C-milk
½ t-ground cinnamon	4 T-raisins
⅛ t-salt	4 T-nuts

Mix the bread crumbs, suet, soda, cloves, cinnamon, salt and baking powder. Add the raisins cut fine, and the nuts. Break the egg into the molasses, beat well, and add the milk. Mix with the first ingredients. Stir and mix thoroughly. Fill a well-buttered pudding mould one-half full. Steam one and a half hours, and serve with yellow sauce.

Yellow Sauce (Four portions)

1 egg	1 T-milk
¼ C-powdered sugar	½ t-vanilla

Beat the egg white until stiff and dry. Add the yolk and beat one minute. Add the powdered sugar and continue beating. Add the milk gradually and the vanilla. Continue beating for one minute. Serve at once over a hot pudding.

CHAPTER XCVIII

CHRISTMAS GIFTS

"SPEAKING of Christmas gifts," said Charlotte, "wouldn't anyone be delighted to receive a little jar of your Russian dressing, Bettina?"

"I'm sure I'd like it!" said Frank Dixon. "Much better than a pink necktie or a white gift book called 'Thoughts at Christmas-Tide!'"

"Mary Owen makes candied orange peel for all of her friends," said Bettina, "and I think that is so nice, for hers is delicious! She saves candy boxes through the year, and all of her close friends receive the same gift with Mary's card. We all know what to expect from her, and we are all delighted, too. And you see she doesn't have to worry over different gifts for each one. I do think Christmas is growing more sensible, don't you?"

"My sister in South Carolina sends out her Christmas gifts a few weeks early," said Frank. "She sends boxes of mistletoe to everyone. They seem to be welcome, too. By the way, Bob, did you and Bettina decide on your Christmas cards?"

"Yes," said Bob, "and they are partly ready. But we are waiting to get a little picture of the bungalow with snow on the roof—a winter picture seems most appropriate—and the snow isn't forthcoming! The weather man seems to be all upset this year."

"Charlotte has been making some small calendars to send out," said Frank. "She has used her kodak pictures, and I'm afraid they're mostly of me! I don't know what some of my friends will say when they see me with an apron around my neck, seeding cherries!"

"They'll be surprised, anyhow," said Charlotte. "I rather like that picture myself!"

For dinner that night Bettina served:

Escalloped Oysters	Baked Potatoes
Head Lettuce	Russian Dressing
Baking Powder Biscuits	Apple Jelly
Prune Whip	Cream
Coffee	

BETTINA'S RECIPES

(All measurements are level)

Escalloped Oysters (Four portions)

2 C-oysters	1 t-salt
2 C-cracker crumbs	¼ t-pepper
3 T-melted butter	1½ C-milk

Look over the oysters carefully and remove any particles of shell. To the melted butter add salt, pepper and cracker crumbs. Place a layer of crumbs in the bottom of a well buttered baking dish, and add the oysters and more crumbs until the dish is filled. Pour the milk over the oysters and crackers. Bake twenty minutes in a moderate oven.

Russian Dressing (Four portions)

1 C-salad dressing	½ t-paprika
1 t-chopped pimento	¼ t-salt
1 t-chopped green pepper	½ C-olive oil
1 t-vinegar	½ C-chili sauce

To the cup of salad dressing, add the oil, chili sauce, seasonings, vinegar and finely chopped vegetables. Beat two minutes. Pour over head lettuce.

Prune Whip (Four portions)

1/3 lb. prunes	1 T-lemon juice
3 egg-whites	½ C-sugar

Look over and wash the prunes. Soak for three hours in

cold water. Cook until soft. Rub through a strainer, and add the sugar and lemon juice. Cook this mixture for five minutes. Beat the egg whites until very stiff, and add the prunes when cold. Pile lightly into a buttered baking dish and bake twenty minutes in a slow oven. Serve with cream.

CHAPTER XCIX

A CHRISTMAS SHOWER

"DEAR Bettina," wrote Polly, "somehow I never do like to write letters—certainly not at this busiest time of the year!—but I simply must tell you about a luncheon that Elizabeth Carter and I gave the other day for one of our holiday brides. (Angeline Carey; do you remember her? A dear girl—rather quiet, but with plenty of good common sense.)

"We had a large Christmas table (aren't they simple and effective?), with a Christmas tree in the center, strung with tiny electric lights, and hung with tinsel and ornaments. Strings of red Christmas bells stretched from the chandelier above the table to the four corners. The favors at each place were several kinds,—Santas, little Christmas trees, snow men and sleds, all of them concealing at their bases the boxes holding the salted nuts. The place-cards were simply Christmas cards.

"Before the guest of honor stood a small Santa, larger, however, than any of the other Santas, and in his hands were the ends of twenty or more narrow green ribbons, each leading to a separate shower-package at the base of the tree. These packages (it was a miscellaneous shower) made an interesting-looking heap, but we didn't ask Angeline to open them until we had reached the salad course. Then she drew each one toward her by the end of a ribbon, opened it, and read the verse on the gift. You have no idea how clever some of the gifts and verses were! Margaret McLaughlin—do you remember her?—had dressed a dishmop in two tea towels, making the funniest old woman! This she introduced as Bridget, Angeline's cook-to-be! One of the girls who sketches cleverly had illustrated her card with pictures of Angeline in her kitchen.

"But I am forgetting our table decorations! We had furnished four rooms for Angeline, doll size, and the furniture of each was grouped along the table. Besides the living room, bedroom, dining room and kitchen, we presented Angeline and Dean with an auto (in miniature, of course), a cow, a horse, several ducks and chickens, a ferocious dog and a sleepy cat. Weren't we good to them? And lo and behold! beside the auto stood Dean himself, disguised as a little china kewpie man; while Angeline, always a lady, stood gracefully in the living room and refused to help him with his menial tasks, or to assist Nora, who was hanging out the clothes in the back yard. Angeline was a kewpie, dressed in style.

"We had the greatest fun finding and arranging these decorations! And now I must tell you about the luncheon itself. I'm even enclosing our recipes, for I know you'll be interested. . . ."

"Hello, there, Bettina!" called Bob at this moment, coming in with a rush, "is dinner ready? What do you suppose I've done? I've absolutely forgotten to send a Christmas gift to Aunt Elizabeth, and I know she'll feel hurt. Will you go with me after dinner to get it?"

Polly's luncheon menu was as follows:

A CHRISTMAS SHOWER

Grapefruit with Maraschino Cherries
Chicken Croquettes   Candied Sweet Potatoes
Creamed Peas
Light Rolls   Butter
Cranberry Jelly
Vegetable Salad   Salad Dressing
Santa Claus Sandwiches
Chocolate Ice Cream a la Tannenbaum
Christmas White Cake
Salted Nuts   Coffee   Candy Canes

"I wish, Bettina," Polly's letter continued, "that you might have seen the cunning sandwiches that we served with the salad. They were cut with a star-shaped cooky cutter, and on each one was perched a tiny Santa Claus. The sandwiches were arranged on a tray decorated with Christmas tree branches.

"And now comes the dessert. The chocolate ice cream was served in small flower pots lined with waxed paper, and in each flower pot grew a miniature Christmas tree. Around the base of the tree, whipped cream was heaped to represent snow. They were really very cunning.

"Served with the ice cream was a large round white cake decorated very elaborately with icing bells and holly. On the top was placed a real candy bell, large and red. This cake was carried in to Angeline to cut. Around the base, inside the cake, were twenty tiny favors wrapped in waxed paper. They were of all sorts: pipes, canoes, flat irons, animals, birds, many things, but all very tiny. Narrow white bows tied on each favor indicated its position in the cake so that the pieces could be cut to give each guest a favor. Angeline cut her piece first and drew her favor by pulling the little white ribbon. It was really great fun drawing and unwrapping the favors, and the girls tried to interpret the meaning of each. Mary Katherine, Angeline's younger sister, drew the ring, and delightedly proclaimed that she would be the next bride. At this the girls looked a little doubtful, for at the table were no less than six engaged girls besides Angeline. Mary Katherine may fool them—who knows?—but I hope not, for she is far too young and silly to 'settle down' for many years.

"With the coffee we served striped candy canes.

"Well, Betty, I believe I've told you everything about our Christmas luncheon. Do write me soon again, for I love to get your letters. Stir Bob up to write occasionally; he has forgotten his sister—now that he has a wife.

"Yours always,

"Polly."

BETTINA'S RECIPES

(All measurements are level)

Chicken Croquettes (Twenty-five croquettes)

A 3-lb. chicken, cooked and cut fine	2 t-salt
	1 C-chicken fat
1 lb. lean veal, cooked and cut fine	½ C-flour
	1 T-salt
4 T-chopped green pepper	2 C-milk
	2 eggs
½ t-paprika	3 T-water
3 C-cracker crumbs	

Melt the chicken fat. Add the flour and salt and mix well. Gradually add the milk, stirring constantly. When the mixture gets thick and creamy, allow it to cook, with an asbestos mat under the pan, for five minutes. This cooks the flour thoroughly. Beat one minute to make it creamy. Add the chicken, veal, green pepper, paprika and salt. Allow the mixture to cool. Take one tablespoon of the cooled mixture, and dip in the beaten egg to which the water has been added. Dip in the crumbs and shape any desired shape, preferably conical. Allow the croquettes to stand at least one hour before frying. Fry in deep fat and drain on brown paper. Keep hot in the oven until serving.

Vegetable Salad (Twenty portions)

10 tomatoes	½ C-green pepper, cut in strips
2 t-salt	20 pieces of lettuce
1 t-paprika	2 C-salad dressing
1 C-cottage cheese	½ C-salad dressing
1 C-pimentoes, cut in strips	½ C-oil from the canned pimento
½ C-whipped cream	

Arrange the lettuce leaves (washed) on salad plates. Place one slice of tomato, two slices of pimento and two slices of green pepper on each. Sprinkle the vegetables with pepper and salt. Add two teaspoons of cottage cheese. Place one teaspoon of salad dressing on each portion.

To prepare the salad dressing, mix boiled dressing and pimento oil together and then add the whipped cream. Mix well, and pile attractively on the salad.

CHAPTER C

BETTINA GIVES A DINNER

"THE Christmas feeling is everywhere now!" said Bettina, as she arranged a small artificial fir tree in the center of the table. "It may be a little early, but I can't keep from using Christmas decorations to-night. Tannenbaum, O Tannenbaum, you look wonderfully festive with snow at your foot and your branches strung with tinsel and ornaments! All that you lack is candles, but I shall use my red shaded candles on the table instead. Let me see, everything is ready, even to the biscuits which are in the ice box waiting to be popped in the oven when the guests arrive. The salad is mixed and waiting, and that Washington pie does look delicious! I'm glad I made it, for Bob is so fond of it. Wonder why Bob doesn't come! I want him to see the table and the tree before the others get here! And build up the fire in the fireplace. It's snowing hard outside, and I want it to be warm and cozy inside. There's someone! Well, off goes my apron!"

The "someone" proved to be Bob, who came in, very pink as to his face, and very white as to his snow-covered shoulders.

"It's growing colder every minute!" said Bob. "Well, a Christmas table! I like that! Makes a fellow feel festive!"

"I couldn't resist the spirit of Christmas," said Bettina.

"I couldn't, either," said Bob, taking a half-dozen gorgeous yellow chrysanthemums from their wrappings. "So I bought you an early Christmas gift. Like 'em?"

For dinner, Bettina served:

Pork Tenderloins   Candied Sweet Potatoes
Creamed Cauliflower
Baking Powder Biscuits   **Butter**
Currant Jelly
Orange and Cherry Salad   Wafers
Washington Pie   Coffee

BETTINA'S RECIPES

(All measurements are level)

Orange and Cherry Salad (Two portions)

2 oranges	½ C-diced celery
½ C-white cherries	⅛ t-salt
	½ C-salad dressing

Remove the white membrane from the pulp of two oranges, and cut each section into half, crosswise. Add the seeded cherries, and celery salt. Mix thoroughly. Add the salad dressing, and serve very cold on lettuce leaves.

Washington Pie (Six portions)

1 1/3 C-sugar	½ t-lemon extract
3 eggs	2 C-flour
½ C-water	2 t-baking powder

Beat the egg-yolks five minutes, add the sugar and beat three minutes. Add the water, lemon extract, flour and baking powder. Mix thoroughly. Fold in the beaten egg whites very carefully. Bake twenty-five minutes in two round shallow pans in a moderate oven. When cool, put the following filling between the layers. Sprinkle the top with powdered sugar.

Cream Filling for Washington Pie

2/3 C-sugar	1½ C-milk
1/3 C-flour	1 egg-yolk
½ t-salt	½ t-vanilla
	½ t-lemon extract

Mix thoroughly the sugar, salt and flour. Gradually add the milk, stirring constantly. Pour into the top of a double boiler, and cook until very thick. Add the egg-yolk, vanilla and lemon extract, and cook two minutes. Beat until creamy and cool. Spread on the cake. Serve Washington pie with whipped cream if desired.

CHAPTER CI

BOB'S CHRISTMAS GIFT TO BETTINA

$\mathbf{B}$OB had walked home from the office through the falling snow—and it was no short distance—with thought for neither snow nor distance. He was distinctly worried,—Christmas only two weeks off, the first Christmas since he and Bettina had been married, and as yet he had no idea what sort of a Christmas gift he ought to purchase for his wife. What did she need? Unfortunately he had heard her say only a few days ago that she didn't need a thing. What did she secretly long for? A glass baking dish! Shucks, what an unromantic present! Surely Bettina had been teasing him when she mentioned such a prosy gift as that! Well, if he didn't have some inspiration by the day before Christmas there would be nothing to do but get her violets, or candy, or perhaps some silly book that she didn't want.

"Hello, Bob!" said a voice almost at his feet.

"Say Mister Bob, Billy," another voice corrected severely.

"Hello, Jacky! Good evening, Marjorie! Coasting good?"

"Oh, pretty good. You don't know what we've got at our house!"

"Four Angora kittens!" interrupted Marjorie eagerly, before Bob had a chance to guess. "Four whole kittens. Can't see a thing, though, but they'll learn after a while! We're going to sell three of 'em, and keep one, and——"

"See here, Marjorie!" exclaimed Bob. "I'd like to buy one myself, for a Christmas present to some one! How about it? You ask your mother to save one for me—I'll stop in to-morrow morning and talk to her about it. Could you take care of it for me till Christmas morning?"

And Bob strode on with a happy grin on his face. Wouldn't Bettina laugh at the idea of an Angora kitten!

For dinner that night Bettina served:

Beef Steak	Baked Potatoes
Cauliflower in Cream	Cranberry Jelly Moulds
Bread	Butter
Burnt Sugar Cake	Confectioner's Icing
Coffee	

BETTINA'S RECIPES

(All measurements are level)

Cranberry Jelly (Three portions)

2 C-cranberries 2/3 C-water

¾ C-sugar

Look over the cranberries, removing any stems and soft berries. Add the water and cook until the skins have burst and all the berries are soft. Press through a strainer, removing all the pulp. Add the sugar to the pulp, and cook until the mixture is thick, stirring occasionally to prevent sticking. When the jelly stands up on a plate it is done. Pour into moulds (preferably of china or glass) which have been wet with cold water.

Burnt Sugar Cake (Sixteen pieces)

½ C-butter	2½ C-flour
1½ C-sugar	4 t-baking powder
2 eggs	1 C-boiling water
¼ t-salt	1 t-vanilla

Caramelize two-thirds of a cup of sugar. When the sugar is melted and reaches the light brown or the "caramel" stage, add the water. Cook until the sugar is thoroughly dissolved in the water. Allow it to cool. Cream the butter, add the rest of the uncooked sugar, and then add the egg-yolks. Mix well. Add the salt, flour, baking-powder, vanilla and the cooled liquid. Beat two minutes and add the egg-whites stiffly beaten. Pour into two pans prepared with buttered paper. Bake twenty-five minutes in a moderate oven. Ice with confectioner's icing.

Confectioner's Icing (Sixteen portions)

2 T-cream or milk   1 T-carmelized syrup
½ t-vanilla   or maple syrup
      1½ C-powdered sugar

Mix the cream, vanilla and syrup. Add the sugar (sifted) until the right consistency to spread. Spread carefully between the layers and on the top. Set aside to cool, and to allow the icing to "set." (More sugar may be needed in making the icing.)

CHAPTER CII

A CHRISTMAS BREAKFAST

O F course a tiny Christmas tree was the centerpiece on Bettina's breakfast table, set for a nine o'clock family breakfast. All of the Christmas gifts except those that were too large were grouped around the base of the tree. Bettina refused to allow even Bob to have a peep at the gifts until the guests, Father, Mother, Uncle John and Aunt Lucy, had arrived.

"Now, don't you give us too much to eat, Bettina," laughed Father. "I know your mother has been making some mighty elaborate preparations for dinner at home, and you must leave us with an appetite."

"Well, you won't have any appetite left if you eat all you want of these waffles of mine!" exclaimed Bob, coming in from the kitchen with a spoon in his hand and an apron tied around his neck.

"Go back to the kitchen, Cook!" said Uncle John. "We don't want to see you, but we're willing to taste your waffles. Bring 'em on!"

"First," said Bettina, "we'll eat our grapefruit. Then we'll open our packages, and then, Bob, you can help me serve the rest of our Christmas breakfast."

"Come on!" said Uncle John. "Then I'll be Santa Claus and deliver the presents!"

For breakfast Bettina served:

Grapefruit with Maraschino Cherries

Oatmeal and Dates   Whipped **Cream**

Ham Cooked with Milk   Creamed Potatoes

Muffins   Orange Marmalade

Waffles   Maple Syrup

Coffee

BETTINA'S RECIPES

(All measurements are level)

Oatmeal with Dates (Six portions)

1 C-oatmeal	1 t-salt
1½ C-water	½ C-dates, cut fine

Mix the oatmeal, salt and water, and cook directly over the fire for three minutes. Add the dates, put in the fireless, and cook all night. Serve with unsweetened whipped cream.

Ham Cooked in Milk (Four portions)

1 lb. ham (a slice two-thirds of an inch thick)
1 C-milk

Pour boiling water over the ham, and allow it to stand ten minutes. Remove the ham, and place in the frying-pan. Add the milk, and allow to cook slowly for twenty-five minutes. Remove from the milk and garnish with parsley.

Muffins (Twelve muffins)

2 C-flour	½ t-salt
4 t-baking powder	1 egg
1/3 C-sugar	1 C-milk
2 t-melted butter	

Mix the flour, baking powder, sugar and salt. Add the egg, beaten, and milk, and beat two minutes. Add the melted butter. Fill well-buttered muffin pans one-half full. Bake twenty minutes in a moderate oven.

Waffles (Six portions)

1¾ C-flour	3 t-baking powder
2 T-sugar	2 well-beaten eggs
1 t-salt	¾ C-milk
1 T-melted butter	

Mix and sift the flour, sugar, salt and baking-powder. Add the eggs and milk. Beat two minutes. Add the butter. Bake in well-greased waffle irons.

CHAPTER CIII

A SUPPER FOR TWO

"WELL, this is something like it!" said Bob, as he sat down to dinner one evening several days after Christmas. "A good plain meal again. I'm so tired of Christmas trees and Christmas flowers and Christmas food that I don't believe I'll care to see any more of them till— well, next year."

"Everything is put away now," said Bettina. "All the presents are in their permanent places. Except Fluff," she added, glancing at the Persian kitten cuddled in an arm chair. "I couldn't put Fluff away, and don't care to. Isn't he a darling? Just the very touch that the living room needed to make it absolutely homelike!"

"Well," said Bob, "we did need a cat, but I think we need a dog, too. About next spring I'll get one, if I can find one to suit me."

"Oh, Bob, won't a dog be a nuisance? And destructive? And do you suppose Fluff could endure one?"

"Fluff can learn to endure one," Bob said. "Every home ought to have a dog in it. Oh, we'll get a good dog some day, Bettina, if I keep my eyes open."

"Have another muffin," said Bettina. "They'll do to change the subject. Some day I may long for a dog, too, but just now—well, Fluff seems to be a pet enough for one house."

For supper that night they had:

Bettina's Scrambled Eggs	Creamed Potatoes
Corn Gems	Plum Butter
Hickory Nut Cake	Confectioner's Icing
	Coffee

BETTINA'S RECIPES

(All measurements are level)

Bettina's Scrambled Eggs (Two portions)

2 eggs	2 T-ham, cooked and cut fine
1 t-onions, cut fine	2 T-milk
⅛ t-celery salt	½ T-butter
1 T-chopped pimento	1/3 t-salt
1 T-green pepper, chopped	⅛ t-paprika

Melt the butter in a frying-pan, and when hot, add the onions, pimento and green pepper. Let cook slowly one minute. Beat the egg, add the milk, celery salt, salt, paprika and chopped ham. Add the mixture to that in the frying-pan. Cook, stirring until it is thick and creamy. (About two minutes.) Serve immediately on a hot platter.

Corn Gems (Six gems)

½ C-corn meal	¼ t-salt
3 T-sugar	1 egg
½ C-white flour	½ C-milk
2 t-baking powder	1 T-melted butter

Mix the cornmeal, sugar, flour, baking-powder, salt, egg and milk. Beat two minutes. Pour into well-buttered muffin pans, filling each half full. Bake twenty minutes in a moderate oven.

JANUARY

Simpler meals and wiser buying,——
 More of planning,—less of hurry,——
More of smiling,—less of sighing,——
 More of fun, and less of worry,
In this New Year's Resolution,
Trouble finds a swift solution.

CHAPTER CIV

ALICE COMES TO LUNCHEON

"I DO love to cook!" exclaimed Alice enthusiastically.

"And we have had such delicious meals since we began to keep house, if I do say it! But oh, the bills, the bills! Bettina, isn't it terrible? But you can't get any meal at all without paying for it, can you? I really do dread having Harry get the first month's grocery bill, though."

"You ought not to have to say that, Alice," said Bettina, laughing nevertheless. "Why don't you have an allowance, and pay the grocery bill yourself?"

"Because I know I could never manage to pay it," said Alice, making a little face. "I do love to have perfect little meals and cooking is such fun, but you just can't have things right without having them expensive; I've found that out. Last night we had a simple enough dinner—a very good steak with French fried potatoes and creamed asparagus on toast. Then a fruit salad with mayonnaise and steamed suet pudding and coffee. Harry said everything was perfect, but——"

"I'm sure it was, Alice. You are so clever at everything

331

you do. But wasn't that expensive for just a home dinner for two? Steak and creamed asparagus! And mayonnaise is so expensive! Then think of the gas you use, too!"

"I didn't think of the gas," said Alice ruefully. "I thought of Harry's likes, and of variety, and of a meal that balanced well. But not much about economy. I'll have to consult you, Bettina. I'll tell you: Couldn't I plan my menus ahead for a week, and bring them over to you to criticise? That would be fun, and I'm sure you could teach me a great deal."

"I'd love to have you, Alice," smiled Bettina.

For luncheon Bettina served:

Chicken Loaf   Creamed Potatoes
Baking Powder Biscuits   Cranberry Jelly
Caramel Custard   Whipped Cream
Coffee

BETTINA'S RECIPES

(All measurements are level)

Chicken Loaf (Two portions)

½ C-cooked chicken	⅛ t-celery salt
½ C-ground, cooked veal	1 t-chopped parsley
½ C-soft bread crumbs	1 egg
½ t-salt	½ C-milk

Mix the chicken, veal and bread crumbs. Add the salt, celery salt, parsley, egg and milk. Mix thoroughly. Bake in a well-buttered pan thirty minutes in a moderate oven.

Caramel Custard (Two portions)

1 C-milk   4 T-sugar
1 egg   ⅛ t-salt
¼ t-vanilla

Melt the sugar to a light brown syrup in a sauce pan over a hot fire, add the milk and cook until free from lumps. Beat the egg, sugar, salt and vanilla, and pour the liquid slowly into the egg mixture. Pour into buttered moulds. Set the moulds in a pan of hot water and bake in a moderate oven until the custard is firm (about forty minutes). Do not let the water in the pan reach the boiling point during the process of baking.

CHAPTER CV

RUTH STAYS TO DINNER

"SEE, Ruth, it's snowing harder—a perfect blizzard. That means that you'll have to stay to dinner."

"I'm only too glad to find an excuse, Bettina, but you must remember that I'll have to get back some time, and I suppose that now is best."

"Well, Bob will take you after dinner. See, I've put on a place for you."

"That's fine, Bettina, and I suppose I may as well stay. I've been anxious to ask you what you were putting in the oven just as I came in."

"A dish of tomatoes, cheese and rice baked together; Bob is fond of it. You know I almost always plan to have two or more oven dishes if I am using the oven at all, and tonight I was making baked veal steak."

"I learned something new yesterday, Bettina, that I have been anxious to tell you. Mother was preparing cabbage for cold slaw (she always chops it, you know), and it suddenly occurred to her that she might easily use the large meat grinder. So she did, and the slaw was delicious. I would have supposed that the juice would be pressed out in the grinding, but it wasn't."

"I must remember that. I suppose that other people may have thought of it, but I never have, and I'm glad to know that it works so well."

"I believe I hear Bob, Bettina. He must be cold, for it is snowing and blowing harder every minute."

"Well, I'm glad I started the fire in the fireplace. There's nothing like an open fire."

For dinner that night Bettina served:

Baked Veal Steak
Baked Tomato, Cheese and Rice
Bread   Butter
Tapioca and Date Pudding   Cream
Coffee

BETTINA'S RECIPES

(All measurements are level)

Baked Veal Steak (Three portions)

1 slice of veal steak (three-fourths of a pound, one-half inch thick	1 t-salt
	¼ t-paprika
	2 T-bacon fat
3 T-flour	2 T-water

Wipe the veal and cut off any rind. Mix the flour, salt and paprika. Roll the steak thoroughly in this mixture. Place the bacon fat in the frying-pan and when hot add the meat and brown thoroughly on both sides. Place the drippings and the meat in a small baking pan. Add the water, cover, and place in the oven. Cook one hour. More water may be added if necessary.

Baked Tomato, Cheese and Rice (Three portions)

1 C-cooked rice	¼ t-paprika
1/3 C-tomatoes	1 T-flour
4 T-cheese, cut fine	½ C-milk
1 T-pimento	1 T-melted butter
1 t-salt	¼ C-cracker or bread crumbs

Mix the rice and flour, and add the tomatoes, cheese, salt and paprika. Add the milk. Pour into a well-buttered baking dish. Melt the butter and add the crumbs. Spread the buttered crumbs on the rice mixture. Bake in a moderate oven for twenty-five minutes.

Tapioca and Date Pudding (Three portions)

4 T-tapioca	8 dates, cut fine
¼ t-salt	1 T-lemon juice
2 T-cold water	1 egg-yolk
1 C-boiling water	1 egg-white
2 T-sugar	1 t-vanilla

Soak the tapioca in cold water for ten minutes. Add the salt and boiling water and cook in a double boiler until transparent. (About twenty minutes.) Add the sugar and the dates cut fine, the lemon juice, egg-yolk and vanilla. Remove from the fire and add the stiffly beaten egg-white. Pile the mixture lightly in glass dishes and serve cold.

CHAPTER CVI

HOW BETTINA MADE CANDY

"I RAN over this morning," said Alice to Bettina, "to get your candy recipes. That was such delicious Christmas candy that you gave Harry! Wasn't it a great deal of work to make so much at a time? Perhaps I can't manage it, but I'd like to make a box of it for Harry's brother; it will be his birthday in a few days."

"It is very easy to make candy for Christmas boxes," said Bettina. "That is, it is no harder to make a large quantity than to fill one box. Bob helped me one evening, and we made four kinds at once. I had already stuffed some dates and made some candied orange peel, so you see when the candy was made, it was fun to fill the boxes with a variety of things. I always save boxes throughout the year for Christmas candy, and then I fill them all at once. Of course, until this year I didn't have Bob to help me; he enjoys it, you know, and two people can make it so much more quickly than one."

"Next year," said Alice, "I think I shall make Christmas candy—a quantity of it, so that I can put a box of it in every family box that I send. Meanwhile, I'll practise and experiment, and perhaps I can improve on the good old recipes, or think of clever ways of arranging and wrapping. Now will you let me write down some of your best recipes? I'll try them for Harry's brother."

The candies that Bettina made were:

Chocolate Fudge	White Fudge
Peanut Brittle	Peanut Fondant

BETTINA'S RECIPES

(All measurements are level)

Chocolate Fudge (One pound)

2 C-sugar	2 squares or two ounces
1 C-sugar, "C"	of chocolate
¼ t-cream of tartar	1 C-milk
	1 T-butter

Mix the ingredients in order named, and cook until a soft ball is formed when a little of the candy is dropped in a glass of cold water. Remove from the fire and allow to cool. Do not stir while cooling. When cool, beat until creamy, add vanilla and pour into a well-buttered pan. Make white fudge and pour on top. When cool cut into squares.

White Fudge (one pound)

3 C-sugar	1/3 t-cream of tartar
½ C-milk	1 T-butter
	1 t-vanilla

Mix and cook the same as chocolate fudge.

Bettina's Peanut Fondant (One and one-half pound)

2 C-"C" sugar	1 T-butter
½ C-milk	2/3 C-roasted, shelled peanuts
¼ t-cream of tartar	¼ t-vanilla

Cook the "C" sugar, milk, cream of tartar and butter until a soft ball is formed in cold water. Remove from the fire and allow it to cool. Beat until thick and creamy and add the nuts and vanilla. Shape into a loaf two inches thick and two inches wide. When cool and hard enough to cut, slice into one-fourth inch slices. Wrap in waxed paper and pack in boxes.

CHAPTER CVII

RUTH'S PLANS

"AND so, Bettina," said Ruth, sitting down on the high stool in Bettina's neat little kitchen, "Fred says we will begin the house early in the spring—as early as possible—and be married in May or June."

"What perfectly splendid news!" said Bettina. "I'm just as glad as I can be!"

"We've waited so long," said Ruth, wistfully. "Of course, if it hadn't been for the war—it did interfere so with business, you know—we would have been married last spring."

"I know," said Bettina, sympathetically, "but you'll be all the happier because you have waited."

"I'll want you to help me a great deal with my plans," said Ruth. "I've had time to do lots of sewing, of course, but I haven't thought anything about the wedding except that it will be a quiet one. And I want to ask you so much about house furnishings—curtains, and all that."

"I'd love to help!" cried Bettina with enthusiasm. "There isn't anything that is such fun. Oh, Ruth!"

"Gracious me! What?" cried Ruth, for Bettina had jumped up suddenly.

"Poor Ruth," laughed Bettina, "I didn't mean to frighten you. I forgot my cake, that was all, and I was afraid it had burned. But it hasn't. A minute longer though—you know a chocolate cake does burn so easily. But it's all right. However, you must admit that I did pretty well not to burn it while I was listening to wedding plans!"

That night Bettina served for dinner:

Swiss Steak   Mashed Sweet Potatoes
Creamed Cauliflower
Bread   Butter
Chocolate Nougat Cake
Coffee

BETTINA'S RECIPES

(All measurements are level)

Swiss Steak (Three portions)

1 lb. of round steak two-thirds of an inch thick	⅛ t-pepper
	½ C-water
5 T-flour	1 T-onion
1 bay leaf	2 cloves
¼ t-salt	1 T-bacon fat

Wipe the steak with a damp cloth, trim the edges to remove any gristle, and pound the flour into the meat, using a side of a heavy plate for the pounding. This breaks up the tendons of the meat. Place the bacon fat in a frying-pan and when hot, add the meat. Brown thoroughly on each side. Lower the flame. Add the bay leaf, salt, pepper, onion and water. Cover with a lid and allow to cook slowly for one and a half hours. More water may be needed if the gravy boils down. Pour the gravy over the meat when serving. This recipe is good for the fireless.

Mashed Sweet Potatoes (Two portions)

3 good-sized sweet potatoes	½ t-salt
	1 T-butter
2 C-water	2 T-milk
¼ t-paprika	

Wash the potatoes and remove any bad places. Add the water, and cook gently until tender. Drain, and peel while still hot, by holding the potatoes on the end of a fork. Mash with a spoon or a potato masher, adding the salt, butter, milk and paprika. Beat one minute. Pile lightly in a buttered baking dish, and place in a moderate oven about twenty minutes until a light brown.

Chocolate Nougat Cake

4 T-butter	1 egg
2/3 C-sugar	½ C-milk
2 squares of chocolate	1 1/3 C-flour
2 T-sugar	2 t-baking powder
2 T-water	½ t-soda
	½ t-vanilla

Cook the two tablespoons of sugar, water and chocolate together for one minute, stirring constantly. Cream the butter, add the sugar, the whole egg and the flour, baking powder and soda sifted together. Add the vanilla. Beat two minutes. Pour into two square layer-cake pans prepared with waxed paper. Bake twenty-two minutes in a moderate oven. Chocolate cakes burn easily and they should be carefully watched while baking.

Ice with White Mountain Cream Icing.

CHAPTER CVIII

A LUNCHEON FOR THREE

"OH, Bettina, what a perfectly charming table!" exclaimed Alice, while her guest from New York, in whose honor Bettina was giving the little luncheon, declared that she had never seen a prettier sight.

"But it's your very own Christmas gift to me that makes it so," declared Bettina, with flushed cheeks. For Alice's deft fingers had fashioned the rose nut cups (now holding candied orange peel), and the rose buds in the sunset shades in the center of the table. "They are almost more real than real ones! I can scarcely believe that they are made of crêpe paper."

The square luncheon cloth on the round table was of linen, decorated with a cross-stitch design in the same sunset shades, so that the table was all in pink and white. A French basket enameled in ivory color held the rose buds, and another Christmas gift to Bettina was the flat ivory basket filled with light rolls. The luncheon napkins matched the luncheon cloth, as the guests noted, and "The menu matches everything else!" exclaimed Alice.

"I'm glad you like it," said Bettina. "I have eaten chicken a la king often at hotels and restaurants, but until recently it never occurred to me to make it myself. And it isn't difficult to make either."

"You must give me the recipe," said Alice. For luncheon Bettina served:

Chicken a la King   Toast
Light Rolls   Butter
Bettina Salad   Salad Dressing
Cheese Wafers
Strawberry Sherbet   Hickory Nut Cake
Coffee
Candied Orange Peel

BETTINA'S RECIPES

(All measurements are level)

Chicken a la King (Three portions)

2/3 C-cold, cooked chicken, diced	2 T-flour
3 T-butter	1½ C-milk
1 T-green pepper, cut fine	¼ t-salt
1 T-pimento, cut fine	1 egg-yolk, beaten
⅛ t-celery salt	3 slices of toast

Melt the butter, add the green pepper, cook slowly for two minutes, and then add the flour. Mix well and add the milk slowly. Cook until creamy. Add the celery salt and the salt. When very hot, add the beaten egg-yolk. Mix well, and add the chicken and pimento. Reheat. Serve very hot on hot toast. (Do not cook the sauce any longer than absolutely necessary after the egg-yolk is added.)

Bettina Salad (Three portions)

3 slices of pineapple	6 halves of nut meats
3 halves of pears	3 T-salad dressing
6 marshmallows	3 T-whipped cream
3 maraschino cherries	3 pieces of lettuce

Wash the lettuce and arrange on salad plates. Lay a slice of pineapple on the lettuce and half a pear, the hollow side up, on the pineapple. Fill the cavity of the pear with salad dressing, and place one tablespoon of whipped cream on top of the salad dressing. Arrange two nut-halves, two marshmallows and one cherry attractively on each portion. Serve very cold.

Hickory Nut Cake

½ C-butter	4 t-baking powder
1½ C-sugar	2 C-flour
2 eggs	¾ C-milk
½ C-chopped hickory nut meats	½ t-vanilla
½ t-lemon extract	

Cream the butter, add the sugar and mix well. Add the egg-yolks, the nut meats, and the flour and baking powder sifted together. Then add the milk, vanilla and lemon extract. Beat vigorously for two minutes. Add the whites stiffly beaten. Mix thoroughly and pour into two layer-cake pans prepared with buttered paper. Bake twenty-five minutes in a moderate oven. Ice with confectioner's icing.

Bettina's Confectioner's Icing

2 T-cream	½ t-vanilla extract
½ t-lemon extract	1 C-powdered sugar

Mix the cream and extracts. Gradually add the powdered sugar sifted through a strainer. Add enough sugar to form a creamy icing which will easily spread upon the cake. (More than a cup of sugar may be needed.)

CHAPTER CIX

THE DIXONS COME TO DINNER

"SHALL I open this jar of grapefruit marmalade?" asked Charlotte, who was helping Bettina to prepare dinner.

"Yes, Charlotte, if you will."

"How nice it is, Bettina! How long do you cook it before you add the sugar?"

"Well, that depends altogether on the fruit. Sometimes the rind is so much tougher than at other times. You cook it until it's very tender, then add the sugar and cook until it 'jells."

"There's another thing I'd like to ask you, Bettina. How on earth do you cut the fruit in thin slices? Isn't it very difficult to do?"

"Not with a sharp knife. I place the fruit on a hardwood board, and then if my knife is as sharp as it ought to be, it isn't at all difficult to cut it thin."

"Well, perhaps I haven't had a sharp enough knife. Oh, Bettina, what delicious looking cake! Is it fruit cake?"

"It's called date loaf cake. It has nuts in it, too, but no butter. I always bake it in a loaf cake pan prepared with waxed paper. Bob is very fond of it. I think it's very good served with afternoon tea."

"I should think it might be."

"Tonight, though, I am serving just sliced oranges with it."

"That will be a delicious dessert, I think. Listen! Is that Bob and Frank coming in?"

For dinner that night they had:

Roast Beef Browned Potatoes
Gravy
Bettina's Jelly Pickle
Bread Grapefruit Marmalade
Date Loaf Cake Sliced Oranges
Coffee

BETTINA'S RECIPES

(All measurements are level)

Bettina's Jelly Pickle (Four portions)

2 t-granulated gelatin
4 T-cold water
¾ C-vinegar from a jar of sweet pickles

2 T-sweet pickles, chopped fine
1 T-olives, chopped fine
1 T-spiced peach, chopped fine
1 T-pickled melon rind

Soak the gelatin in cold water for ten minutes. Heat the vinegar and when very hot pour into the gelatin mixture. Stir until dissolved. When partially congealed so that the fruit will not stay on the top, add the pickles, olives, peaches and rind. Pour into a well-moistened layer mould or four small ones. Set in a cold place one hour. Unmould.

Grapefruit Marmalade (One and one-half pints)

6 grapefruit 1 orange
4 lemons 1 lb. sugar for each lb. of fruit
6 C-cold water for each lb. of fruit

Wash the grapefruit, lemons and orange carefully. Cut each in quarters. Slice the quarters through the rind and pulp, making thin slices. Weigh the fruit, and for each pound allow six cups of cold water. Allow to stand with the water on the fruit for twenty-four hours. Let all boil gently until the rind is very tender. No particular test can be given for this, as some fruit is much tougher than others. Set aside for four hours. Drain off the liquid. Weigh the fruit mixture, and for each pound allow a pound of sugar. Let cook slowly until the mixture thickens or "jellies" when tried on a dish. Be careful not to get the mixture too thick, as it will thicken somewhat more upon cooling.

Date Loaf Cake (Twelve pieces)

1 C-flour	2 eggs
2 t-baking powder	1 t-vanilla
½ t-salt	1 C-dates, cut fine
1 C-sugar	½ C-nut meats, cut fine

Mix the flour, baking powder, salt and sugar thoroughly. Add the dates, nut meats and vanilla. Mix thoroughly, add the egg-yolks and mix well. Beat the egg-whites until very stiff. Cut and fold these into the mixture. Pour into a loaf cake pan prepared with waxed paper. Bake in a slow oven for fifty minutes.

FEBRUARY.

Cold and snowy February
Does seem slow and trying, very.
Still, a month made gay by Cupid
Never could be wholly stupid.

CHAPTER CX

A STEAMED PUDDING

"THIS was a splendid dinner, Bettina," said Ruth, as the two of them were carrying the dishes into the kitchen and Fred and Bob were deep in conversation in the living-room. "Such a delicious dessert! Suet pudding, wasn't it? I couldn't guess all that was in it."

"Just a steamed fig pudding, Ruth. The simplest thing in the world!"

"Simple? But don't you have to use a steamer to make it in, and isn't that awfully complicated? I've always imagined so."

"You don't need to use a steamer at all. I steamed this in my fireless cooker, in a large baking powder can. I filled the · buttered can about two-thirds full, and set it in boiling water that came less than half way up the side of the can. Of course, the cover of the can or the mould must be screwed on tight. And the utensil in which it is steamed must be covered. I used one of the utensils that fit in the fireless, of course, and I brought the water to a boil on the stove so that I was sure it was boiling vigorously when I set it in the cooker on the sizzlinz hot stone. You see it is very simple. In fact, I think steaming anything is very easy, for you don't have to keep watching it as you would if it were baking in the oven, and basting it, or changing the heat."

349

"We haven't a cooker, you know. Could I make a steamed pudding that same way on the stove?"

"Yes, indeed the very same way. Just set the buttered can filled two-thirds full in a larger covered utensil holding boiling water. Keep the water boiling all the time."

"I shall certainly try it tomorrow, Bettina!"

For dinner that night Bettina served:

Breaded Veal   Creamed Potatoes
Browned Sauce
Spinach with Hard Cooked Eggs
Bread   Butter
Spiced Peaches
Fig Pudding   Foamy Sauce
Coffee

BETTINA'S RECIPES

(All measurements are level)

Breaded Veal (Four portions)

    1 lb. veal round steak, cut one-half an inch thick
    1 T-egg (either the white or the yolk)
    1 T-water
    2/3 C-cracker crumbs, or dry bread crumbs
    2 T-lard
    ¼ t-salt
    1 T-butter
    ⅛ t-paprika

Wipe the meat with a damp cloth, and cut into four pieces. Mix the egg, water, salt and paprika, and dip each piece of meat into the egg mixture. Roll in the crumbs and pat the crumbs into the meat. Place the lard in the frying-pan, and when hot, add the meat. Brown well on one side, and then turn, allowing the other side to become the same even color. Lower the flame under the meat, and cook thirty minutes, keeping the pan covered. When the meat has cooked twenty-five minutes, add the butter to lend flavor to the lard.

Browned Gravy (Four portions)

    1 T-butter   ½ t-salt
    2 T-flour   ½ C-water
        ¼ C-milk

Remove the breaded veal from the pan, and place on a hot platter. (Keep in a warm place.) Loosen all the small pieces of crackers and meat (if there are any) from the bottom of the pan. If there is no fat left, add butter. Allow the fat to get hot, and add flour and salt. Mix well with the heated fat, and allow to brown. Stir constantly, and add the water. Mix well, and add one-fourth cup of milk. Allow to cook one minute, stirring constantly. If a thinner sauce is desired, add another one-fourth of a cup of milk. If a thicker sauce is desired, allow to cook for two minutes.

Bettina's Steamed Fig Pudding (Four portions)

1 C-flour	½ C-molasses
½ t-soda	½ C-milk
½ t-ginger	½ C-suet, chopped fine
2/3 t-cinnamon	1/3 C-chopped figs
¼ t-nutmeg	1/3 C-stoned raisins
½ t-lemon extract	

Mix the flour, soda, ginger, cinnamon, nutmeg, and suet. Add the figs, raisins, molasses and milk. Stir well. Add the lemon extract. Fill a well-buttered pudding mould two-thirds full. Steam an hour and a half, with the water boiling. Serve hot with foamy sauce.

Foamy Sauce (Four portions)

1 egg	½ C-hot water
½ C-sugar	1 T-lemon juice or 1 t-lemon extract

Beat the egg vigorously. Add the sugar and mix well. Add the hot water and stir vigorously. Add the lemon juice. Serve. (This sauce may be reheated if desired.)

CHAPTER CXI

ON VALENTINE'S DAY

"**B**OB, the flowers are lovely!" said Bettina, looking again at the brilliant tulips on the dinner table. "They make this a real valentine dinner, although there is nothing festive about it. I had intended to plan something special, but I went to a valentine luncheon at Mary's, and stayed so late——"

"A valentine luncheon? With red hearts everywhere, I suppose?"

"Yes, everything heart-shaped, and in red, too, as far as possible. Mary had twelve guests at one large round table. Of course, there were strings and strings of red hearts of various sizes decorating the table—not a very new idea, of course, but so effective. And everything tasted so good; cream of tomato soup, the best stuffed tenderloin with mushroom sauce (I must find out how that is made), and the best sweet potato croquettes!"

"Sweet potato croquettes? That's a new one on me!"

"I'll have to try them some time soon. And Mary had peas in heart-shaped baking powder biscuits—the cunningest you ever saw!—heart-shaped date bread sandwiches with her salad, and heart-shaped ice cream with individual heart cakes."

"That was Valentine's day with a vengeance; wasn't it?"

"Yes, but it was lovely, Bob!"

That night Bettina served:

Broiled Steak   Baked Potatoes
Macaroni with Tomatoes and Green Peppers
Bread   Butter
Cornstarch Fruit Pudding
Cherry Sauce
Coffee

BETTINA'S RECIPES
(All measurements are level)

Macaroni, Tomatoes and Green Peppers (Three portions)

1/3 C-macaroni	¼ t-celery salt
3 C-water	⅛ t-onion salt
1 t-salt	3 T-cheese, cut fine
1 C-canned tomatoes	2/3 C-meat stock or milk
3 T-chopped green pepper	¼ C-crumbs
¼ t-salt	1 T-butter

Boil the water, add the salt. Add the macaroni cut in small pieces. Boil until tender (about fifteen minutes) and drain. Butter a baking dish. Add a layer of macaroni, a layer of tomatoes and some green pepper. Sprinkle with salt, celery and onion salt. Add the cheese, and continue with the layers until the dish is full. If available, use meat stock, if not, milk. Pour the liquid over the mixture. Melt the butter, add the crumbs and place on the top of the food. Place the dish in a moderate oven, and allow to bake twenty-five minutes, or until brown.

Corn Starch Fruit Pudding (Three portions)

½ C-water	⅛ t-salt
½ C-cherry juice	3 T-sugar
3 T-corn starch	1 egg-yolk
1 egg-white	

Mix thoroughly the corn starch, sugar and salt. Gradually add the cold water and then the juice. Cook over hot water until the mixture becomes quite thick. Add the egg-yolk. Mix well, cool slightly and add the egg-white stiffly beaten. Pour into a well-moistened custard mould. Allow to stand for half an hour or more. Serve with cherry sauce.

Cherry Sauce (Three portions)

½ C-cherry juice	½ t-lemon extract
½ C-water	⅛ t-salt
1 T-flour	2 T-sugar
¼ C-cherries, cut fine	

Mix the flour, salt and sugar. Add slowly the cherry juice and water. Cook two minutes. Add the cherries and extract. Serve hot over the cold pudding.

CHAPTER CXII

RUTH GIVES A DINNER FOR FOUR

BETTINA and Bob arrived at half-past six, as Ruth had requested.

"She wouldn't let me come earlier, Bob," explained Bettina as they rang the bell. "I wanted to help her, you know, but she said her father and mother were out of town and Fred was to be the only guest besides ourselves, so she was sure that she could manage alone. There she is now!"

But it was not Ruth after all.

"Why, Fred; hello!" said Bob. "Did you come early to assist the cook?"

"I did," said Fred, "but she informed me at once that she wanted no inexperienced 'help' around. So I've been sitting in the living-room alone for the last half hour. She did say that I might answer the bell, but as for doing anything else—well, she was positively rude!"

And Fred raised his voice so that its penetrating tones would reach the kitchen. "The worst of it all is that I've been hungry as well as lonesome. I might endure sitting alone in the living-room if I hadn't gone without lunch today in anticipation of this banquet. And now——"

"Shame on you, Fred!" interrupted Ruth, coming in with flushed cheeks above her dainty white apron. "Did he receive you properly?"

"I leave it to you, Bettina, to say that I've received harsh treatment! Here I went and purchased four good seats for the Duchess theatre tonight."

"You did, Fred," cried Ruth. "Why, you dear boy! For that, I'll see that you are certainly fed well! Dinner is ready, people! Will you walk into the dining-room?"

Ruth's dinner consisted of:

Pigs in Blankets   Candied Sweet Potatoes
Escalloped Egg Plant
Bread   Butter
Date Pudding   Cream

BETTINA'S RECIPES

(All measurements are level)

Pigs in Blankets (Four portions)

1 C-oysters   ¼ t-salt
8 slices thin bacon ⅛ t-paprika

Remove the rind from long, thin slices of bacon. Place two or more oysters upon each slice of bacon. Sprinkle the oysters with salt and pepper. Roll up and tie with a white string. Sautè in a hot frying-pan until nicely browned. Garnish with parsley.

Candied Sweet Potatoes (Six portions)

6 large sweet potatoes ½ C-water
1 C-brown sugar   1 t-salt
1 T-butter

Wash the potatoes thoroughly. Cook in boiling water until tender when pierced with a knitting needle. Drain and peel when cool enough to handle. Cut in slices lengthwise, three-fourths of an inch thick. Make a syrup by boiling the sugar, butter and water five minutes. Lay the potatoes in a pan, sprinkle with salt and pour the syrup over them. Cook in a moderate oven until the potatoes are browned, basting frequently.

Escalloped Egg Plant (Six portions)

2 C-cubed egg-plant ½ t-salt
3 T-butter   ¼ t-pepper
3 T-flour   1½ C-milk

Remove the skin from the egg-plant, and cut into slices a

quarter of an inch thick. Sprinkle the slices with salt, pile one above the other, and place a weight on the top to extract the juice. Allow to stand one hour. Wash off, and cut into quarter of an inch cubes. Melt the butter, add the flour, salt and pepper. Mix well, gradually add the milk and cook two minutes. Add the egg-plant and pour the whole mixture into a buttered baking dish. Bake thirty minutes in a moderate oven.

Date Pudding (Four portions)

1 C-flour	⅛ t-salt
2 t-baking powder	1 egg
¼ C-"C" sugar	1/3 C-milk
10 dates, cut fine	½ t-vanilla
3 T-melted butter	

Mix the flour, baking powder, "C" sugar, dates and salt. Add the egg, milk and vanilla. Stir vigorously and beat one minute. Add the melted butter. Bake twenty minutes in a moderate oven, and serve hot with cream.

ALICE PRACTISES ECONOMY

"OH, Bettina," said Alice, delightedly, as she opened the door. "I'm so glad to see you! I've just been thinking about you! What do you suppose I'm doing?"

"Getting dinner? That is what I must be doing very soon. I stopped in for only a minute on my way home."

"I am getting dinner, and I want to tell you that it is a very economical dinner. And it's going to be good, too. I thought and thought about your advice, and decided to practise it. So I searched through all my cook books for the recipes I wanted, and finally decided on this particular menu. But, Bettina, now I can tell you the flaw in your system of economy!"

"What is that? Harry doesn't like it?"

"Goodness no! Harry was delighted with the idea! My argument is this: It's going to take me an endless amount of time to plan economical meals that are also good, time that I ought to spend in polishing silver and making calls, and sewing on buttons, and——"

"I don't believe it'll be as bad as you think, Alice, dear," laughed Bettina. "For instance, if this meal tonight is good and economical, and Harry is pleased, don't forget the combination, but write it down in a note-book. You can repeat the menu in two or three weeks, and you have no idea how soon you will collect the best combinations, and ideas of economy! Tell me what you are having tonight."

That night Alice served:

Baked Eggs
Potatoes Escalloped with Bacon
Baking Powder Biscuits   Butter
Peach Cup with Peach Sauce
Tea

357

BETTINA'S RECIPES

(All measurements are level)

THE RECIPES ALICE USED

Baked Eggs (Two portions)

2 eggs	1 T-butter
½ C-milk	¼ t-salt
2 T-soft bread crumbs	⅛ t-paprika

Butter two individual moulds, and break an egg into each. Mix the salt and pepper in the milk, and pour half of the mixture over each egg. Melt the butter, and add the crumbs. Place the buttered crumbs on top of each egg. Bake in a moderate oven twenty minutes. Serve in the moulds.

Potatoes Escalloped with Bacon (Two portions)

3 medium-sized potatoes	⅛ t-paprika
3 slices of bacon	2 T-flour
¼ t-salt	1 C-milk

Broil the bacon, cut each piece in three parts. Butter a casserole and place in it a layer of peeled sliced potatoes. Sprinkle part of the flour, salt and paprika over the potatoes, and add three pieces of bacon. Continue in this manner until the dish is filled. Pour the milk over the contents, and bake forty minutes in a moderate oven.

Peach Cup (Two portions)

4 halves of canned peaches, sweetened	1½ t-baking powder
	⅛ t-salt
1 T-egg	1 t-melted butter
3 T-milk	¼ t-vanilla
2/3 C-flour	2 T-sugar

Mash two peach halves, add the egg, milk, vanilla, melted butter, flour, baking powder and salt. Mix thoroughly. Place a tablespoon of the mixture in the bottom of a well-buttered baking cup. Add a peach half, and cover with the batter. Sprinkle one tablespoon of granulated sugar on the top and bake twenty minutes in a moderate oven. Turn from the cups and serve hot with peach sauce.

Peach Sauce (Two portions)

2/3 C-peach juice   1 T-flour
1 T-lemon juice   ½ t-butter
¼ t-salt

Mix one tablespoon of the peach juice with the flour. Gradually add the rest of the peach and lemon juice. Add the salt. Cook one minute. Add the butter. Serve hot.

CHAPTER CXIV

A COMPANY DINNER FOR BOB

"SOME dinner tonight," remarked Bob, as he sat down at the table. "Were you expecting company that didn't show up?"

"No, indeed," laughed Bettina. "I expected just you and nobody else. But maybe I did cook a little more than usual. You see I was over at Alice's this afternoon inspecting her list of next week's menus. You know she is trying to economize, and she is really doing it, but in spite of economy, Harry is having elaborate meals. I do hope he appreciates it. Nearly all of her dinners are three-course affairs, most carefully planned to look like 'the real thing' as she calls an expensive dinner. I tell her that hers are the real thing, only almost too elaborate. You see, she is trying to disguise her economy so that Harry won't miss the first meals she gave him. She makes me almost afraid that I'm not feeding you enough."

"No danger of that," said Bob, emphatically. "But what are all these economical things she is serving?"

"Wait, I wrote some of them down. Listen. Here is one:

Peanut Croquettes	Olive Sauce
Duchess Potatoes	Creamed Beets
Parker House Rolls	
Orange Marmalade	
Pea and Cheese Salad	Wafers
Apricot Ice	Sponge Cake

"How's that? And here's another:

Creamed Tuna
Stuffed Potatoes   Mock Egg Plant
Whole Wheat Muffins   Grape Jelly
Russian Salad
Fairy Gingerbread   Hard Sauce

"Well," said Bob, "they sound good, but not so good as the dinners you give me."

That evening Bettina served:

Escalloped Salmon   Baked Potatoes
Creamed Cabbage
Egg Rolls   Currant Jelly
Chocolate Kisses
Coffee

BETTINA'S RECIPES

(All measurements are level)

Escalloped Salmon (Two portions)

2/3 C-flaked salmon	1 hard-cooked egg
1 T-butter	1 t-lemon juice
1 T-flour	3 T-chopped sour pickle
2/3 C-milk	½ t-minced parsley
½ t-salt	4 T-cracker crumbs
¼ t-paprika	1 T-butter

Melt the butter, add the flour and mix well. Add the milk and cook one minute. Add the salmon, salt, paprika, egg diced, lemon juice, pickle and parsley. Mix thoroughly with a silver fork, being careful not to let the mixture get pasty. Pour into a well-buttered baking dish, melt the butter and add the crumbs. Place buttered crumbs on the top. Bake twenty-five minutes in a moderate oven.

Egg Rolls (Two portions)

1½ C-flour	2 T-lard
2 t-baking powder	1 T-egg
¼ t-salt	½ C-milk

For the Top

1 T-milk   1 t-sugar

Mix and sift the flour, baking powder and salt. Cut in the fat with a knife. Add the egg and milk, using the knife to make a soft dough. Toss onto a floured board. Roll out to a thickness of one-fourth an inch. Cut out with a round cooky cutter, three inches in diameter. Brush over with milk. Fold over like pocket-book rolls. Place in a tin pan and brush over the top with one tablespoon of milk to which has been added one teaspoon of sugar. Bake in a moderate oven for twenty minutes.

Chocolate Kisses (Fourteen kisses)

1 C-powdered sugar	2 ounces melted chocolate
2 egg-whites	1 t-cinnamon
1 C-fine bread crumbs	1 t-vanilla
	1 t-baking powder

Beat the egg-whites very stiffly. Add very carefully the powdered sugar. Cut and fold in the bread crumbs and the baking powder. Add the chocolate, cinnamon and vanilla. Drop the mixture from the tip of a spoon, two inches apart upon a well-greased pan. Bake in a moderate oven twelve to fifteen minutes.

CHAPTER CXV

SUPPER AFTER THE THEATRE

"NOW, Bob, you start the fire in the fireplace while I go into the kitchen and get a little lunch."

"Mrs. Bob," said Donald, an old school-friend of Bob's, "I don't want you to do any such thing! We don't need any lunch! Stay in here and we'll all talk."

"You'll talk all the better for something to eat," said Bettina, "and so will Bob. Won't you, Bob?"

"Well," said Bob, with a grin, "I will admit that coming home in the cold has given me something of an appetite. Then too, I'll tell you, Donald, that Bettina's after-theatre suppers aren't to be lightly refused! Yes, on the whole, I think we'd better have the supper. We couldn't get you for dinner to-night, and you're leaving so early in the morning that you see you won't have had any real meal at our house at all!"

Meanwhile, Bettina was busying herself with the little supper, for which she had made preparations that morning. When she had creamed the oysters and placed them in the ramekins, she popped them in the oven. Next she put on the coffee in her percolator, and placed in the oven with the oysters the small loaf of bran bread that she had steamed that morning. "Bob likes it better warm," she said to herself.

Then she arranged her tea-cart with plates, cups, silver, napkins and peach preserves, not forgetting the rice parfait from the refrigerator.

When she wheeled the little supper into the living-room, Bob and Donald welcomed her with delight. "I take it back; I am hungry after all!" said Donald.

Bettina served:

Creamed Oysters in Ramekins
Steamed Bran Bread   Peach Preserves
Rice Parfait
Coffee

BETTINA'S RECIPES

(All measurements are level)

Creamed Oysters in Ramekins (Three portions)

1 doz. oysters	⅛ t-paprika
2 T-butter	2 T-crumbs
3 T-flour	2 t-butter
¼ t-salt	1 hard-cooked egg
	2 t-chopped parsley

Heat the oysters until they are plump. Drain. Melt the butter, add the flour, salt and paprika. Mix well. Add the milk slowly and cook until creamy. (About two minutes.) Add the oysters, and place one-third of the mixture in each well-buttered ramekin. Melt the butter (two teaspoons) and add the crumbs, stirring well. Place the buttered crumbs on top of the mixture in each ramekin. Brown in the oven for fifteen minutes. Sprinkle with parsley, and garnish with hard-cooked egg cut in slices.

Steamed Bran Bread (One small loaf)

1 C-bran	4 T-raisins
½ C-white flour	2 T-chopped nuts
½ t-soda	1 T-sugar
⅛ t-salt	2 T-molasses
1 t-baking powder	½ C-milk
	2 T-water

Mix the bran, flour, soda, baking powder, salt, raisins and nuts. Add the molasses, sugar, milk and water. Stir well for two minutes. Fill a well-buttered mould one-half full of the mixture. Cover with the lid, well-buttered, and steam for two hours. The steaming may be done in the fireless cooker, if desired.

Rice Parfait (Three portions)

1 C-cooked rice	2 T-chopped nut meats
½ C-hot milk	½ C-brown sugar
2 C-cold water	¼ t-salt
1 T-granulated gelatin	½ C-whipped cream

Soak the gelatin in cold water for five minutes. Add the hot milk and allow it to dissolve thoroughly. Add the sugar, salt, nut meats and rice, and mix well. When thoroughly cooled, add the whipped cream. Pour into a well-buttered mould, and allow to stand in a cool place for two hours. Serve cold. Whipped cream may be served with the parfait if desired.

CHAPTER CXVI

WASHINGTON'S BIRTHDAY PLANS

"**G**OOD bran bread," said Bob, reaching for another piece. "I like that recipe," said Bettina, "and it is so easy to make."

"What have you been doing all day?" Bob asked, "Cooking?"

"No, indeed. Charlotte was here this afternoon and we made plans for the tea we are going to give at her house on Washington's birthday. Oh, Bob, we have some of the best ideas for it! Our refreshments are to be served from the dining-room table, you know, and our central decoration is to be a three-cornered black hat filled with artificial red cherries. Of course we'll have cherry ice, and serve cherries in the tea, Russian style. The salad will be served in little black three-cornered hats; these filled with fruit salad, will be set on the table and each guest will help herself. The thin bread and butter sandwiches will be cut in hatchet shape. And—oh, yes, I forgot the cunningest idea of all! We'll serve tiny gilt hatchets stuck in tree-trunks of fondant rolled in cocoanut and toasted brown. Isn't that a clever plan? Charlotte saw it done once, and says it is very effective."

"It sounds like some party! And I'll feel especially enthusiastic if you don't forget to plan for one guest who won't appear—or perhaps I should say two, for I know Frank won't want to be forgotten."

For dinner that night Bob and Bettina had:

Corned Beef au Gratin	Baked Tomatoes
Apple Sauce	
Gluten Bread	Butter
Cream Pie	Coffee

BETTINA'S RECIPES

(All measurements are level)

Corned Beef au Gratin (Three portions)

1½ C-milk	2 T-butter
½ slice of onion	1 egg
1 piece of celery	1 t-salt
2 T-flour	¼ t-paprika
1 C-chopped corned beef	

Place the milk, onion and celery over the fire. Allow to get very hot. Remove from the fire and let stand for ten minutes. Remove the celery and·onion from the milk. Melt the butter, add the flour. Mix well and slowly add the milk. Cook until the consistency of white sauce. Add the egg, well beaten, the salt, paprika, and beef. Pour into well-buttered individual dishes.

Place in a moderate oven and bake twenty-five minutes. Remove from the oven and allow to stand two minutes. Remove from the moulds and garnish with parsley.

Baked Tomatoes and Cheese (Three portions)

1 C-canned tomatoes	¼ C-fresh bread crumbs
½ t-salt	3 T-cheese, cut fine
¼ t-paprika	¼ C-cooked celery
1 T-butter	

Mix the tomatoes, salt, paprika, cheese and celery. Add half the bread crumbs. Pour into a well-buttered baking dish. Melt the butter, add the remaining crumbs and place on top of the mixture. Bake twenty minutes in a moderate oven.

Gluten Bread (Ten slices)

1 C-gluten flour	2 T-sugar
1½ t-baking powder	1/3 C-milk
¼ t-salt	1/3 C-water
¼ C-bran	1 t-melted butter

Mix the flour, baking powder, salt, bran and sugar. Add the milk and water. Beat vigorously for one minute and then add the butter. Pour into a well-buttered bread pan and bake forty minutes in a moderate oven.

CHAPTER CXVII

AN AFTERNOON WITH BETTINA

WHEN Bettina pushed her tea cart into the living-room, Alice and Ruth laid aside the mending at which they had been busy.

"What delicious toast, Bettina!" said Alice, taking one bite. "Why, it has cinnamon on it! And sugar! I wondered what on earth you were making that smelled so good, and this is something new to me!"

"It is cinnamon toast," said Bettina, "and so easy to make. I was busy all morning, and didn't have time to make anything but these date kisses for tea, but cinnamon toast can be made so quickly that I decided to serve it."

"I like orange marmalade, too, Bettina," said Alice. "I wish I had made some. I have spiced peaches, and a little jelly, but that is all. Next summer I intend to have a perfect orgy of canning. Then my cupboard will be even better stocked than Bettina's—perhaps! I opened a jar of spiced peaches last evening for dinner, and what do you think! Harry ate every peach in the jar! I had expected them to last several days, too."

"I hoped you saved the juice," said Bettina.

"I did, but I don't know why. It seemed too good to throw away, somehow."

"Have you ever eaten ham cooked in the juice of pickled peaches? It's delicious. Just cover the slice of ham with the juice and cook it in the oven until it is very tender. Then remove it from the juice and serve it."

"It sounds fine. I'll do it tomorrow."

That afternoon Bettina served:

Cinnamon Toast   **Tea**
          Orange Marmalade
          Date Kisses

BETTINA'S RECIPES

(All measurements are level)

Cinnamon Toast (Six portions)

6 slices of slate bread   1/3 C-powdered sugar
2 T-butter   ½ t-cinnamon

Make a delicate brown toast and butter each slice. Mix the sugar and cinnamon, and place in a shaker. Shake the desired quantities of sugar and cinnamon over the hot buttered toast. Keep in a warm place until ready to serve.

Bettina's Date Kisses (One dozen)

1 egg-white   ¼ t-baking powder
⅛ t-salt   ¼ C-chopped dates
½ C-powdered sugar   ¼ C-chopped nut meats
          ½ t-lemon extract

Add the salt to the white of an egg, and beat the egg-white very stiff. Then add the sugar, baking powder, nuts, dates and lemon extract. Drop from a teaspoon onto a buttered pan. Bake in a slow oven until delicately browned. (About twenty-five minutes.)

Orange Marmalade (One pint)

3 oranges   ½ grapefruit
2 lemons   Sugar

Wash thoroughly the rinds of the fruits. Weigh the fruit, and slice it evenly. To each pound of fruit, add one quart of cold water. Let the mixture stand for twenty-four hours. Cook slowly for one hour. Drain. Weigh the cooked fruit, and add an equal weight of sugar. Cook with the sugar for thirty minutes, or until it stiffens slightly when tried on a dish. Pour into sterilized jelly glasses. When cool seal with hot paraffin.

CHAPTER CXVIII

A WASHINGTON'S BIRTHDAY TEA

WHEN the tea guests were ushered into Charlotte's dining-room that afternoon, they were delighted with the table and its red, white and blue decorations. In the center was a large three-cornered hat made of black paper, and heaped with artificial red cherries. The cherry ice was tinted red, and served in sherbet glasses. A large white cake, uncut, was one of the chief decorations, for halves of red cherries were placed together on it to represent a bunch of cherries, while tiny lines of chocolate icing represented the stems.

Bettina poured the tea and placed in each cup a red cherry. The guests helped themselves to trays, napkins, forks and spoons, and each took a portion of Washington salad, served in a small, black, three-cornered hat, lined with waxed paper. Each took also a rolled sandwich, tied with red, white and blue ribbon, and a nut bread sandwich in the shape of a hatchet.

The Washington fondant, rolled in cocoanut and toasted to represent tree trunks, with small gilt hatchets stuck in them, occasioned great delight. "How did you ever think of it?" Ruth asked, and Bettina gave Charlotte the credit, though she in turn disclaimed any originality in the matter.

"One thing is lacking," said Bettina. "Charlotte and I should be wearing colonial costumes. We did think of it, but happened to be too busy to make them."

That afternoon Charlotte and Bettina served:

George Washington Salad
Rolled Sandwiches   Nut Bread Sandwiches
Cherry Ice
Cherry Cake   Washington Fondant

BETTINA'S RECIPES

(All measurements are level)

Washington Salad (Twelve portions)

1 C-diced pineapple
1 C-marshmallows, cut fine
1 C-grapefruit, cut in cubes
1 C-canned seeded white cherries
¼ C-filberts

¼ C-Brazil nuts, cut fine
1½ C-salad dressing
½ C-whipped cream
6 red cherries
12 tiny silk flags

Mix the pineapple, marshmallows, grapefruit, white cherries and nuts. Add the salad dressing. Serve immediately. Place waxed paper in the paper cups of the small, black, three-cornered hats. Place one serving of salad in each cup. Put one teaspoon of whipped cream on top and half a cherry on that. Stick a tiny silk American flag into each portion.

Nut Bread for Sandwiches (Twenty-four sandwiches)

2 C-graham flour
1 C-white flour
3 t-baking powder
1 egg

2/3 C-sugar
1½ t-salt
½ C-nut meats, cut fine
1½ C-milk

Mix the flours, baking powder, salt, nut meats and sugar. Break the egg in the milk and add to the dry ingredients. Mix thoroughly, pour into a well-buttered bread pan and allow to rise for twenty minutes. Bake in a moderate oven for fifty minutes.

Nut Bread Sandwiches

24 pieces bread   2/3 C-butter

When the nut bread is one day old, cut in very thin slices. Cream the butter and spread one piece of bread carefully with butter. Place another piece on the top. Press firmly. Make all the sandwiches in this way. Allow to stand in a cool, damp place for one hour. Make a paper hatchet pattern. Lay the pattern on top of each sandwich and with a sharp knife, trace around the pattern. Cut through carefully and the sandwiches will resemble hatchets. This is not difficult to do and is very effective.

Washington's Birthday Sandwiches

1 loaf of white bread one day old
8 T-butter
2 yards each of red, white and blue ribbon

Cut the bread very thin with a sharp knife. Remove all crusts. Place a damp cloth around the prepared slices when very moist, and tender. Spread with butter which has been creamed with a fork until soft. Roll the sandwiches up carefully like a roll of paper. Cut the ribbon into six-inch strips, and tie around the sandwiches. Place in a bread box to keep moist. Pile on a plate in log cabin fashion.

CHAPTER CXIX

ANOTHER OVEN DINNER

BETTINA heard a step on the porch, and quickly laying aside her kitchen apron, rushed to the door to meet Bob. Her rather hilarious greeting was checked just in time, at sight of a tall figure behind him.

"Bettina, this is Mr. MacGregor, of MacGregor & Hopkins, you know. Mr. MacGregor, my wife, Bettina. I've been trying to get you all afternoon to tell you I was bringing a guest to dinner and to spend the night. The storm seems to have affected the lines."

"Oh, it has! I've been alone all day! Haven't talked to a soul! Welcome, Mr. MacGregor, I planned Bob's particular kind of a dinner tonight, and it may not suit you at all, but I'm glad to see you, anyhow."

Mr. MacGregor murmured something dignified but indistinct, as Bob cried out heartily, "Well, it smells good, anyhow, so I guess you can take a chance; eh, MacGregor?"

Bettina had a hazy idea that Mr. MacGregor, of MacGregor & Hopkins, was somebody very important with whom Bob's firm did business, and although she knew also that Bob had know "Mac," as he called him, years before in a way that was slightly more personal, her manner was rather restrained as she ushered them into the dining-room a few minutes later. However, the little meal was so appetizing, and the guest seemed so frankly appreciative, that conversation soon flowed freely. Bob's frank comments were sometimes embarrassing, for instance when he said such things as this:

373

"Matrimony has taught me a lot, MacGregor! I've learned —well, now, you'd never think that all this dinner was cooked in the oven, would you? Well, it was: baked ham, baked potatoes, baked apples, and the cakes—Bettina's cakes, I call 'em. You see, my wife thinks of things like that—a good dinner and saving gas, too!"

"Oh, Bob!" said Bettina, with a scarlet face.

"You needn't be embarrassed, Bettina, it's so! I was just telling 'Mac' as we came in, that two can live more cheaply than one provided the other one is like you—always coaxing me to add to our bank account. It's growing, too, and I never could save before I was married!"

The dinner consisted of:

Baked Ham	Baked Potatoes
Head Lettuce	Roquefort Cheese Dressing
Bread	Butter
	Baked Apples
	Bettina's Cakes

BETTINA'S RECIPES

(All measurements are level)

Bettina's Baked Ham (Three portions)
(Bob calls it "great")

1 lb. slice of ham three-fourths of an inch thick	
14 cloves	½ C-water
½ C-vinegar	2 T-sugar
2 t-mustard	

Remove the rind from ham. Stick the cloves into both sides. Place in a pan just the size of the meat. Pour the vinegar, water, sugar and mustard (well mixed) over the ham. Baste frequently. Bake in moderate oven until crisp and tender (about forty-five minutes).

Head Lettuce with Roquefort Cheese Dressing (Three portions)

1 head of lettuce	⅛ t-pepper
½ t-salt	¼ C-Roquefort cheese
3 T-oil	1 T-vinegar

Cream the cheese, add salt, pepper and vinegar. Add the oil gradually. Mix well, shake thoroughly. Pour over the lettuce and serve.

Baked Apples (Four portions)

4 apples	1 t-cinnamon
6 T-brown sugar	4 marshmallows
4 T-granulated sugar	1 t-butter

Wash and core apples of uniform size. Mix the sugar and cinnamon together. Fill the apples. Press a marshmallow in each apple also. Dot the top with a piece of butter. Place the apples in a pan, add the remaining sugar, cover the bottom with water, and bake until tender (twenty-five to thirty minutes), basting often. Serve hot or cold.

Bettina's Cakes (Eight cakes)

1 C-flour	½ t-soda
½ t-cinnamon	¼ t-baking powder
¼ t-powdered cloves	⅛ t-salt
1/3 C-sugar	1 egg
2 T-melted butter	1/3 C-sour milk

Mix and sift the dry ingredients. Add the egg and the sour milk. Beat two minutes. Add the melted butter; beat one minute. Fill well-buttered muffin pans one-half full. Bake in a moderate oven twenty minutes.

CHAPTER CXX

BOB MAKES POP-OVERS

BETTINA was busily setting the table in the dining-room when Bob appeared.

"Oh, Bettina," said he in a disappointed tone, "why not eat in the breakfast alcove? I'd like to show MacGregor how much fun we have every morning."

"Won't he think we're being too informal?"

"I want him to think us informal. The trouble with him is that he doesn't know that any simple brand of happiness exists. His life is too complex. Of course we're not exactly primitive—with our electric percolator and toaster——"

"Sorry, Bob, but you can't use the toaster this morning; I'm about to stir up some pop-overs."

"Well, I'll forgive you for taking away my toy, inasmuch as I do like pop-overs. Let me help you with them, Bettina; this is one place where you can use my strong right arm."

"Yes, indeed I can, Bob. I'll never forget those splendid pop-overs that you made the first time you ever tried. They look simple, but not very many people can make good ones. The secret of it is all in the beating," said she, as she stirred up the smooth paste, "and then in having the gem pans and the oven very hot."

"Well, these'll be good ones then," said Bob, as he set about his task. "You light the oven, Betty, and put the gem pans in it, and then before you have changed things from the dining-room to the alcove, I'll have these pop-overs popping away just as they ought to do!"

The percolator was bubbling and the pop-overs were nearly done when they heard Mr. MacGregor's step. "He's exactly on time," chuckled Bob. "That's the kind of a methodical fellow he is in everything."

"Well, there's no time when promptness is more appreciated than at meal-time," said Betty, decidedly. "I like him."

"Come on out here!" called Bob, cheerfully. "This is the place in which we begin the day! We'll show you the kind of a breakfast that'll put some romance into your staid old head. I made the pop-overs myself, and I know they're the best you ever saw—likewise the biggest—and they'll soon be the best you've ever eaten!"

When Bob had finished removing the pop-overs from their pans, the two men took their places at the table to the merry tune of the sizzling bacon Bettina was broiling.

"I never entertained a stranger so informally before," said she.

"And I was never such a comfortable guest as I am at this minute," said Mr. MacGregor, looking down at his breakfast, which consisted of:

Grapefruit
Oatmeal
Bacon   Pop-Overs
Coffee

BETTINA'S RECIPES

(All measurements are level)

Pop-Overs (Eight)

1 C-flour	½ t-salt
1 C-milk	1 egg, beaten well

Add the milk slowly to the flour and salt, stirring constantly, until a smooth paste is formed. Beat and add the remainder of the milk, and the egg. Beat vigorously for three minutes. Fill very hot gem pans three-fourths full. Bake thirty minutes in a hot oven. They are done when they have "popped" at least twice their size, and when they slip easily out of the pan. Iron pans are the best.

MARCH.

Weary are we of our winter-time fare;
  Hasten, O Springtime, elusive and arch!
Bring us your dainties; our cupboards are bare!
  Pity us, starved by tyrannical March!

CHAPTER CXXI

IN MARCH

"**S**PRING is in the air," thought Bettina, as she opened the casement windows of her sun room. "I believe we'll have dinner out here tonight. If Bob would only come home early, before the sun goes down! Now I wonder who that can be!" (For she heard a knock at the kitchen door.)

"Why, Charlotte. Come in!" she cried a moment later, for it was Mrs. Dixon with a napkin-covered pan in hand, whom she found at the door.

"I've brought you some light rolls for your dinner, Bettina," said Charlotte. "I don't make them often, and when I do, I make more than we can eat. Will they fit into your dinner menu?"

"Indeed they will!" said Bettina. "I'm delighted to get them. Now I wish I had something to send back with you for your dinner, but I seem to have cooked too little of everything!"

"Don't you worry," said Charlotte, heartily. "When I think of all the things you've done for me, I'm only too glad to offer you anything I have! Well, I must hurry home to get our dinner. That reminds me, Bettina, to ask you this: When you escallop anything, do you dot the crumbs on top with butter?"

"No, Charlotte, I melt the butter, add the crumbs, stir them

379

well, and then spread them on the top of the escalloped oysters, or fish, or whatever I am escalloping."

"I'm glad to know the right way of doing, Bettina. Goodbye, dear."

For dinner Bob and Bettina had:

Ham Timbales		Macaroni and Cheese
	Baked Apples	
Light Rolls		Butter
	Grapefruit Salad	
Chocolate Custard		Coffee

BETTINA'S RECIPES

(All measurements are level)

Ham Timbales (Three timbales)

1 C-ground, cooked ham	¼ t-paprika
1/3 C-soft bread crumbs	1 egg
¼ t-salt	½ C-milk

Mix the ham, salt, crumbs and paprika. Add the egg, well beaten, and the milk. Pour into a well-buttered tin or aluminum individual moulds. Place in a pan of hot water and bake in a moderate oven for thirty minutes. Unmould on a platter. Serve hot or cold.

Grapefruit Salad (Two portions)

1 C-grapefruit, cut in cubes	2 T-cottage cheese
¼ C-marshmallows, cut in squares	¼ t-paprika
¼ C-diced celery	3 T-salad dressing
¼ t-salt	2 lettuce leaves

Place the lettuce leaves on the serving plates. Arrange carefully portions of grapefruit, marshmallows, celery and cheese upon the lettuce. Sprinkle with salt and paprika. Pour the salad dressing over each portion and serve cold.

Chocolate Custard (Two portions)

1 C-milk	1/3 square of chocolate, melted
1 large egg	1 T-water
4 T-sugar	½ t-vanilla
⅛ t-salt	

Cook half the sugar, the chocolate and the water until smooth and creamy (two minutes). Add the milk while the mixture is hot. Stir until smooth. Beat the egg, add the rest of the sugar and the salt. Add to the custard mixture. Mix well. Pour into two well-buttered custard moulds. Place the moulds in a pan surrounded by hot water. Set in a moderate oven and cook until a knife piercing it will come out clean. (Generally thirty minutes.) Allow to stand fifteen minutes in a warm place. Unmould and serve cold.

CHAPTER CXXII

A FIRELESS COOKER FOR AUNT LUCY

"WELL, Uncle John! Hello!" said Bob, as he came into the kitchen. "Is Aunt Lucy here, too?"

"No, she isn't," said Uncle John, shaking his head solemnly, "and the fact is, I shouldn't be here myself if it weren't for a sort of conspiracy; eh, Bettina?"

"That's so, Bob," said Bettina, coming in from the dining-room, her hands full of dishes, "and now I suppose we'll have to let you in on the secret. Uncle John has just bought a beautiful new fireless cooker for Aunt Lucy. Haven't you, Uncle John?"

"Well!" said Bob, heartily. "That's fine! How did you happen to think of it?"

"Well Bob, she's been dreading the summer on the farm—not feeling so very strong lately, you know—and this morning she was just about discouraged. It's next to impossible to get any help out there—she says she's given up that idea—and at breakfast she told me that if the spring turned out to be a hot, uncomfortable one, she believed she'd go out and spend the summer with Lem's girl in Colorado. I naturally hate to have her do that, so I concluded to do everything I could to keep her at home. I telephoned to Bettina, and she promised to help me. The very first thing she suggested was a fireless cooker, and we bought that today. I believe your Aunt Lucy'll like it, too."

For dinner Bettina served:

Meat Balls with Egg Sauce
Baked Potatoes
Creamed Peas
Marshmallow Pudding   Chocolate Sauce

BETTINA'S RECIPES

(All measurements are level)

Meat Balls (Three portions)

1 C-raw beef, cut fine	⅛ t-paprika
¼ C-bread crumbs	1 t-chopped parsley
2 T-milk	¼ t-onion salt
1 egg-yolk	¼ t-celery salt
¼ t-salt	3 T-bacon fat

Soak the crumbs, milk and egg together for five minutes. Add the beef, salt, paprika, parsley, onion and celery salt. Shape into flat cakes one inch thick, two and a half inches in diameter. Place the fat in the frying-pan and when hot, add the cakes. Lower the flame and cook seven minutes over a moderate fire, turning to brown evenly. Serve on a hot platter. Garnish with parsley. Serve with egg sauce.

Egg Sauce for Meat Balls (Three portions)

3 T-flour	¼ t-salt
2 T-butter	¼ t-paprika
1 t-chopped parsley	1 hard-cooked egg,
1 C-milk	cut fine

Melt the butter, add the flour, salt and paprika. Mix well, add the milk, and cook for two minutes. Add the hard-cooked egg sliced, or cut in small pieces. Serve hot with the meat balls.

Marshmallow Pudding (Three portions)

2 t-granulated gelatin	½ C-boiling water
2 T-cold water	1 t-lemon extract
1/3 C-sugar	1 t-vanilla
	1 egg-white

Soak the gelatin in cold water for three minutes. Add the boiling water, and when thoroughly dissolved add the sugar. Allow to cool. Beat the egg-white stiff. When the gelatin begins to congeal, beat it until fluffy, add the extracts and then the egg-white. Beat until stiff. Pour into a moistened cake pan. When hard and cold, remove from the pan, cut in one inch cubes and pile in a glass dish.

CHAPTER CXXIII

THE DIXONS DROP IN FOR DESSERT

"COME in! Come in!" cried Bob to the Dixons. "You're just in time to have dessert with us! Bettina, here are the Dixons!"

"Do sit down," said Bettina, "and have some Boston cream pie with us!"

"Frank won't need urging," said Charlotte. "Our dessert tonight was apple sauce, and Boston cream pie (whatever it is) sounds too enticing to be resisted."

"It looks a little like the Washington pie my mother used to make," said Frank. "Only that wasn't so fancy on the top."

"Washington pie needs whipped cream to make it perfect," said Bettina, "and as I had no whipped cream I made this with a meringue."

"Dessert with the neighbors!" said Frank, laughing. "Charlotte read me a suggestion the other day that sounded sensible. A housewife had introduced a new custom into her neighborhood. Whenever she had planned a particularly good dessert she would phone a few of her friends not to plan any dessert for themselves that evening, but to stroll over after dinner and have dessert with her family. Wasn't that an idea? It might lead to cooperative meals! We haven't done our share; have we? We should have telephoned to you to have the main course with us tonight. Say, Bettina, I like this Boston cream pie! It's what I call a real dessert!"

Lamb Chops   Creamed Carrots
Baked Potatoes
Rolls   Butter
Baked Apples
Boston Cream Pie   Coffee

BETTINA'S RECIPES

(All measurements are level)

Creamed Carrots (Two portions)

1 C-carrots	½ C-milk
1 T-flour	¼ t-salt
1 T-butter	⅛ t-paprika

Carrots

Wash and scrape the carrots thoroughly, cover with boiling water, and allow to boil until tender when pierced with a knitting needle or a fork. (About twenty minutes.) Drain and serve with sauce. Carrots may be cut into three-fourth inch cubes or any fancy shapes, and will cook in less time.

White Sauce for Carrots

Melt butter, add the flour, salt and paprika. Mix well. Gradually add the milk, and cook the sauce until creamy.

Baked Potatoes (Two, portions)

2 potatoes

Wash thoroughly two medium-sized potatoes. With the sharp point of the knife, make a small cut around the potato to allow the starch grains to expand. Bake the potato in a moderate oven until it feels soft and mealy, when pressed with the hands. (About forty-five minutes.) Break open the potato to allow the steam to escape. (Turn the potato about in the oven to insure evenness in baking.)

Bettina's Baked Apples (Two portions)

2 apples	1 t-cinnamon
½ C-"C" sugar	½ t-vanilla
½ C-water	A few grains of salt

Wash and core the apples. Mix the sugar, cinnamon, vanilla and salt, and fill the cavity with the mixture. Place the apples in a small pan, and pour a little water around them. Bake twenty-five minutes in a moderate oven.

Boston Cream Pie (Six portions)

3 T-butter	¼ C-milk
8 T-(one-half C-sugar)	⅞ C-flour
1 egg	1½ t-baking powder
	¼ t-vanilla

Cream the butter, add the egg. Mix well. Add the sugar and mix thoroughly. Add the milk alternately with the flour and baking powder. Mix thoroughly. Add the flavorings. Bake in two layer-cake pans, fitted with waxed paper, in a moderate oven for twenty minutes. Spread the following filling between the layers.

Filling

7 T-sugar	1 egg-yolk
3 T-flour	1 C-milk
⅛ t-salt	½ t-vanilla

Mix the sugar, flour and salt. Add slowly the egg-yolk, beaten, and the milk. Stir well. Cook ten minutes in a double boiler, stirring occasionally to prevent lumping. Add vanilla and remove from the fire. When partially cool, spread part of the filling over one layer of the cake. Allow to stand five minutes and then add more filling. Allow to stand two minutes. Place the other layer on the top. Spread a meringue over the whole and place in a hot oven long enough to brown it delicately.

Meringue

3 egg-white	2 T-sugar
⅛ t-salt	⅛ t-baking powder

Add salt to the egg, beat until thick and fluffy, add the sugar and baking powder and beat one minute.

CHAPTER CXXIV

RUTH PASSES BY

"**M**—M!" said Ruth, walking into Bettina's kitchen late one afternoon. "What is it that smells so perfectly delicious?"

"Lamb stew," said Bettina. "Bob is particularly fond of it, and we haven't had it for a long time. This is such a cold day that I thought lamb stew would taste very good tonight."

"And what are you making now?"

"Soft gingerbread. It's just ready to pop into the oven, and then I can go into the living-room with you and we'll visit in state."

"Don't, Bettina. I'd much rather talk in your shining little kitchen with the kettle bubbling on the hearth (only it's a gas stove and you won't let it bubble long if you think of your gas bill). 'Kitchen Konfidences!' What a name for a nice little domestic science book!"

"Well, we'll stay in the kitchen then, and exchange kitchen konfidences. Where have you been this afternoon in your big woolly coat?"

"Down town to the market. And I did get something besides food—a small purchase that you advised me to buy. A box of labels—plain label stickers, you know—to stick on the boxes that I put away—out of season things and all that. I've noticed how neatly all your stored-away things are labeled."

"It saves so much time in finding things. And a label looks better than writing on the box, for the labels are white and very often the box is dark pasteboard, and pencil marks are difficult to see."

"Well, good-bye, Betty dear, I must run along now."

Bettina's menu that night consisted of:

Lamb Stew

Apple Sauce Rolls

Gingerbread

Coffee

BETTINA'S RECIPES

(All measurements are level)

Lamb Stew (Four portions)

1½ lbs. lamb (from the shoulder)	⅛ t-powdered cloves
3 T-lard	1 C-tomato
3 C-boiling water	2 medium-sized potatoes
1 small onion	2 T-rice
2 t-salt	½ C-diced carrots

Wipe the meat with a damp cloth, and cut into two-inch pieces. Place the lard in a frying-pan, and when hot, add the onion cut fine and allow to brown. Add the meat and brown. Add the boiling water to the meat and onion, and cook one minute. Pour all of the contents of the frying-pan into a sauce pan, and let it cook slowly for one hour. Increase the heat a little to allow the stew to boil occasionally. Add the potatoes cut in one-inch cubes, and the diced carrots. In twenty minutes, add a cup of canned tomato pulp or fresh tomatoes to the stew. Add the seasoning (salt and cloves), and cook ten minutes. This allows two hours for the entire stew. If at this time the stew does not seem thick enough, mix four tablespoons of water very slowly with two level tablespoons of flour, stir thoroughly, and pour slowly into the stew. Allow to cook two minutes and serve.

Soft Gingerbread (Twelve pieces)

1 C-molasses	1 t-soda
2 T-sugar	2 t-ginger
1/3 C-butter and lard	1 t-cinnamon
¼ C-warm water	1 t-salt
2 C-flour	

Cream the butter and lard, add the sugar, molasses and warm water; mix well. Mix and sift the soda, ginger, cinnamon, salt and flour and add to the first mixture. Beat one minute and pour into a well-buttered pan. Bake in a moderate oven twenty-five minutes. Serve hot or cold.

CHAPTER CXXV

BETTINA ENTERTAINS A SMALL NEIGHBOR

"INDEED I will keep Kathleen for you," said Bettina to Mrs. Fulton. "I'll enjoy it. We'll have to invent some new plays and have such a jolly time that she won't miss her mother at all."

"You're sure you don't mind?" asked Mrs. Fulton, anxiously. "If mother were only stronger, I would leave her there——"

"Go right on, Mrs. Fulton, and don't worry one bit! Kathleen and I are going to have the time of our lives! Let's see—it's nearly three. Shall I feed her anything?"

"Well, she had an early lunch, and has just wakened from her nap. Perhaps she is a little hungry. Are you?"

"Bed'n delly," replied Kathleen with emphasis.

"Oh, I know something that's better for little girls than bread and jelly!" said Bettina, lifting the roly-poly little mite onto the kitchen table. "I'll make her some good cream toast! May I, Mrs. Fulton?"

"Indeed, you may, if you will," said Mrs. Fulton. "I'm afraid she won't always eat it, though. Well, I'll have to go, I suppose, if I get to sister Annie's train on time. Then we'll do a little shopping down town, and I'll be back for Kathleen at six o'clock sharp."

"Just whenever it's convenient for you, Mrs. Fulton. Goodbye!"

"Doodby," echoed Kathleen, apparently without the least regret.

When Kathleen was established with her cream toast at the

kitchen table, Bettina said, "Now, when you're all through eating, you and Aunt Bettina will make a beautiful graham cracker cake for Uncle Bob. But first we'll clean some white gloves! Shall we?"

Kathleen nodded solemnly, her mouth full of "dood tream toast."

"Well, watch me then, honey-lamb. See, I'll put these dirty old gloves in this nice Mason jar of clean gasoline, and let 'em soak awhile. Then once in a while I'll shake 'em up like this. Then by and by I'll rinse 'em in nice new gasoline, and they'll be just as white as new. Did you know that, Kathleen?"

" 'Es," said Kathleen, staring wisely.

"Oh, you little owl! You knew more than Aunt Bettina then—at least than I knew till yesterday, for I always thought it necessary to rub white gloves to get them clean. See? This way I'll drop them down in the gasoline, and won't need to soil my hands at all! I'll get them out with a clean little stick or a long fork. There! Now, are we all ready to make the cake?"

BETTINA'S RECIPES

(All measurements are level)

Cream Toast (Two portions)

½ T-butter ½ C-milk
½ T-flour ⅛ t-salt
2 pieces of toast

Melt the butter, add the flour, mix well, add the milk slowly. Add the salt and boil two minutes. Dip the toasted bread into the white sauce, and when soft, remove to the serving dish. Pour the rest of the sauce over the toast and serve hot. One teaspoon of sugar may be added to the sauce.

Graham Cracker Cake (Twelve pieces)

1/3 C-butter 3 t-baking powder
2/3 C-sugar 2 egg-whites, beaten
2 egg-yolks ½ t-ground cinnamon
1 C-milk ½ t-vanilla
2/3 lb. graham crackers rolled fine

Cream the butter, add the sugar and heat. Add all the dry ingredients mixed together alternately with the milk. Beat two minutes. Add the vanilla and the egg-whites, stiffly beaten. Bake in square tin pans for twenty-five minutes in a moderate oven.

White Icing

¼ C-sugar   Sifted powdered sugar
¼ C-water   ½ t-vanilla

Boil the sugar and the water five minutes without stirring. Remove from the fire. Add the flavoring, and sufficient sifted powdered sugar to spread evenly on the cake.

CHAPTER CXXVI

A SUNDAY NIGHT TEA

"STIR this chicken a la king a moment for me, will you, Ruth?" said Bettina. "I'll warm the plates in the oven."

"What is that brown paper for?"

"To put under the dishes I'm warming. It breaks the heat and prevents cracking. There, that cream sauce has cooked enough now. I'll take it and beat it for a minute. See? There, now it's ready for the egg and the chicken mixture."

"Shall I stir it now? Don't you put it back over the fire?"

"Just for a minute. You see, if any custard or egg sauce is allowed to cook more than a minute after the egg has been added, it will curdle."

"Oh, is it done now? Let me toast the bread for it, will you, Bettina? I like to make cunning little light brown triangles."

"I hope I have made enough of this chicken a la king."

"For eight people? I'm sure that you have, Bettina. Even for people with as good appetites as Fred and I have! Are you ready to serve it now?"

That Sunday evening Bettina served:

Chicken a la King   Toast
Cakes with Bettina Icing
Coffee

BETTINA'S RECIPES

(All measurements are level)

Chicken a la King (Eight portions)

1½ C-cold boiled chicken, cut in 2/3-inch cubes
½ t-salt
1/3 C-button mushrooms, cut in fourths
4 T-pimento, cut in hallf-inch lengths
2 T-green pepper, cut fine
5 T-butter or chicken fat

6 T-flour	2 C-milk
1½ t-salt	2 egg-yolks
½ t-paprika	8 pieces of toast

Boil the green pepper slowly for five minutes. Drain off the water. Melt the butter, add the flour, salt and paprika, mix thoroughly, and add the milk, stirring constantly. Cook three minutes or until quite thick. Remove from the fire, beat one minute, reheat, add the egg-yolk, mix thoroughly, and add the chicken mixture. Heat again. Serve immediately by pouring over slices of toast.

To prepare the chicken mixture, thoroughly mix the chicken, half a teaspoon of salt, the mushrooms, the cooked green pepper and the pimento.

Small Cakes (Fourteen cakes)

1¼ C-sugar	⅛ t-salt
1/3 C-butter	2/3 C-milk
2 C-flour	1 t-vanilla
4 t-baking powder	½ t-lemon extract
2 egg-whites	

Cream the butter, add the sugar slowly and continue creaming. Mix and sift the flour, baking powder and salt and add these and the milk, vanilla and lemon extracts to the butter and sugar. Mix well and beat two minutes. Beat the egg-whites till very stiff and fold these very carefully into the cake mixture. When thoroughly mixed, fill the cake pans (which have been prepared with waxed paper) two-thirds of an inch deep with the mixture.

Bake twenty-five minutes in a moderate oven, allow to stand five minutes, then slip a knife around the edges and remove the cake carefully from the pan. Turn over, remove the paper and allow the cake to cool. Ice on the bottom side. When ready for serving, cut in two-inch squares.

Bettina Icing

1 egg-white	1 t-vanilla
1 T-cream	½ t-lemon extract
2 C-powdered sugar	

Beat the egg-whites, add part of the sugar. Add the cream, vanilla and lemon extracts. Keep beating. Add the rest of the sugar gradually. (A little more sugar may be needed.) Beat the icing till very fluffy and until it will spread without running off the cake. Spread each layer.

CHAPTER CXXVII

A SHAMROCK LUNCHEON

BETTINA was entertaining "the crowd" at a shamrock luncheon, and each guest, to show her enthusiasm for the charms of "ould Ireland," was wearing somewhere upon her gown, a bit of green.

A green basket filled with white carnations and green foliage stood in the center of the table. White glass candlesticks with green shades also carried out the color scheme, while white crocheted favor baskets, filled with dainty green candies, were at each plate. The table was set for six.

The name cards were white shamrocks outlined with green ink and edged with gilt, and the name on each was written in green.

Bettina used green ferns for decoration in every possible place where they might add to the attractiveness of the table, under the glass dishes and around the baskets containing rolls, cakes and croutons.

"You might be Irish yourself, Bettina," said Mary, "you have such a feeling for green! And isn't the table lovely, girls!"

For luncheon Bettina served:

<pre>
                 Grapefruit Cocktail
Cream of Celery Soup   Shamrock Croutons
    Bettina Meat Timbales   Brown Sauce
                Asparagus on Toast
            Mashed Sweet Potato Croquettes
    Shamrock Rolls   Mint Jelly
        Pepper Salad   Sandwiches
            Bombe Glace   Shamrock Cakes
                    Coffee
                Shamrock Candies
</pre>

BETTINA'S RECIPES

(All measurements are level)

Grapefruit Cocktail (Six portions)

2 grapefruit	6 green cherries
1/3 C-sugar	Smilax or fern leaves

Peel the grapefruit, remove the white part and the tough membrane, leaving the fruit. Cut with the scissors into one-inch cubes. Place in a bowl, add the sugar and allow to stand in a cold place for one hour. Arrange the servings in six sherbet glasses. Place one green cherry on the top of each and garnish the plate with smilax or a fern leaf. Stand the sherbet glasses on a paper doily on a small serving plate. Arrange a bit of the green leaf under the sherbet glass (on top of the doily) so that the green color will be visible through the glass.

Cream of Celery Soup (Six portions)

2/3 C-celery, cut fine	2½ C-milk
1½ C-water	2 t-salt
4 T-butter	¼ t-paprika
6 T-flour	1 t-chopped parsley
2 T-whipped cream	

Wash the celery thoroughly, and cut into small pieces. Add the small leaves and the water. Simmer for thirty-five minutes. Strain through a coarse strainer, rubbing all of the pulp through. Melt the butter, add the flour, salt and paprika. Add the milk and cook two minutes, stirring to prevent scorching. Add the celery stock and the pulp. Cook one minute. Fill bouillon cups three-fourths full, add two pinches of parsley and one teaspoon of cream to each serving.

Shamrock Croutons (Six portions)

6 slices bread	2 T-butter
¼ t-salt	

Cut the slices of bread half an inch thick and cut pieces out of each with a shamrock cooky cutter. Toast on each side until a delicate brown. Butter and sprinkle with salt, serve warm with soup.

CHAPTER CXXVIII

AT DINNER

"**M**ARY gave a waffle party today," announced Bettina at the dinner table.

"A waffle party in the afternoon?" said Bob. "That was queer! Usually at afternoon parties you women serve tiny little cups of tea and dainty olive sandwiches, almost too small to be visible; don't you? Waffles are more sensible, I think, but it seems a shame that we men had to miss such a party."

"Well, I'm afraid I'll have to acknowledge that we had a very good time without you," laughed Bettina, wickedly. "It has been cold today, you know, and Mary's kitchen was so warm and bright and cozy! We all went out there and took turns baking the waffles. We consumed a large number of them, and had a very jolly informal kind of time. We housekeepers compared notes and gave each other advice and really learned a great many things."

"Such as——"

"Well, Alice tells me that when she makes a devil's food cake she removes all of the melted chocolate from the pan by adding a little flour which mixes in thoroughly and saves any waste of chocolate. Surely that is worth knowing."

"It certainly is, though I'll admit that I don't quite understand your language."

"Well, cheer up, Bob! There are times when I confess that I don't quite understand the automobile explanations you so often give me of late!"

Their dinner that evening consisted of:

Pork Chops	Mashed Potatoes
Creamed Carrots	Bettina Salad
Orange Dessert	
Coffee	

397

BETTINA'S RECIPES

(All measurements are level)

Pork Chops (Two portions)

2 pork chops	1 T-egg
½ C-cracker crumbs	1 T-water
	1 T-bacon fat

Wipe the chops with a damp cloth. Mix the crumbs and the salt. Beat the egg and the water together. Dip the chops in the crumbs, then in the egg mixture and then in the crumbs. Place the bacon fat in the frying-pan and when hot add the chops. Brown thoroughly on both sides, add half a cup of water, and cook over a moderate fire until tender. (About thirty minutes.) Cover with a lid while cooking. More water may be needed to prevent burning.

Bettina Salad (Two portions)

1 tomato	1 t-salt
1 green pepper	¼ t-onion salt
2 T-pimento cut in	¼ t-celery salt
small pieces	⅛ t-paprika
2 T-grated cheese	½ C-salad dressing
2 pieces of lettuce	

Arrange the lettuce leaves on a plate. Place a slice of tomato, two slices of green pepper, one tablespoon of pimento and one tablespoon of cheese on each serving. Mix the salad dressing with salt, paprika, celery and onion salts. Pour half of the mixture over a portion of the salad.

Orange Dessert (Two portions)

2 slices of sponge cake	2 T-nut meats, cut fine
1 orange	2/3 C-whipped cream
2 T-sugar	1 t-vanilla

Add the vanilla and the sugar to the whipped cream. Arrange the slices of cake on the plates. Place one-fourth of the orange, divided into sections and sprinkled with sugar, on each slice. Pile the whipped cream on the orange. Place one tablespoon of nut meats and the remaining fourth of the orange (cut small) on each portion. Do not arrange this dessert until just ready to serve.

CHAPTER CXXIX

AN ANNIVERSARY DINNER

"THIS is some dinner, Bettina!" said Bob, over his dessert. "It's like a celebration, somehow, with the pink candles on the table, and the flowers, and the company menu. Why, Bettina, I do believe it is an anniversary! Isn't it? Let me see! The second anniversary of our engagement!"

"I've been waiting to see if you would remember that, Bob, and I must say that I'm a little ashamed of you! After all, it took the pink candles and the company dinner to make you think of it! Well, I suppose men are all alike!" And she sighed the sigh of deep disillusionment.

Bob waited for a moment to see the dimple reappear in her cheek, and the twinkle in her eyes, and then he, too, sighed—a sigh of relief.

"Bless your heart, Bettina, don't you sigh like that again! You almost had me thinking that you were in earnest. Now you took the very nicest way to remind me of that anniversary. Instead of feeling neglected like some women——"

"What do you know about 'some women,' Bob?"

"Only what I've read in books——"

"Well, the books don't know. But I give you fair warning, Bob, that on the next anniversary you fail to remember, I'll feed you bread and milk, and not chicken."

"This is a fine dessert," said Bob meekly and tactfully.

"Do you like it? I enjoy making it, it looks so light and fluffy. I pile it very lightly into the glass dish to make it that way. I prefer gelatin in glass dishes, don't you, Bob?"

"You bet I do! Everything about this anniversary dinner is fine except for my own stupidity!"

That night Bettina served:

Bettina's Chicken En Casserole
Whole Wheat Bread   Butter
Cranberry Jelly
Head Lettuce with Salad Dressing
Bettina's Sponge
Coffee

BETTINA'S RECIPES

(All measurements are level)

Bettina's Chicken En Casserole (Two portions)

4 pieces of chicken	½ C-cooked potatoes, cut in cubes
2 T-flour	
1 T-lard	½ C-cooked carrots
1 C-boiling water	¼ C-cooked celery
1 t-salt	1 T-raw onion
2 T-butter	1 t-salt

Roll the chicken in the flour. Place the lard in the frying-pan, and when very hot, add the chicken, browning thoroughly on all sides. Season with the salt. Place in the casserole and add the boiling water. Cover, and place in a moderate oven for one hour. Melt the butter, and when hot, add the potatoes, carrots, onion, celery and salt. Stir constantly, and when well-browned, add to the chicken mixture. Allow to cook for half an hour. More water may be needed. Serve in the casserole.

Bettina's Sponge (Three portions)

2 t-granulated gelatin	1 C-boiling water
1 T-cold water	½ C-whipped cream
4 T-sugar	6 cocoanut macaroons, crushed
1 T-lemon juice	8 candied cherries, cut fine
2 T-nut meats, cut fine	

Add the cold water to the gelatin and allow it to stand

five minutes. Add the sugar and the lemon juice. Mix well, and add boiling water. When thoroughly dissolved, allow to cool. When the mixture begins to congeal, or thicken, add the whipped cream, crushed macaroons, cherries and nut meats. Beat until the mixture begins to thicken. Pile lightly into a glass dish and set away to harden for one hour.

CHAPTER CXXX

RUTH COMES TO DINNER

"HOW do you like this kind of meat, Ruth?" asked Bob. "It is a little invention of Bettina's own. I call it a symphony and no 'mis-steak.'"

"It is an economy, not a symphony," said Bettina, "but if it leads you to make such dreadful puns as that, I'll wish I had fed you something else for dinner."

"To me," said Ruth, "this dish is a delicacy and a despair. How can you think of things like this? I know I never could do it in the wide world!"

"I can't compose symphonies or poems," said Bettina, "so I express myself in this way. And most of my music is played in a simple key. It is difficult to think of a variety of inexpensive meat dishes, and sometimes I have to invent them in order to keep within my allowance, and still vary my menus. Creamed onions are economical and healthful, too, so you see that my whole dinner is inexpensive."

"And also delicious," said Ruth. "I don't see how you manage to keep cooked onions from having a strong smell, and to keep the house so free from the odor."

> "O that someone would patent
> That someone would patent and sell
> An onion with an onion taste
> And with a violet smell,"

quoted Bob.

"Well," said Bettina, "I'm afraid that a house in which onions have recently been cooking, can't be entirely free from the odor, but I largely overcome the difficulty by peeling them under cold water, and then cooking them in an uncovered vessel. Then, too, I wonder if you know that boiling them for five minutes and then draining them and covering them with boiling water again—even draining them twice and finishing the cooking in fresh boiling water —is a splendid thing for taking away the strong taste."

"No, I didn't know that. Bettina, dear, your kind of apple sauce is as fine a dessert as I ever ate."

"You're good to say so, Ruth. I was afraid when I urged you to stay tonight that you might think this meal very plain and simple for a guest, but I know it is healthful and economical and Bob seems to thrive, so I'll not be remorseful."

"Just let me ask you what gives this apple sauce such a delicate flavor. It isn't a bit like common, ordinary apple sauce."

"I don't know; maybe it's the butter. I always put that in, and a few grains of salt. This has also a thin slice of lemon cooked in it—rind and all—and of course there is a little cinnamon, though some people prefer nutmeg. Then I try to be careful in putting in the sugar, for I know that some apples require more than others. These were tart apples; I like them better for apple sauce."

> "The reason why I'm never cross
> Is 'cause I'm fed on apple sauce,"

remarked Bob complacently.

> "But I am sure you'd fret and cry
> If fed instead on apple pie,"

added Ruth.

"Not Bettina's apple pie!" said Bob decidedly. "You may just be sure that it would improve any disposition!" Dinner that night consisted of:

Bettina Steak
New Potatoes with Maitre d'Hotel Sauce
Creamed Onions
Apple Sauce
Bread   Butter

BETTINA'S RECIPES

(All measurements are level)

Bettina Steak (Four portions)

1 lb. ground beef from the round	½ t-onion juice or onion salt
¼ C-bread crumbs	½ t-chopped green pepper
¼ C-milk	1 t-salt
1 egg, well beaten	¼ t-paprika
⅛ t-grated nutmeg	½ t-chopped parsley

Soak the crumbs in milk for three minutes, add the meat, egg, nutmeg, onion juice, parsley, salt, green pepper and paprika. Mix well. Pat into shape one and one-half inches thick in a well buttered tin pan. Cook five minutes under a very hot broiler. Turn down the heat a little and cook ten minutes more. Turn the steak into another buttered pan the same size and cook that side ten minutes. Pie tins may be used to cook the meat in.

Creamed Onions (Four portions)

6 onions   1½ C-vegetable white sauce

Peel six medium sized onions under cold water. Place in a stew-pan and cover with boiling water. Boil five minutes, drain, cover again with boiling water and cook ten minutes. Drain, recover with boiling water and cook ten minutes longer or until tender. Serve with hot white sauce.

Apple Sauce

6 tart apples	1 thin slice of lemon
½ C-water	⅛ t-cinnamon
½ C-sugar	½ t-butter
A few grains of salt	

Wash, peel, quarter and core the apples. Add the water, cover the kettle with a lid and cook till apples are soft. Add other ingredients. Cook enough longer to dissolve the sugar. Mash or put through a colander, if desired.

APRIL.

Tell me, housewife blithe and fair,
How does your garden grow?
Crisp and green the lettuce there,——
Onions, row by row,——
Radishes beyond compare!
Spring and I with tender care
Watch them well, you know!

CHAPTER CXXXI

MILDRED'S SPRING VACATION

"I WAS so afraid Father wouldn't let me come, Aunt Bettina!" exclaimed Mildred, after the first greetings. "And your letter sounded so jolly—about the cooking and all—well, if Father had said 'no,' I should simply have died."

"Died, Mildred?" asked Bob. "I must say you look fairly healthy to me, too much so to pine away soon!"

"I don't intend to die now, Uncle Bob! I'm going to live and have the most fun helping Aunt Bettina! I like that so much better than lessons. I brought two aprons in my suit case; Mother said I acted as if I wouldn't meet anybody in a three day visit but your kitchen stove. And to tell the truth, Aunt Bettina, I just hope I won't! I'd rather help you cook than see sights or meet people."

"Oh, dear!" exclaimed Bob tragically. "Just when I was counting on you to climb to the dome of the capitol with me, too! Why was I ever born?"

"You'll have to do your climbing alone, I'm afraid," Mildred replied cheerfully. "Now, Aunt Bettina, may I set the table for you? Do show me what you are going to have for dinner! Little custards? Oh, how cunning! Made in moulds and served cold with maple syrup? Aunt

Bettina, I just believe I could make that dessert myself!
Will you teach me while I'm here?"

The dinner consisted of:

Round Steak En Casserole	Baked Potatoes
Lettuce Salad	Bettina Dressing
Steamed Custard	Maple Syrup
Coffee	

BETTINA'S RECIPES

(All measurements are level)

Round Steak En Casserole (Three portions)

1 lb. round steak, cut one inch thick	2 T-green pepper, cut fine
	1 C-diced carrots
½ C-flour	2 C-water
1 T-onion, cut fine	2 t-salt

Place the meat, which has been wiped with a damp cloth,
upon a meat board. Cut into four pieces. Pound the flour
into the meat on both sides, using a meat pounder or the
side of a heavy saucer. Butter the casserole, add a layer of
meat, then onions and green peppers. Add the carrots.
Add the salt to the water and pour over the meat. Cover
closely. Place in a moderate oven and allow to cook slowly for
two hours. More water may be needed before the meat
is done. Serve in the casserole.

Lettuce Salad (Three portions)

6 pieces of lettuce   ½ t-salt

Arrange the lettuce, which has been washed and chilled,
upon three plates. Sprinkle the lettuce with salt and serve
with the following dressing:

Bettina Dressing

2/3 C-salad dressing	1 T-pimento catsup
1 t-olive oil	¼ C-celery, cut fine
2 T-chopped pickle	2 T-nut meats, cut fine
1 T-chopped pimento	¼ t-salt
	¼ t-paprika

Beat the salad dressing, add the oil, pickle, pimento, catsup, celery, nut meats, salt and paprika. Beat one minute. Pour three tablespoons of the mixture over each portion of the lettuce. Serve very cold.

Steamed Custard (Four custards)

1½ C-milk	¼ t-salt
2 eggs	¼ t-vanilla extract
3 T-sugar	¼ t-lemon extract
⅛ t-grated nutmeg	

Beat the eggs, add the sugar, salt, vanilla, and lemon extract. Mix thoroughly. Butter four custard cups. Fill a pan four inches deep with hot (not boiling) water. Set the cups in the pan and place in a moderately slow oven for thirty-five or forty minutes (or until a knife inserted in the custard comes out clean). Serve cold with maple syrup poured over it.

CHAPTER CXXXII

HELPING BETTINA

"MILDRED helped me get the dinner tonight," said Bettina, as they sat down at the table.

"Indeed I did, Uncle Bob!" exclaimed the little girl delightedly. "And I'm having so much fun that I don't ever, ever, ever want to go home! Aunt Bettina is going to show me how to make cookies tomorrow!"

"Is she?" said Bob. "Well, don't eat 'em all up before I get here. Save me six fat ones, with raisins in. Don't forget the raisins."

"I set the table, Uncle Bob, and I made the rice croquettes into that cunning shape, and when they were fried, I put in the jelly! Don't they look nice?"

"The most artistic rice croquettes, I ever ate!" declared Bob.

"And wait till you see the dessert! I fixed that; Aunt Bettina showed me how. But I won't tell you what it is— yet. I know you'll like it, though."

"Well, you're a great little helper, Mildred, aren't you!"

"That's just what Aunt Bettina says. And I've learned so many things! I didn't know before that it was easier to cut up marshmallows with the scissors than any other way. Oh, Aunt Bettina! I almost told him about our dessert!"

"Marshmallows? Marshmallows?" said Bob. "A clue,

I do believe! I have it: 'Marshmallows served with scissors!' "

"Oh, Uncle Bob, you're too funny!" cried Mildred, shouting with laughter.

"Appreciated at last!" said Bob.

For dinner that night they had:

Lamb Chops   Rice Croquettes

Creamed Peas

Bread   Butter

Sponge Cake   Whipped Cream

Coffee

BETTINA'S RECIPES

(All measurements are level)

Broiled Lamb Chops (Three portions)

3 lamb chops	1 t-salt
1 T-butter	¼ t-paprika
⅛ t-parsley	

Wipe and trim the chops. Place on a hot tin pan four inches from a direct hot flame (under a broiler). Cook two minutes, turn and thoroughly cook the other side for two minutes. Lower the flame a little, add the salt and pepper, and cook for eight minutes more. (A little longer if the chops are very thick.) Remove to a warm platter, dot with butter, add the parsley and serve immediately.

Rice Croquettes with Jelly (Three croquettes)

1 C-steamed rice	¼ t-salt
1 egg-yolk	1 t-chopped parsley
1 T-butter	3 T-flour
⅛ t-paprika	2 T-grape jelly

Mix the steamed rice, egg-yolk, butter, paprika, salt and parsley. Shape into flat disks one inch thick and three inches in diameter. Roll in flour. Make an indentation in the center of each with a spoon, to hold the jelly. Fry in hot deep fat until brown. Drain, the wrong side up. Heat in a hot oven and serve hot. Place a cube of jelly in the center of each.

Sponge Cake with Whipped Cream (Three portions)

3 slices of stale cake (three by three by one inch)	3 T-cherry juice
8 marshmallows cut in cubes	4 T-whipping cream
3 T-canned cherries	½ t-vanilla
	1½ T-sugar

Beat the cream until stiff, add the vanilla, marshmallows and sugar. Arrange the cake in glass sherbet dishes. Place a tablespoon of cherries and a tablespoon of juice on each slice. Place one and a half tablespoons of the whipped cream mixture on each portion. Allow to stand in a cold place for five minutes.

CHAPTER CXXXIII

HELPING WITH A COMPANY DINNER

"COOKING a company dinner is such fun!" sighed Mildred. "I like the dinner part, but I always wish that the company would stay away at the last minute."

"Oh, you'll like Mr. Jackson, Mildred. He's one of Uncle Bob's best friends, and so nice and jolly!"

"The jolly men always like to tease, and the ones who aren't jolly are always cross. I don't intend to get married myself. I'm going to live in a nice little bungalow like this one and do my own cooking."

"Will you live all alone?" asked Bettina.

"I'll adopt some children—seven or eight, I think,—all girls. I don't want any boys around."

"Your bungalow will have to be larger than this to accommodate them all if you adopt seven or eight."

"I don't want a large one; that would spoil the fun. I'll let the children take turns sleeping on the floor. Children always love to sleep on the floor, and mothers never like to have them do it! I wonder why? Now, will you let me brown the flour for the gravy?"

"Yes, dear. Put half a cup of white flour in that frying-pan over the fire and keep stirring it constantly until it is a nice brown color, about like powdered cinnamon."

"This way?"

"Yes, Mildred; a little darker than that, but keep stirring it so that it won't burn. There, that's exactly right!"

That evening Bettina served:

Leg of Lamb with Browned Potatoes
Gravy
Lettuce and Egg Salad
Strawberry Shortcake   Cream
Coffee

BETTINA'S RECIPES

(All measurements are level)

Leg of Lamb and Browned Potatoes (Four portions)

3 lb. leg of lamb	¼ t-paprika
6 potatoes	2 T-bacon fat
1 T-salt	1/3 C-boiling water

Allow the lamb to stand in cold water for ten minutes. Remove and wipe dry. Place the fat in a frying-pan. Add the meat and cook until thoroughly browned on all sides. Place in the fireless cooker (or a slow oven) and surround the meat with the potatoes. Sprinkle with the salt and paprika. Add the water. (If in the cooker, place the heated disks under and over the meat.) Cook two hours.

Gravy (Four portions)

4 T-browned flour	¼ t-white pepper
1 T-butter	1½ C-meat stock and
1 t-salt	water

Remove the meat from the pan in which it was cooked (also remove the potatoes) and add sufficient water to the stock in the pan to make one and a half cups all together. Melt the butter, add the browned flour and a tablespoon of the stock. Mix well, and add the salt and pepper. Add the remaining stock; cook, stirring constantly for two minutes. Pour into a heated gravy dish. Serve at once.

Egg and Lettuce Salad (Four portions)

8 pieces of lettuce	2 t-salt
4 hard-cooked eggs	½ t-paprika
4 radishes	¼ t-celery salt
4 young onions	8 T-salad dressing

Arrange two pieces of lettuce on each plate. Slice an egg, a radish and an onion and arrange these upon the lettuce leaves. Sprinkle each portion with a fourth of the seasoning. Place two tablespoons of salad dressing on each portion. Have all the ingredients cold before combining.

CHAPTER CXXXIV

MILDRED'S DAY

"**I** HELPED to make the cunning little biscuits, Uncle Bob," explained Mildred at dinner.

"You did?" said Bob, feigning astonishment. "You rolled them out with a rolling pin, I suppose, and——"

"Oh, no, Uncle Bob! You ought never to use a rolling pin, Aunt Bettina says!" said Mildred in a horrified tone, as if she had been cooking for the First Families for a score of years. "Good cooks always pat down the dough—they never roll it out."

"Well, what do you do first? Stir up the dough with a spoon?"

"No, indeed; you use a knife. Then you pat the dough down, and cut out the dear little biscuits with a biscuit cutter."

"And put them side by side in a nicely buttered pan? I know how!"

"But you don't butter the pan," said Mildred triumphantly. "Or flour it, either. Aunt Bettina says that lots of people think the pan has to be buttered or floured, but they're wrong. It's lots better to put the biscuits into a nice clean pan."

"But don't they stick to it, and burn?"

"No, indeed! They don't burn a bit! Look at these!" said Mildred, delighted to find the opportunity to impart some of her newly acquired knowledge.

"Well, what else did you help Aunt Bettina to make?"

415

"These nice stuffed onions. It was fun to make them, even though I don't like onions. I ground up the dry bread that Aunt Bettina keeps in the jar by the stove."

"Well, you can tell Mother Polly that Aunt Bettina will make a good cook of you yet!"

For dinner that night they had:

Rolled Stuffed Steak   Potatoes au Gratin
Stuffed Onions
Sour Cream Biscuits   Currant Jelly
Sliced Bananas   Cream
Coffee

BETTINA'S RECIPES

(All measurements are level)

Stuffed Onions (Four portions)

4 onions	1 t-parsley
½ C-bread crumbs	1 T-pimento
1 T-tomato pulp	1 egg-yolk
1 T-butter	¼ C-cooked celery
	½ t-salt

Wash and peel the onions. Cook for ten minutes in boiling water. Rinse with cold water to make them firm. Push out the centers. Place the onions in a well-buttered baking pan and fill each onion with filling. Place in a moderate oven for twenty minutes.

Filling

Mix the crumbs, tomato pulp, butter, parsley, pimento, salt, egg yolks and celery. Cook for one minute. Fill each onion case carefully with the mixture. Then pour the following sauce about the onions before placing them in the oven:

White Sauce (Four portions)

2 T-butter	¼ t-salt
2 T-flour	1/6 t-paprika
	1 C-milk

Melt the butter, add the flour, salt and paprika. Mix well, add the milk, and cook for one minute.

Sour Cream Biscuits (Four portions)

2 C-flour	3 T-fat
½ t-salt	¼ t-soda
3 t-baking powder	2/3 C-sour milk

Mix the flour, salt and baking powder. Cut in the fat with a knife. Add the soda to the milk, and when the effervescing ceases, add slowly to the dry ingredients. (All the milk may not be needed.) When a soft dough is formed, toss onto a floured board. Pat into shape, cut with a biscuit cutter, and place side by side on a tin pan or baking sheet. Bake fifteen minutes in a moderately hot oven.

CHAPTER CXXXV

POLLY COMES FOR MILDRED

"SO you've been teaching Mildred to cook?" asked Polly as they sat down to dinner.

"Oh, Mother, I've learned so much!" cried Mildred with enthusiasm. "And when I'm married, I'm going to have a dear little kitchen just like Aunt Betty's! Aunt Betty does know the very best way to do everything! Why, Mother, I think she's a better cook even than Selma, and not half so cross when I bother!"

"Bother!" said Bettina. "Why, Mildred, you've been a real help to me!"

"I hope so," laughed Polly, "but I'm not so sure. Children never worry me—it's fortunate, isn't it?—but I don't see how on earth anyone can cook with a child in the kitchen! I wanted Selma to teach Mildred, but I hadn't the heart to insist when she objected to the plan."

"H—m, Selma!" said Mildred with scorn. "Why, Mother, Selma doesn't even know enough to line her cake pans with waxed paper! She butters 'em! And I don't believe we have a spatula in the whole house!"

"A—what?" said Polly in a puzzled tone. "I don't believe I——"

"Don't you know what a spatula is, Mother?" asked Mildred didactically. "Why, it's one of those flattened out spoon-things to use in the kitchen. We ought to have one. And—Mother, you ought to see how much mayonnaise Aunt Bettina makes at a time! It'll keep, you know."

"Goodness!" said Polly tragically. "What a dreadful thing it will be to live with a child who knows more than I do!"

For dinner that night they had:

Veal Chops

Baked Potatoes   Escalloped Onions
Bread   Butter
Mocha Cake   Mocha Icing
Coffee

BETTINA'S RECIPES

(All measurements are level)

Escalloped Onions (Four portions)

1 C-onions	1 t-salt
1 qt. water	¼ t-pepper
2 T-butter	1 C-milk
2 T-flour	¼ C-buttered crumbs

Wash and peel the onions. Cook in one quart of water. Allow to boil five minutes. Change the water and continue boiling ten minutes. Change the water again, and when thoroughly cooked (about fifteen minutes more), remove from the fire and drain.

Melt the butter, add the flour and salt and mix thoroughly. Add the milk and cook one minute. Add the onions, and pour the mixture into a well-buttered baking dish. Place the buttered crumbs on the top of the onions and bake in a moderate oven for twenty minutes.

Mocha Cake (Twelve portions)

1/3 C-butter	1 C-strong coffee
1 C-sugar	½ t-vanilla
2 eggs	2 C-flour
3 t-baking powder	

Cream the butter, add the sugar and cream the mixture, add the egg-yolks, mix well and add the coffee, vanilla, flour and baking powder. Beat two minutes. Add the stiffly beaten egg-whites. Pour the mixture into two layer-cake pans prepared with waxed paper. Bake twenty-five minutes in a moderate oven. When cool, spread with the mocha icing.

Mocha Icing (Twelve portions)

4 T-strong boiling coffee   1 t-vanilla
1½ C-powdered sugar

Mix the vanilla with the coffee. Add the powdered sugar slowly until the proper consistency to spread. Spread over one layer and place the upper layer on the lower. Place the icing on the top layer and on the sides. More sugar may be needed.

CHAPTER CXXXVI

MILDRED'S PLANS

"**I** SUPPOSE that when we get home again, Mildred will be insisting that we reorganize our household along the lines of yours, Bettina," laughed Polly. "I can just hear Selma's outbursts at the idea of any changes in her department."

"But you can always smile Selma out of her 'spells,' Mother," coaxed Mildred. "And just think, Selma doesn't even know what a fireless cooker is! We'll have to explain it to her."

"What can you make in a fireless cooker, Mildred?" asked Polly of her little daughter, who was fairly bursting with her newly acquired information.

"Oh, Mother, this roast! Isn't it good? Aunt Betty kept it in the cooker almost four hours, and think how much gas that saved!"

"Well, I'll admit that such an item would appeal to your father, Mildred," Polly replied, "so I think I'll leave it to you to get around him and Selma. I'm sure," she continued, turning to Bob, "that such an undertaking can reasonably be expected to occupy Mildred for some time. But I do like the roast."

"The roast?" said Bob. "It is good, Polly, but you needn't think that this is a company meal, especially. Why, Bettina gives me company dinners every day!"

For dinner that night they had:

Pot Roast   Gravy
Boiled Rice
Apple and Nut Salad
Chocolate Pie
Coffee

421

BETTINA'S RECIPES

(All measurements are level)

Pot Roast (Four portions)

2½ lbs. of beef (a rump roast	2 t-salt
	½ t-pepper
2 T-bacon drippings	¼ C-diced carrots
3 T-flour	¼ C-diced turnips
1 bay leaf	2 T-chopped onions
4 cloves	¼ C-celery
3 C-boiling water	

Place the bacon drippings in a frying-pan. Roll the beef in the flour, and when the fat is hot, add the beef and brown thoroughly on all sides. Place the meat in a kettle, and add the vegetables. Pour the water in the frying-pan to remove any fat. Pour all over the meat. Add the bay leaf, cloves and salt. Cover closely and allow to cook very slowly for three and a half hours. Turn the meat after the second hour. This is a good fireless cooker recipe.

Gravy

1 C-stock   1 T-flour
1 T-water

Remove the meat from the kettle. Strain the stock into a bowl. To the flour, add the water. Mix well, and gradually add the stock. Mix and cook one minute. Pour the gravy over the meat and reserve the remaining stock and vegetables for soup.

Soup

Strain the vegetables through the strainer, pressing thoroughly to remove all the pulp. Add the stock and one-half a cup of water. Reheat and serve for dinner with croutons or salted wafers.

Rice

½ C-rice   1 t-salt
2 C-boiling water ⅛ t-paprika
1 T-butter

When the water is boiling, add the salt. Add the rice and allow it to boil twenty minutes. More water may be needed. Stir occasionally with a fork. Pour into a strainer, and rinse thoroughly with cold water. Toss into a buttered vegetable dish. Sprinkle with paprika and dot with butter. Set in a moderate oven for fifteen minutes.

CHAPTER CXXXVII

A LUNCHEON FOR POLLY

"NOW that this delicious little luncheon is over, Bettina," said Alice, "I want to ask you something. How did you make the croquettes that cunning shape?"

"With a conical ice cream mould, Alice," Bettina answered. "It is very simple. And I'll tell you another thing. I made those croquettes yesterday, not today."

"You don't mean that you fried them yesterday?"

"Yes, I did, Alice. In deep fat."

"But they were warm, not cold."

"Yes, for I reheated them in the oven a few minutes before I served them. They really are as good as new when treated that way. I had always supposed that croquettes had to be served immediately after they were fried, and you know frying in deep fat is really a nuisance when it has to be done at the last minute. For instance, today I had the biscuits to make, and the soup and sweet potatoes to prepare. And I believe in being leisurely when giving a luncheon, so I certainly would not serve croquettes if they had to be made that day. I tried reheating them once when Bob and I were here alone and discovered that they were delicious. So I've always, ever since, fried my croquettes the day before."

"Hereafter I'll serve croquettes at luncheon myself," said Alice. "You have taught me something."

For luncheon that day Bettina served:

Cream of Pea Soup   Toasted Sticks
Pork Croquettes   Glazed Sweet Potatoes
Creamed Green Beans
Biscuit   Cherry Butter
Head Lettuce   French Dressing
Date Pudding   Cream
Coffee

BETTINA'S RECIPES

(All measurements are level)

Cream of Pea Soup (Four portions)

1 C-peas	2 T-butter
1 C-water	2 C-milk
¼ t-sugar	1 t-salt
2 T-flour	¼ t-paprika

Cook the peas, water and sugar slowly for fifteen minutes. Strain, and rub all the pulp through the strainer. Melt the butter, add the flour, salt and paprika. Mix thoroughly and gradually add the milk. Boil one minute and add the pulp and liquid from the peas. Cook one minute. Serve in hot soup plates or bouillon cups.

Toasted Sticks (Four portions)

3 slices of bread   1 T-butter
½ t-salt

Cut the slices of bread one-half an inch thick. Butter, and sprinkle with salt. Cut into strips, the length of the slice and half an inch wide. Place on a tin pan, and cook directly under a fire or in an oven until a delicate brown. Serve warm.

Ground Pork Croquettes (Four croquettes)

1 C-chopped, cooked pork	½ T-butter
⅛ t-paprika	1 T-flour
¼ t-celery salt	1/3 C-milk
⅛ t-onion salt	1/3 C-crumbs
¼ t-salt	2 T-egg
1 T-pimento, cut fine	1 T-water

Melt the butter, add the flour, paprika, celery salt, onion salt, salt and pimento. Gradually add the milk and cook thoroughly for one minute. Add the meat and allow the mixture to cool. When cool, shape into the desired shape, preferably conical. Roll in the crumbs, dip in the egg and water mixed, then dip in the crumbs and allow to stand for fifteen minutes or more. Fry in deep fat.

Date Pudding (Four portions)

2 egg-whites	1 t-baking powder
½ C-sugar	½ C-dates, cut fine
4 T-flour	½ C-nut meats, cut fine
⅛ t-salt	¼ t-vanilla

Beat the egg whites thoroughly, add the sugar, flour, salt and baking powder. Mix well, add the dates, nuts and vanilla. Pile lightly in a well-buttered baking-dish. Place the dish in a pan of hot water and bake thirty minutes in a moderate oven. Allow the pudding to remain in the oven a little while after the heat is turned off. If cooled slowly, it will not fall. The pudding may be baked in individual moulds if preferred, and may be served with whipped cream.

CHAPTER CXXXVIII

FURS TO PUT AWAY

"**A** PENNY for your thoughts!"

Bettina started in surprise. "Why, Ruth, I didn't see you coming up the walk!"

"I knew you didn't. But what on earth are you doing out here on your front steps? Enjoying the weather?"

"Indeed I am! Isn't it a wonderful spring day? But my thoughts weren't very poetic, I must admit. I was just wondering if it was too early to put away my furs for the summer. I'm always tempted to do that when the first signs of spring appear, and then I'm generally sorry a few days later."

"I'll have to put mine away soon, too. Do tell me, Bettina, just how you go about it."

"Well, I always hang mine in the sun for a while, then I beat them well, comb them out with a steel comb, and wrap them up."

"With moth-balls?"

"That is a good way, but not at all necessary. I always wrap mine in a newspaper—a good tight package. Moths don't like printer's ink, you know, and furs so wrapped are perfectly safe."

"Then, Bettina, you don't need to add that you label the package, for I know that you do, you thoroughly thorough housekeeper!"

Bettina laughed. "Well, Ruth, I do label it. Labelled packages are so much better to have, for very often you need to get something out in a hurry."

For dinner that night Bettina served:

Broiled Steak Lyonnaise Potatoes
Bean Salad
Bread Butter
Date Rocks Coffee

BETTINA'S RECIPES

(All measurements are level)

Lyonnaise Potatoes (Two portions)

2 T-onion
2 T-butter
¼ t-paprika
½ t-salt
1 C-cold boiled potatoes, cut in ½-inch cubes
1 t-chopped parsley

Place one tablespoon of butter in a frying-pan and when hot add the onion. Let the onion cook until it is brown. Add the salt and parsley, the rest of the butter, the potatoes and the paprika. Stir well. Cook until the potatoes are well browned.

Bean Salad (Two portions)

1 C-kidney beans 1 t-salt
½ C-celery, cut fine 3 T-chopped pickle
2 T-nut meats 1/3 C-salad dressing
2 pieces of lettuce

Mix the beans, celery, nut meats, green pepper, pickles and salt. Add the salad dressing. Serve very cold on lettuce leaves.

Date Rocks

1 C-sugar 1 t-cinnamon
½ C-lard and butter mixed ½ t-powdered cloves
1½ C-flour ½ t-vanilla
½ t-baking powder ½ C-dates, cut fine
2 eggs ½ C-nut meats, cut fine
⅛ t-salt

Cream the butter and lard, add the sugar, and mix well. Add the two eggs well beaten. Mix and sift thoroughly the flour, baking powder, salt, cloves and cinnamon. Add the dates and nuts. Stir these dry ingredients into the first mixture. Add the vanilla. Mix thoroughly and drop from the end of the spoon upon a well larded and floured baking pan. Bake fifteen minutes in a moderate oven.

CHAPTER CXXXIX

PLANNING A CHILDREN'S PARTY

"OF course, I'll help you, Ruth," said Bettina. "I'd love to. A children's party! What fun it will be! How many children will be there?"

"Twelve or fifteen, I think. Now let me tell you Ralph's own idea for entertainment. I suppose I'm a doting aunt, but it sounds very possible to me."

"Did Ralph suggest the kind of a party he wished? Well, isn't he a clever boy! And he's only eleven years old, too."

"He suggested that the invitations invite the children to a circus. You see, we could write a little rhyme to that effect on animal paper, or with an animal picture pasted in the corner. When the children arrive, we'll have the parade. We'll have ready the horns, drums, and so forth, for the band, and some of the children will represent the various wild animals. The parade will lead to the refreshment table (after some circus games, perhaps), which will be set outdoors if it is warm enough. The table must represent a circus ground (I've seen those paper circuses downtown, haven't you?), and the refreshments must carry out the scheme. So, Bettina, do help us to plan the details!"

Bettina's dinner that night consisted of:

Sliced Ham and Potatoes en Casserole
Baked Creamed Cabbage
Bread   Butter
Plum Pudding
Cocoanut Pudding

429

BETTINA'S RECIPES

(All measurements are level)

Sliced Ham and Potatoes en Casserole (Four portions)

1 lb. slice of ham two-thirds of an inch thick	12 cloves
	¼ t-paprika
4 new potatoes	1 t-chopped parsley
1 C-water	2 T-flour

Have a frying-pan very hot. Add the ham and brown thoroughly on both sides. Add the water and let boil for one minute. Remove the ham. Stick the cloves into it, and place it in the bottom of a casserole. Add the parsley and paprika to the water in the pan, and pour the liquid over the meat. Cover and bake in a moderate oven for half an hour. Roll the potatoes (which have been washed and peeled) in the flour, and add to the casserole. Baste with the liquid. Cover and cook three-fourths of an hour. Serve in the casserole.

Creamed Cabbage Baked (Four portions)

3 C-cabbage, cut or chopped fine	1 t-salt
1 qt. water	1 C-milk
3 T-flour	¼ C-cracker or dry bread crumbs
2 T-butter	1 T-butter

Wash the cabbage and chop into half inch pieces. Cook in boiling water fifteen minutes. Drain and rinse with cold water. Make a white sauce by melting the butter, adding the flour and salt, and then adding the milk. Cook two minutes, stirring constantly. Add the cabbage, and pour into a well-buttered open baking dish. Melt the one tablespoon of butter, add the crumbs and mix well. Spread the buttered crumbs over the top of the cabbage. Bake fifteen minutes in a moderate oven. Serve in the dish.

Cocoanut Pudding (Four portions)

1 C-milk	½ t-lemon extract
¼ t-salt	½ t-vanilla
3 T-corn starch	3 T-cocoanut
2 T-sugar	

Mix the corn starch and salt in the upper part of **the**

double boiler. Add the milk slowly, stirring all the time. Add the sugar. Place the upper in the lower part of the double boiler and cook, stirring occasionally to prevent lumping. When very thick, add the egg-yolk, the vanilla and lemon extracts and the cocoanut. Beat one minute. Cook again for three minutes. Place in a buttered baking dish. Beat the egg-white and when very stiff, add the two tablespoons of sugar. Pile lightly on the top of the pudding and place in a moderate oven for ten minutes to brown the meringue.

CHAPTER CXL

THE PARTY CIRCUS

R UTH and Bettina led "the parade," the band at its head, to the cheerful sunroom, where the table had been set. At sight of the "party" spread before them, the young musicians and the others gave a sudden shriek of delight.

"It's a circus!" explained Ralph to curly-headed Margery, who was adding her own piping voice to the general din.

A small American flag floated from a flag pole in the center of the table, and around it were arranged paper circus tents and circus wagons of the five and ten cent store variety. Animal crackers were all about, and the animal sandwiches and animal cakes in flat baskets looked almost too real to be eaten.

Smooth boards on supports represented circus seats, and on these the children soon clambered, eager to eat as children always are.

The paper napkins, decorated with animals, were folded before the places to represent tents. The salad faces, which Ralph called "clowns," leered up from the plates.

But the joy was not to be all in seeing. There was a favor for each child to carry away, the favors from the table being claimed by matching the numbers on each one with a corresponding number on the pieces of candy passed at the close of the meal.

The refreshments consisted of:

Clown Salad   Animal Sandwiches
    Picnic Lemonade
 Brick Ice Cream   Fancy Cakes
     Candies

BETTINA'S RECIPES

(All measurements are level)

Sandwiches (Forty)

3 loaves bread	3 hard-cooked eggs
½ lb. butter	3 T-chopped pickles
1½ C-ham, minced or ground fine	2/3 C-salad dressing
	1/3 t-salt

Chop the ham, eggs and pickles very fine. Add the salt and salad dressing. Cut the bread very thin and match the pieces in pairs. Spread one of a pair with the ham mixture and spread the other side with butter which has been mixed and softened with a wooden spoon. Place the two pieces of bread together and press firmly. Moisten the cooky cutter with water and cut evenly the desired shape.

Clown Salad (Twelve portions)

12 rounds of sliced pineapple	24 filberts
12 T-salad dressing	2 canned pimentos
	12 pieces of lettuce

Wash the lettuce carefully. Roll and cut into fine shreds. Arrange a portion on each serving plate. Place a slice of pineapple on each portion and very carefully place the salad dressing on it so that it just covers the circle of pineapple. Arrange two filberts on top to represent eyes, and cut the pimento in a strip to represent the mouth. Cut small triangular pieces of pimento to represent the nose. Arrange these as features on the pineapple and serve at once.

Fancy Cakes (Eighteen cakes)

½ C-butter	½ C-milk
1 C-sugar	1¾ C-flour
8 egg-yolks	2 t-baking powder
	2 t-lemon extract

Cream the butter, add the sugar and mix well. Beat the egg-yolks until very thick, and add to the first mixture.

Mix and sift together the flour and baking-powder and add the milk alternately with the flour mixture, beating well. Beat two minutes after mixing. Add the extract. Pour to the thickness of one inch into flat pans lined with buttered paper. Bake twelve minutes in a moderate oven. Remove from the fire and when cool, cut into shapes with fancy animal cutters. The individual cakes may be iced if desired.

CHAPTER CXLI

PLANNING A LUNCHEON

"I T won't be hard, Ruth, if you plan it out in detail several days before. Decide on the menu, and if you find that some one dish is going to cause more trouble than it's worth, plan something else in its place."

"If it weren't for Aunt Gertrude I shouldn't worry at all, but she is such a wonderful housekeeper! And I am determined that Mother sha'n't have one bit of the responsibility. She's to feel herself just as much a guest as Aunt Gertrude."

"I think it's a lovely thing for you to do, Ruth. Now let me tell you how I think you should go about it. Make a visit to your grocery store or to the market tomorrow, and notice the good things that are in sea· n and inexpensive. Build your menu around them. When you get home, sit down with a paper and pencil and plan everything out. Go into detail, even if it takes several hours of planning. It will be well worth it. I don't mean by that an elaborate luncheon; it ought to be a simple and delicious one, but complete in every detail. When I plan, I write down the things that I can do the day before, and even the day before that. You know there are always so many things to see to —polishing the silver and writing the name cards and seeing that the table linen is in order. It ought to be planned so that the day of the party won't be crowded full of 'last minute things.' Come into the kitchen with me, Ruth; I must baste my pork tenderloin."

That night Bettina served:

Pork Tenderloin	Baked Potatoes
Bread	Butter
Raspberry Jam	
Vegetable Salad	Salad Dressing
Tapioca Pudding	
Coffee	

BETTINA'S RECIPES

(All measurements are level)

Pork Tenderloin (Three portions)

1 lb. pork tenderloin	¼ t-paprika
1 t-salt	1 t-chopped parsley
2 T-water	1 T-lemon juice

Have the tenderloin cut in two-inch pieces and flattened. Place these in a small baking dish. Sprinkle with salt and paprika and add the water. Cover, and cook in a moderate oven for thirty-five minutes. Turn and baste frequently. When done, place on a heated platter, pour the parsley and lemon juice over the top and serve immediately.

Vegetable Salad (Three portions)

1 tomato	1 t-salt
9 slices of cucumber	¼ t-paprika
2 T-chopped onion	2 T-chopped green pepper
1 T-chopped pimento	2 T-nut meats
3 lettuce leaves	

Wash the lettuce carefully and arrange on individual serving dishes. Place upon each lettuce leaf a slice of tomato, three slices of cucumber and one-third of each of the other ingredients. Sprinkle with salt and paprika. Pour the salad dressing over the top and serve very cold.

Bettina Salad Dressing

2 egg-yolks	¼ C-vinegar
1 T-sugar	1/3 C-sour cream
½ t-salt	2 T-pimento liquor (the
2 T-flour	juice from the can)

Beat the egg-yolks, add the sugar, salt and flour. Mix well and add the vinegar, pimento liquor and water. Cook in a double boiler until very thick. When cool, add the sour cream, and pour over the salad.

CHAPTER CXLII

THE NEW CAR

"DO stay to dinner, Ruth!" begged Bettina. "Bob is going to drive the new car out when he comes, and we'll have him take us for a spin after dinner."

"Oh, Bettina, has Bob really bought it? Will you really have a car of your own?"

"Yes, indeed, we will. I can hardly realize it myself, and although I'm so happy over it, I have a little haunting fear that perhaps it is too great an extravagance. But we'll enjoy it so!"

"Of course you will. I'm so glad! Won't the summer be delightful when you can get out into the country every day!"

"Ruth, you must stay to dinner and see the car for yourself! I planned a special little celebration dinner, a kind of salad that Bob particularly likes, and a good dessert, too. And now, if you'll come into the kitchen with me, I'll show you how to make peanut butter rolls. You never heard of them? Well, they're a little like pinwheel biscuit. Don't you remember the pinwheel biscuit that I make sometimes—baking powder biscuit dough rolled out and spread with butter and sugar and cinnamon—then rolled up and cut like cinnamon rolls and baked?"

"Of course, I remember, Bettina! They're the best little things, and so easy to make!"

"Well, these peanut butter rolls are like them, but spread

437

with butter and peanut butter.   Come into the kitchen and I'll show you how they're made."

For dinner they had:

Lamb Chops   Sautèd Potatoes
Creamed Peas
Peanut Butter Rolls
Pear Salad   Cheese Wafers
Chocolate Pie
Coffee

BETTINA'S RECIPES

(All measurements are level)

Peanut Butter and Fruit Rolls (Eight rolls)

1½ C-flour	½ C-milk
3 t-baking powder	2 T-peanut butter
2 T-lard	3 T-currants
¼ t-salt	½ T-butter

Mix the flour, baking powder and salt thoroughly, cut in the lard with a knife until the consistency of cornmeal. Add the milk, mxing with a knife until a soft dough is formed.   More milk may be needed; this depends on the consistency of the flour.   Pat into a rectangular shape, on a floured board or on a paper.   The dough should be half an inch thick.   Cream the butter, add the peanut butter and spread on the biscuit dough.   Sprinkle the currants on the top.   Roll up carefully, over and over like a cinnamon roll.   Cut off pieces half an inch wide and pat them down in a tin pan.   Bake eighteen minutes in a moderate oven.

Pear Salad (Three portions)

3 halves of pears	2 T-nut meats
½ C-cottage cheese	2 dates, cut fine
¼ t-salt	1 T-pimento, cut fine
⅛ t-paprika	5 T-salad dressing
	3 lettuce leaves

Mix the cottage cheese, salt, paprika, nut meats, dates and pimento thoroughly.   Add two tablespoons of salad dressing.   Arrange the pears on the lettuce leaves and place one tablespoon of the mixture on each portion.   Place a tablespoon of salad dressing on the top. Serve very cold.

Cheese Wafers

6 salted wafers	½ T-pimento, cut fine
½ T-butter	⅛ t-salt
2 T-yellow cream cheese	⅛ t-paprika

Cream the butter, add the cheese, pimento, salt and paprika and mix into a paste. Spread carefully on top of the wafers. Place in a moderate oven until a delicate brown. Serve with the salad.

MAY.

Scrub and polish,—sweep and clean,——
 Fling your windows wide!
See, the trees are clad in green!
 Coax the spring inside!
Home, be shining fair to-day
For the guest whose name is May!

CHAPTER CXLIII

IN HOUSECLEANING TIME

"**G**OODNESS gracious, Ruth!" said Bettina. "Surely it can't be half-past five already!"

"Yes, it is, Bettina. Exactly that!" said Ruth, glancing at her tiny wrist watch. "But Bob won't be home till six, will he?"

"No, but I want to have dinner ready when he arrives. You see, as I told you before, I simply shouldn't have gone to Mary's this afternoon. My curtains are down and my rugs are up, and my house isn't an attractive place for a man to come home to, to say the least. And then to come straight from a party and give Bob a pick-up lunch instead of a full meal, will be——"

"The last straw? What had you planned for lunch?"

"Well, I have some soup all made, ready to reheat. Then I think I'll have banana salad, tea, and hot baking-powder biscuits."

"De-licious!" said Ruth, with a Teddy-fied grin. "I believe I'll invite myself to stay!"

"Good! You can make the salad while I'm mixing the biscuits. I also have some chocolate cookies, and I'll open a jar of canned peaches——"

"And I'll be so bright and scintillating that old Bobbie won't even miss the curtains and the rugs!"

That night Bettina served:

Bettina Soup   Oyster Crackers
Banana Salad
Hot Biscuits
Canned Peaches   Chocolate Cookies
Tea

BETTINA'S RECIPES

(All measurements are level)

Bettina Soup (Three portions)

3 C-meat stock (left over)   1 T-sliced onion
½ C-cooked rice   ½ t-salt
½ C-tomato pulp   ¼ t-paprika
3 celery leaves

Add the rice, tomato pulp, onion, salt, paprika and celery leaves to the meat stock. Cook for twenty minutes over a slow fire. Strain and serve in hot soup dishes or bouillon cups.

Banana Salad (Three portions)

2 bananas   1 T-lemon juice
½ C-shelled peanuts,   ½ t-salt
broken in halves   ¼ t-paprika
½ C-celery, cut small   ½ C-salad dressing
3 lettuce leaves

Cut the bananas in one-fourth inch cubes. Add the lemon juice, mixing thoroughly. Add the peanuts, celery, salt and paprika. Add the salad dressing, mixing lightly with a silver fork. Pile on the lettuce leaves which have been washed and arranged on a serving dish. Serve immediately.

Baking Powder Biscuits (Eight biscuits)

1½ C-flour   ¼ t-salt
3 t-baking powder   1½ T-lard
½ C-milk

Mix and sift well the flour, baking powder and salt. Cut in the lard with a knife until the consistency of cornmeal. Add the milk slowly, stirring with a knife until the dough is soft enough to be handled without sticking to the fingers. Place on a floured board, pat into shape, with the hands, to a thickness of two-thirds of an inch. Cut with a biscuit cutter. Place the biscuits side by side in a tin pan. Bake in a moderate oven fifteen minutes. Serve on a folded napkin.

CHAPTER CXLIV

MRS. DIXON HAPPENS IN

"I MUST hurry home to get dinner," said Mrs. Dixon. "See, Bettina, I've been to the market! Isn't this a fine big cantaloupe? I have two more just like it. Frank is very fond of them, but——" she added ruefully, "I like them cold, of course, and after I've fixed them and had them in the refrigerator a while, everything in it—milk, butter and eggs—has the cantaloupe taste!"

"I'll tell you how you can prevent that, Charlotte. Of course they must be very cold when served, but I never prepare them till just before the meal. I put them in the ice box whole, in a paper sack, taking care that the mouth of the sack is closed. They become very cold that way, and at the same time can't affect the other food."

"I'm so glad you told me that, Bettina. I've learned a great many things from you, haven't I? Oh, yes, another thing puzzles me. I like chipped ice served in and with the cantaloupe, and I don't own any tool for preparing the ice. I do fix it somehow, of course, but I've wondered how other people manage."

"Well, there are regular ice shavers, you know; but I haven't one, either. I keep a salt sack that I use for that purpose whenever I need just a little chipped ice. It isn't hard to break off a piece small enough to go in a salt sack; in fact, you usually have one in your ice box already. I put it in the sack and break it fine with the flat side of a small hatchet."

"Well, I've learned something more, and I'll use the knowledge tomorrow evening. I must be going now. How lovely those asters are on your dinner table! They seem to prophesy an especially good meal! Do tell me what you are going to have! I never can think of a variety—simple meat dishes are my bugbear."

"We have veal chops for tonight—just plain veal chops and boiled new potatoes and carrots with Bechamel sauce."

"Gracious me! Here comes Bob. I must hurry along or Frank will be home before I am."

Bettina's dinner that evening was made up of:

Veal Chops	New Potatoes
Carrots	Bechamel Sauce
Bread	Butter
Peaches	Custard Sauce

BETTINA'S RECIPES

(All measurements are level)

Veal Chops (Two portions)

2 chops   ¼ t-paprika
1 t-salt   4 T-flour
1 T-fat

Trim and wipe chops one-half inch thick, which are cut from the thick part of the leg. Season with salt and pepper and roll in flour. Put the fat (bacon fat or lard) in the pan, and when hot, add the chops. Brown both sides evenly and allow to cook ten minutes.

Creamed Carrots (Two portions)

1 C-carrots   3 C-boiling water
1 t-salt

Carrots should not be peeled, but after being scrubbed well they should be scraped with a knife. Cut into one-half inch cubes, cook in boiling water (salted) twenty-five minutes, or until soft when pierced with a knitting needle. Drain and serve with Bechamel sauce.

Bechamel Sauce (Two portions)

1 T-butter	⅛ t-pepper
1 T-flour	1 egg-yolk
¼ t-salt	2/3 C-milk

Melt the butter, add the flour, salt and pepper and mix well. Gradually stir in the milk. Cook until it thickens slightly. Add the beaten egg-yolk, cook one minute and serve immediately with one cup of diced carrots.

CHAPTER CXLV

ENGAGEMENT PRESENTS

"RUTH has had some of the loveliest engagement presents," said Bettina to Bob across the dinner table. "And some that are so practical and sensible!"

"Did you see her this afternoon?"

"Yes, and we walked over to the new house. She has had Fred put up a shelf in the kitchen for her cook-books and recipe card box, and she finds that she really has quite a library! And the various engagement gifts are all put away.. In fact the bungalow is nearly ready for use. I've told Ruth that she might write a magazine article on 'Engagement Presents,' using her own for illustrations."

"What does she have?"

"Well, a dear old Aunt of Bob's presented her with some wonderful kitchen scales—an aid to economy. Then it seems to me that every friend who has some favorite kitchen device has given one to her—she has egg-beaters, waffle-irons, cream-whippers, silver-polishers, cases for linen and silver—oh, everything you can think of!"

"What did you give her?"

"The cards and card box for her indexed recipes. I included many of my own recipes, you know. That is to be my own particular engagement gift to all my friends."

That night Bettina served:

Salmon Loaf   Salmon Sauce
Baked Potatoes
Bread   Butter
Marble Pudding   Whipped Cream
Iced Tea

BETTINA'S RECIPES

(All measurements are level)

Salmon Loaf (Two portions)

2/3 C-flaked, canned salmon   ¼ t-paprika
1/3 C-cracker crumbs   1 egg
½ t-salt   1/3 C-milk

Flake the salmon apart with a silver fork, add the crumbs, salt and paprika. Beat the egg and add the milk. Add to the first mixture. Place in a well-buttered mould and bake in a moderate oven for twenty-five minutes. Allow to stand three minutes, remove from the mould, and place on a warmed platter. Pour salmon sauce around the loaf and serve at once.

Salmon Sauce (Two portions)

3 T-flour   1 egg, hard-cooked and
2 T-butter   chopped fine
¼ C-liquor from the   ½ t-salt
    salmon   1 T-pickle, chopped fine
2/3 C-milk   ½ t-chopped parsley
          ¼ t-paprika

Melt the butter, add the salmon liquor. Add the flour, salt and paprika and mix well. Add the milk and cook two minutes. Add the egg, pickle and parsley, mix well, and pour around the loaf.

Baked Marble Pudding

1 C-flour   1 egg
2 t-baking powder   2 T-melted butter
¼ t-cinnamon   ¼ C-water
⅛ t-salt   ½ t-vanilla
½ C-sugar   ½ square of chocolate, melted

Mix and sift the sugar, flour, salt, baking powder and cinnamon. Add the egg-yolk, water and vanilla. Beat one minute. Add the egg white stiffly beaten. Mix well. Add the butter, melted. Divide the mixture, and to half add the melted chocolate. Prepare a loaf-cake pan or a small round tin with waxed paper. Fill it with both mixtures, first placing in it a tablespoon of the plain mixture, then a tablespoon of the chocolate mixture, then the plain, until all is used, and the pudding has a marbled appearance. Bake thirty minutes in a moderate oven. Serve warm with whipped cream.

CHAPTER CXLVI

WITH HOUSECLEANING OVER

"**B**ROILED steak and French fried potatoes! Whew!" said Bob, strolling into Bettina's shining kitchen. "Why so festive?"

"Because I've just finished house-cleaning, Bob, and I want to celebrate. Doesn't everything look splendid?"

"Well, it looked good to me before, but now that I think of it, I believe there is an extra shine on things. What makes that nickel there look so bright and silvery?"

"I cleaned it with a damp cloth dipped in powdered borax. That always makes nickel bright and clean."

"I might have done that for you, Betty. Why didn't you suggest it to me?"

"Oh, this house is so small and dear that I enjoyed every minute of my house-cleaning. And I didn't want to bother you with it at all."

"Well, I'll help now with dinner. What can I do?"

"Will you cut the bread, dear? There's the steel bread knife; doesn't it look bright and shiny, too? I cleaned all my steel knives by dipping them into the earth in a flower pot I keep filled for that purpose. Well, I think dinner is ready now, Bob."

For dinner they had:

Broiled Steak		French Fried Potatoes
	Stuffed Onions	
Bread		Currant Jelly
Orange Tapioca		Whipped Cream
	Coffee	

449

BETTINA'S RECIPES

(All measurements are level)

Stuffed Onions (Two portions)

2 large Spanish onions	½ t-salt
3 T-soft bread crumbs	2 t-melted butter
1 t-egg	½ t-celery salt
½ t-chopped parsley	¼ C-milk

Cook the whole onions in boiling water until tender, but not broken. When the fork pierces them easily, drain off the water and rinse in cold water. This makes them firm for stuffing.

Remove the centers carefully. Add the removed portion, chopped fine, to the crumbs, egg, parsley, salt, butter and celery salt. Mix thoroughly. Fill the holes with the mixture. Place the onions in a small pan. Sprinkle the salt over the onion and pour over it the milk. Bake in a moderate oven for twenty minutes.

Orange Tapioca (Two portions)

4 T-orange juice	2/3 C-boiling water
2 t-lemon juice	2 T-powdered tapioca
5 T-sugar	¼ t-salt
	1 orange

Stir the tapioca into the orange and lemon juice. Add the sugar and salt. Let it stand for three minutes while boiling the water. Add the water. Place directly over the fire. Stir constantly and cook till thick (about three minutes). Peel the orange and break apart in sections. Line a glass serving dish with it and pour the tapioca over the sections. Serve cold with whipped cream.

Whipped Cream

1/3 C-thick cream	½ t-lemon extract
2 T-sugar	½ t-vanilla extract

Place the cream in a round-bottomed, chilled bowl. Beat until thick and fluffy. Add the sugar, lemon and vanilla. Mix well. Pile lightly on the orange tapioca and serve very cold.

CHAPTER CXLVII

SPRING MARKETING

"I 'VE been to the market, Bettina," said Charlotte, "and I thought I'd stop here just a moment to rest."

"Come in," said Bettina, "and set that heavy basket down. Why didn't you leave it for Frank to bring?"

"Because I needed the things for dinner."

"What did you get?"

"Oh, the same old fresh vegetables," said Charlotte wearily. "A month ago they seemed so wonderful—strawberries, asparagus, new potatoes and all—but there are no new ways to cook them! One day I cream the asparagus and the next day I serve it on toast."

"Do you ever make asparagus salad?" asked Bettina. "We are very fond of it. Cold cooked asparagus is good with any kind of salad dressing, but we like best a very simple kind that I often make—oil and lemon juice and cheese."

"Cheese?" echoed Charlotte in surprise.

"Yes, cottage cheese and Roquefort cheese are equally good. And, Charlotte, if you want some delicious strawberry desserts——"

"Oh, I do! We're so tired of shortcake and plain strawberries!"

"I know several good strawberry dishes. Come, let me show you one that I made today!"

Bettina's dinner consisted of:

451

Veal Steak   New Potatoes in Cream
Bread   Butter
Asparagus Salad   Salad Dressing
              Strawberry Tapioca

BETTINA'S RECIPES

(All measurements are level)

Asparagus Salad (Three portions)

18 stalks of asparagus   3 C-water
½ t-salt   3 pieces of lettuce

Wash the asparagus and cut it in six-inch pieces. Cook
for ten minutes in boiling salted water (longer if necessary).
Rinse with cold water, handling carefully. Arrange six
stalks on each piece of lettuce. Serve with salad dressing.

Asparagus Salad Dressing (Three portions)

4 T-olive oil   ¼ t-salt
2 T-lemon juice   ¼ t-paprika
       1 T-cottage cheese

Beat the oil, and add the lemon juice slowly. Add the
salt and paprika. Beat one minute. Add the cheese. Serve
very cold, poured over the asparagus salad.

Strawberry Tapioca

3 T-granulated tapioca   ⅛ t-salt
4 T-sugar   ½ t-vanilla
1¼ C-hot water   1 C-strawberries
              ¼ C-sugar

Wash and hull the strawberries, and cut in halves with a
spoon. Add the sugar, mix well, and set in a cold place.
Mix the tapioca, the sugar and the salt. Add the boiling
water slowly. Cook ten minutes in the upper part of the
double boiler. Add the vanilla. When cold, add the strawberries. Serve very cold with plain or whipped cream.

CHAPTER CXLVIII

PLANS FOR THE WEDDING

"OH, Bob!" cried Bettina, "don't you hope it won't rain?"

"Rain? When? Tonight?" asked Bob, absent-mindedly, for he was busily eating the first cherry cobbler of the season, and enjoying it, too.

"No, stupid! I'm thinking about the wedding—Ruth's wedding."

"And Fred's wedding, too," added Bob. "You talk as if Ruth were the only one who is vitally interested."

"Fred's wedding, then. For, you see, the ceremony is to be in that darling summer house if it doesn't rain. If it does it will have to be in the solarium. The bridesmaids and matrons (if it is an outdoor wedding) are to carry the prettiest green silk parasols that you ever saw. They will be Ruth's gifts to us. Over our arms we'll carry plain soft straw hats filled with pink peonies, and lots of trailing greenery. Won't that be lovely? For you know we are all to wear short white dresses and white shoes."

"And what am I to do?"

"You're to be an usher and help carry the green ropes that form the aisle."

"Ropes?"

"Yes, plain ropes covered with greenery. Will you have some more cherry cobbler, Bob?"

That night for dinner Bettina served:

Pork Tenderloin	Creamed New Potatoes
Cauliflower with Butter Sauce	
Vegetable Salad	French Dressing
Cherry Cobbler	Cream
Coffee	

453

BETTINA'S RECIPES

(All measurements are level)

Vegetable Salad (Four portions)

2 tomatoes	½ t-celery salt
12 slices of cucumber	1 t-salt
4 T-cottage cheese	¼ t-paprika
8 pieces of lettuce	

Arrange two pieces of lettuce on each salad plate. Cut the tomatoes in half and arrange on the lettuce. Place three slices of cucumber on each piece of tomato. Add a tablespoon of cheese to each portion. Sprinkle with celery salt, salt and paprika. Serve at once with French dressing.

Bettina's French Dressing (Four portions)

2 T-lemon juice	1 t-salt
5 T-olive oil	¼ t-paprika
1 t-chopped parsley	

Mix the lemon juice, salt, paprika and parsley. Add the oil slowly, beating vigorously with a Dover egg-beater or a fork. Beat until the mixture becomes a little thick. Pour over the salad.

Cherry Cobbler (Four portions)

2 C-cherries, stemmed and pitted	1 C-flour
	1 t-baking powder
2/3 C-sugar	¼ t-salt
2 t-flour	1 T-sugar
1 T-water	2 T-butter
⅛ t-salt	6 T-milk

Mix the cherries, sugar, flour and salt. Allow to stand five minutes. Add the water. Pour the mixture into a deep glass or china baking dish. Mix and sift the flour, baking powder, salt and sugar. Cut in the butter with a knife. Add the milk, mixing until a soft dough is formed. Shape it with the hands to fit over the cherries. Make three slits in the dough to permit the steam to escape. Place in a moderate oven and bake for thirty minutes. Serve in the baking dish. Plain cream or whipped cream should be served with the cobbler.

CHAPTER CXLIX

ENTERTAINING THE WEDDING GUESTS

"IF you girls only would, my dear," Ruth's mother had responded to Bettina's suggestion that she and Alice entertain Ruth's house guests the entire day before the wedding, "you have no idea what a load would be taken off my mind!"

"And Alice and I would so enjoy helping you," Bettina had replied. "And remember, we mean the whole day, breakfast and all!"

Luckily, the day before the wedding dawned warm and clear At eight o'clock Harry and Bob drove them all in automobiles to a lovely country spot in which the girls served an outdoor breakfast. The morning was spent in motoring and luncheon was eaten at a charming downtown tea-room. Then they were whisked off to Bettina's little home for an informal afternoon, and Harry and Bob, feeling that they had indeed been model husbands, departed for their respective offices.

"The girl from Kentucky has volunteered to sing," whispered Alice to Ruth. "She's a dear. Do you suppose we can keep Aunt Jenny from talking for half an hour?"

That afternoon the following refreshments were served on trays:

Fruit Salad   Bettina Sandwiches
Orange Sherbet
Bettina Cake, White Mountain Cream Icing
Coffee
Nuts   Candy

BETTINA'S RECIPES

(All measurements are level)

Fruit Salad (Twelve portions)

3 C-diced pineapple	½ C-marshmallows, cut fine
1 C-nut meats, cut in small pieces	½ C-red cherries, cut fine
	1/3 C-figs, cut fine
½ C-oranges, cut in small pieces	1 C-salad dressing
	½ C-whipped cream
12 pieces lettuce	

Mix the pineapple, nut meats, oranges, marshmallows, cherries and figs. Mix the whipped cream and the salad dressing. Pour this over the fruit. Serve on lettuce leaves which have been washed and placed on serving plates. Serve immediately.

Bettina Sandwiches (Twelve portions)

½ C-creamed cheese	½ C-pimento olives, chopped fine
3 T-pickles, chopped fine	2 T-salad dressing
¼ t-salt	

Mix the cheese, pickles, olives and salt. Add the salad dressing. Spread this mixture between two thin pieces of buttered bread. Press firmly together and cut into fancy shapes.

Bettina Cake (Twelve squares)

¼ C-butter	1 t-baking powder
½ C-sugar	¼ C-strained orange juice
4 egg-yolks	½ t-orange extract
⅞ C-flour	½ t-lemon extract

Cream the butter, add the sugar and mix well. Add the egg-yolks which have been well beaten. Mix and sift the flour, baking powder and salt, and add these, with the orange juice and the orange and lemon extracts to the first mixture. Beat vigorously for two minutes. Fill a twelve-inch square pan which has been prepared with waxed paper, with the mixture. Bake thirty minutes in a moderate oven. When cool, cover with the icing and cut into twelve pieces.

CHAPTER CL

THE BRIDESMAIDS' DINNER

R UTH'S wedding colors were to be pink and green, and pink and green were, therefore, the colors which decorated the charming dinner table laid for the wedding party and close relatives the night before the wedding. A bud vase holding a half-opened pink rose bud stood before every two places. A large, low dish in the center of the table held pink roses, while at either end was another low arrangement of the same flowers.

Tiny paper slipper nut cups at each place held the pecans, and at the places laid for the best man and the ushers, silver pencils, Fred's gifts to the groomsmen, were found.

"They are cunning, of course," chattered Bernadette, Ruth's cousin and maid-of-honor, "but you men just wait till you see the green parasols that we bridesmaids are to carry! Ruth is giving them to us, you know!"

The dinner menu was as follows:

Watermelon Balls

Celery Bouillon   Bread Sticks

Veal Birds

Creamed New Potatoes   Buttered New Beets

Rolls   Butter Balls

Mint Frappe

Blackstone Salad   French Dressing

Thin Bread and Butter Sandwiches

Brick Ice Cream   White Cake

Coffee

Salted Pecans

457

BETTINA'S RECIPES

(All measurements are level)

Blackstone Salad (Eighteen portions)

36 pieces of head lettuce	½ t-paprika
9 grapefruit	½ t-salt
9 T-Neufchatel cheese	2 T-cream
9 T-cottage cheese	1 T-salad dressing

Arrange two pieces of lettuce on each salad plate. Carefully peel the grapefruit and remove all the tough fibres and the white skin. Cut the grapefruit into one-inch pieces. Arrange the pieces in a circle upon the lettuce leaves. In the center of the circle, place the cheese mixture. Pour the salad dressing over the lettuce, cheese and grapefruit.

Cheese Mixture

Mix the Neufchatel and cottage cheese, the salt, paprika, cream and salad dressing. Stir until very creamy. Spread on a piece of waxed paper to the thickness of one inch. Place in the refrigerator, on the ice if possible. When cold and hard, cut in pieces three-fourths of an inch square. Place a cube in the center of the grapefruit circle on each side plate.

French Dressing

8 T-lemon juice	½ t-paprika
2 t-salt	1 C-olive oil

Mix and beat thoroughly the lemon juice, salt and paprika. Add the oil very slowly. Beat for three minutes. Add one tablespoon to each portion of the salad. Serve at once.

CHAPTER CLI

A MORNING WEDDING IN JUNE

AFTER the solemn and beautiful ceremony had taken place in the rose-embowered summer house, there was the usual hush for a moment, and then Ruth and Fred were engulfed in a sudden rush of chattering friends, eager to offer congratulations. Bettina and Bob were swept off with the others to the house, where the wedding breakfast was waiting to be served.

"The morning is after all the happiest time for a wedding," whispered Ellen to Bettina, as they found their places at the bride's table. "Everything seems so fresh and new and green and hopeful! Isn't the table lovely, Bettina?"

And indeed it was. Rose-decorated again, with the graceful flowers in baskets, and the white bride's cake in the center of the table, Bettina felt that it made the proper setting for the flushed and smiling little bride.

"And the wedding cake is to be passed in darling little baskets," continued Ellen. "Little baskets with handles—and the cake in tiny packages tied with white ribbon! Pink and green candy all around them, too!"

The wedding breakfast consisted of:

Watermelon Balls in Halves of Cantaloupe
Chicken Croquettes   Creamed Potatoes
Mushroom Sauce
New Peas   Butter Sauce
Parker House Rolls   Loganberry Jam
Fruit Salad   Wafers, Bettina
Brick Ice Cream   White Cake
Coffee
Nuts   Candy

459

BETTINA'S RECIPES

(All measurements are level)

Mushroom Sauce (Thirty portions)

1 C-chicken fat	2 t-salt
¼ C-water	½ t-paprika
1¼ C-flour	7 C-milk

Mix the fat and flour carefully, add the water, salt and paprika. Cook one minute, stirring constantly, add one-half of the milk and cook until the mixture gets very thick. Beat one minute, add the rest of the milk and cook again, still stirring continuously. When the sauce is very thick and creamy, add the mushrooms. Stir over a hot fire for one minute. This allows the mushrooms to get hot. Serve one tablespoonful of the mixture around each croquette. The sauce may be reheated by adding two tablespoons of milk, and placing over a hot fire.

Fruit Salad (Thirty portions)

30 slices of pineapple	120 pecan meats
120 white cherries	30 T-salad dressing
30 red maraschino cherries	30 pieces of head lettuce
2 t-salt	

Arrange the pieces of lettuce on the salad plates. Sprinkle with salt, arrange on each portion a slice of pineapple, four white cherries, four pecan nuts and one maraschino cherry. Place one tablespoon of salad dressing on each slice of pineapple, then arrange the fruits and nuts in any desired design. Serve immediately.

Wafers Bettina (Thirty portions)

30 double wafers	3 T-chopped nut meats
¼ lb. cream cheese (white)	3 T-butter
¼ t-salt	

Mix the cheese, nuts, butter and salt thoroughly. Spread evenly over the double wafers. Bake in a moderate oven until a delicate brown on the top.

CHAPTER CLII

THE FIRST YEAR ENDS

"AND a whole year has gone since then," said Bob, as his eyes met Bettina's across the little table set for two. "That's the queer part of it," Bettina replied. "That year seems unbelievably short in some ways and unbelievably long in others, and stranger yet, I don't feel that it is really gone. I feel as if we had it, captured, held forever, with all of its fun and all of its little sad times. We own it, even more than we own a collection of snapshots in a camera book—because that year is a part of us now."

"And the little hard places only make the bright spots all the brighter by contrast. Do you know, Bettina, that I've found you wiser than I ever imagined a young wife could be?"

"Bob,"—and Bettina laughed and blushed at the same time.

"Don't interrupt. This is our anniversary and I'm making a speech. You are wise because from the first you've realized that we get out of life just what we put into it. You've faced things. You've realized that marriage isn't a hit-or-miss proposition. It's a business——"

"A glorified business, Bobby. Dealing in materials that can't all be felt and seen and tasted, but that are, nevertheless, just as real as others. More truly real, I sometimes think. I know that the more love we give the more we receive, but we can't forget that we were given intelligence, too. So we mustn't turn the rose-colored lights of romance too beautifully low to let us see the wheels go round. And after all, romance is really in everything that we do lovingly, and intelligently. I find it in planning and cooking the best and most economical meals that I can, and in getting the mending done on time, and in keeping the house clean and beautiful. And—in having you appreciate things."

"If you knew how I *do* appreciate them!" said Bob. "Let's make our second year even happier than the first. If that is possible!"

For that anniversary dinner Bettina served:

Broiled Steak   New Potatoes in Cream
Hot Biscuits   Butter
Currant Jelly
Tomato Salad
Charlotte Russe
Coffee

BETTINA'S RECIPES

(All measurements are level)

Currant Jelly (Five glasses)

2 qts. of currants   1 C-water
Sugar

Pick over the currants, leaving the berries on the stems. Wash and drain. Place in an enamel preserving kettle and add one cup of water. Cook slowly until the currants are white. Strain through a jelly bag. Boil the juice five minutes in a shallow pan. It is better to boil small quantities at a time, as this makes the jelly much clearer. When the juice has all been boiled, measure, and add an equal amount of heated sugar. Boil three minutes, or until it jells when tried on a cold saucer. Pour into sterilized glasses. Allow to stand in the sun twenty-four hours. Cover with boiling paraffin and put away in a cool, dark place. This recipe makes about five glasses or two and a half pints.

Tomato Salad (Two portions)

4 slices tomato, ½ inch thick	⅛ t-celery salt
3 T-chopped green pepper	2 T-olive oil
½ t-salt	2 T-lemon juice
¼ t-paprika	2 pieces lettuce

Mix the salt, paprika, celery salt, olive oil and lemon juice. Beat one minute. Add the tomatoes and green pepper. Place in the ice box for half an hour. Arrange the lettuce leaves on salad plates. Place two slices of tomato on each portion. Pour the oil mixture over the tomatoes.

Charlotte Russe (Two portions)

2 t-granulated gelatin	1 C-whipped cream
2 T-cold water	½ t-vanilla
¼ C-hot milk	4 thin pieces sponge cake
¼ C-sugar	

Place the sponge cakes around the edges of a moistened mould. Soak the gelatin in cold water five minutes. Add the hot milk. Stir until it dissolves. Add the sugar and vanilla. Allow the gelatin mixture to cool. When it begins to thicken, fold in the cream. Beat until the mixture holds its shape. Pour into the mould. Allow to remain two hours in a cold place.

INDEX

Bread, Rolls, etc.

Cakes and Cookies.

Cereals.

Desserts.

Ice Creams and Ices.

Icing.

Jellies and Preserves.

Nuts and Candies.

Pastry.

Pickles, Relishes, etc.

Puddings.

Salads.

Salad Dressing and Sauces.

Sandwiches.

Soups.

Vegetables.

Bettina's Suggestions.